W9-ARX-100

THE POLITICS OF CRUELTY

Also by Kate Millett

Sexual Politics

The Prostitution Papers

Flying

Sita

The Basement

The Loony-Bin Trip

THE POLITICS OF CRUELTY

An Essay on the
Literature of
Political
Imprisonment

KATE MILLETT

W · W · Norton & Company
New York   London

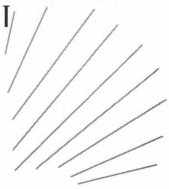

The text of this book is composed in 11/13 pt. Sabon,
with the display set in Radiant Bold Condensed.
Composition and manufacturing by the Haddon Craftsmen, Inc.
Book design by Margaret M. Wagner.

*Because the permission credits cannot be legibly accommodated on this
page they have been placed on pp. 317–318.*

Library of Congress Cataloging-in-Publication Data
Millett, Kate.
The politics of cruelty : an essay on the literature of
imprisonment / by Kate Millett.
p.   cm.
Includes index.
1. Torture.   2. Imprisonment.   3. Oppression (Psychology)
I. Title.
HV8593.M55   1994
365—dc20   93-34406

ISBN 0-393-03575-1

W.W. Norton & Company, Inc., 500 Fifth Avenue, New York, N.Y. 10110
W.W. Norton & Company Ltd., 10 Coptic Street, London WC1A 1PU

1 2 3 4 5 6 7 8 9 0

For all political prisoners:
past, present, and to come

The author would like to thank the Hamburg Institute for Social Research for their material and spiritual support during the writing of this book.

CONTENTS

Preface   11

Introduction   15

**PART ONE
THE MECHANISM**

1   Solzhenitsyn and the Creation of
the Gulag   23

2   The Nazi Camp System   44

3   Henri Alleg and Colonialism in Algeria   74

4   The British in Ireland   97

5   The Apartheid System in South Africa   117

9

CONTENTS

PART TWO
THE IMAGINATION

6 Photography: The Experience of Shock   137

7 *Closet Land:* State and Sexual
   Authority   168

8 The Extreme Experience of Solitude:
   Aurobindo, Ngũgĩ, Nien Cheng   194

PART THREE
RECENT POLITICS OF CRUELTY IN ACTION

9 The Little School: Argentina and Brazil   225

10 The Death of a Guatemalan Village.
    El Salvador   253

11 State Torture and Religion. The Torture of
    Children   280

12 Conclusion   296

Acknowledgments   315

Permissions   317

Index   319

PREFACE

PARTIAL and imperfect as it is,* this essay is the result of years of study inside a profoundly disturbing subject. Nothing in the world frightens as much as torture, nothing so outrages, cries out as hard to be cried out against. It was for that reason that I chose it, had to choose it. It is a logical outgrowth of *Sexual Politics* and *The Basement,* both examinations of power and domination, oppression and abnegation, but also of courage and endurance as well. It has been a long and harrowing journey; many times I felt despair while merely reading about what other persons actually endured. In asking the reader to accompany me over this ground, I have the same motive that first drove me: if we know these things, there is some hope that they can be changed; if we care, there is the possibility of action against this evil.

I had meant to begin this book, arbitrarily, perhaps even

---

*There is only one mention here of Bosnia, none of East Timor, the Philippines, Iraq, or scores of other locations where torture is widely practiced today.

unjustifiably, with the sight of a big earthenware jug full of yellow tulips at the foot of my bed one morning as I began to plan an outline of the text, an image of life that would stand in opposition to what I would discover, represent freedom and vitality, sustain by contradicting the pain and horror in what I would have to confront. Evanescent as this reference point might be, I needed a starting place, some emblem of what one lives for, endures for, an icon of the joy of living against the death and terror of incarceration . . . Would someone who has undergone all that agree in principle? . . . perhaps nod at the intention but then select another object altogether: reunion with one's family, the company of friends, sex, sunshine, a glass of wine, the sight of a coastline. We are posing life against death here, and the sweetness of life. For that sweetness one chooses it, for its endless possibilities and varieties and pleasures. So different from fear and pain, so immeasurably different that one hits upon something to illustrate that difference and represent peace, safety, repose, beauty, civilization. Everything that the politics of cruelty is not.

Merely opposites, ends of a spectrum? Not inevitably, for the politics of cruelty is finally unnecessary, an excrescence, neither part of nature nor the human condition, a negation of life, dull and mechanical as bureaucratic thought: consider "ethnic cleansing" as an idea. The many forms of state terrorism are now a global situation, there for this generation and the next to face, and possibly, with fortitude and determination, to dismantle and abolish.

K.M.

From the United Nations Declaration on the Protection of All Persons from Torture, 9 December 1975, Article 1:

> Torture means any act by which severe pain or suffering, whether physical or mental, is intentionally inflicted by or at the instigation of a public official on a person for such purposes as obtaining from him or a third person information or confession, punishing him for an act he has committed or is suspected of having committed, or intimidating him or other persons.

INTRODUCTION

THE French, who have a word for this kind of writing, call it *témoignage,* the literature of the witness; the one who has been there, seen it, knows. It crosses genres, can be autobiography, reportage, even narrative fiction. But its basis is factual, fact passionately lived and put into writing by a moral imperative rooted like a flower amid carnage with an imperishable optimism, a hope that those who hear will care, will even take action.

The witnesses in this study, whether the writer in person or a fictional character, have this in common: they describe the experience of torture, frequently having undergone it themselves. With the immediacy and detail of literature, they make clear to us what life is like in a culture which practices torture, both the individual and the collective effect of its reintroduction on social and political existence.

Torture is practiced now on a scale the world has never seen before, diminishing even the centuries of the Inquisition. This is true despite that recent moment in Western history which

witnessed the widespread abolition of torture in criminal procedure. As such traditional legal or judicial torture was outlawed, a hope arose that torture itself would become a thing
of the past: the Tsar relinquished torture in 1801, the Emperor
of Japan in 1847. Throughout Europe, torture was officially
prohibited in country after country during the eighteenth and
early nineteenth centuries; statutory abolition of torture in
criminal law was so complete by 1874 that Victor Hugo could
proclaim that "torture had ceased to exist." Although skeptics
see torture as a historical constant, a legal historian like Nigel
Rodley in his *Treatment of Political Prisoners Under International Law** puts emphasis on the phenomenon of official abolition: "In the space of half a century, torture was abolished as
part of the legal process, and was virtually gone from Europe
by the end of the eighteenth century." Centuries of agitation
and reform were behind the formal renunciations as political
ideas such as the proscription of torture in the Declaration of
the Rights of Man and the constitutional state were experienced in one place after another.

The hiatus was short-lived, but even a century's formal
abolition of a practice as ancient and widespread as civilization, and assumed (as had been slavery) to be endemic to
human nature, is a monumental change. After so long a campaign to end torture, the fact of its return, its transformation
and proliferation under different circumstances, is monumental as well. For as the legal historian Edward Peters *(Torture)*†
interprets the event, when torture continues and increases, it
does so as the political weapon of the state against what it
imagines to be subversion, rather than the confession of ordinary criminal activity. For ordinary crime, traditional judicial
torture—open, public, regulated by statute, and acknowledged—was indeed abolished: as legal process was improved

*Nigel Rodley, *The Treatment of Political Prisoners Under International Law* (London and New York: Oxford University Press, 1987).
†Edward Peters, *Torture* (Oxford: Basil Blackwell, 1985).

and the rules of evidence refined, confessions were less important. But for "political crime," procedures of an unacknowledged state "necessity" begin to emerge instead from the late nineteenth century and into the twentieth, instruments of a vastly amplified state power, with no judicial review or supervision.

THE Tsar published his ban in the *Ukaz* of 27 September 1801, decreeing that "finally the very name of torture, bringing shame and reproach on mankind, should be forever erased from the human memory." Even though technically abolished and effectively reduced, torture did not disappear entirely in Russia or elsewhere, particularly in the climate of political dissent and repression which followed at the end of that century and the beginning of the next; there was still Siberia and interrogation by the *Okhrana* or political police. The Russian revolutionaries could remember their own torture before 1917. Nevertheless, by the 1920s Lenin had already restored torture both in interrogation and treatment, and had begun to populate the places of suffering with political prisoners.

The abolition of torture in one area, criminality, was a triumph for reform and the rights of the individual against the state, but its reappearance in another area, political dissent and subversion, is a greater triumph for state power over individual rights. Curbed in one place, the force of the state contracted only briefly, then expanded into another arena with greater violence, brutality, and oppressive might: the suspected criminals tortured had been few in number; the number of "political enemies" was and is vast and endless. The offenses alleged against criminals were against a nearly universal social and moral code and the rule of law, through real and specific acts, capable of evidence and proof. The offenses of the politicals were far more theoretical, abstract, ideological, or heretical, sometimes even imaginary insults to power rather than to fellow citizen or moral principle. In this they resemble the uses to which the Inquisition in the twelfth century had, after many centuries of relative forbearance, reappropriated ancient Roman law's practices of torture. When the Inquisition ended, torture was reduced again to the torture of criminal suspects. When this too was eliminated, the use of torture was transformed in the fields of political control, where it has spread and proliferated.

THERE was one great difference in the modern practice of torture: those who practiced it kept it secret. Not only was torture covert, it was still generally and expressly forbidden. This remains central to its practice today. Stalin and Hitler, building upon Lenin's model of total state power and its demands for security and surveillance, created a system that lives on in many parts of the world. Imitated by colonial powers and Western democracies as well, honed by technological advances, this system of rule is most notable in Central and South America, Iran, and South Africa, but Amnesty International locates its practices in parts of Africa, Asia, Eastern Europe, and the Middle East as well. In 1985, Peters estimated that one out of three countries practiced torture; the figure may now be higher.

States which practice torture also resort to legal fictions and conveniences, the by now customary "emergency" statutes, which suspend constitutional rights, including the writ of habeas corpus, and facilitate arrest, detention, and interrogation, circumstances created for the practice of torture. Yet torture itself remains forbidden, therefore secret, therefore more powerful still.

Torture is the ultimate act of state power. In arrogating to itself the capacity to torture its citizens, the state has assumed absolute power over them. If, in addition to its other powers over the person—arrest, confinement, trial process, judgment, and sentence—it adds torture as well, it annihilates. Because torture cannot be withstood. It was for this reason, perhaps above all others, that the reforming spirit of the Enlightenment and the movement for the rights of man outlawed torture categorically.

Its reinstitution therefore is a return to absolute power, cancelling the most fundamental reforms of the last two hundred years and threatening a world movement toward human rights and democratic governmental forms. Witnessing the return of torture in our time, we witness not only widespread suffering under barbarous force, but the overturning of hundreds of years of social and political development. Circumstances not only for pity but for terror.

PART ONE

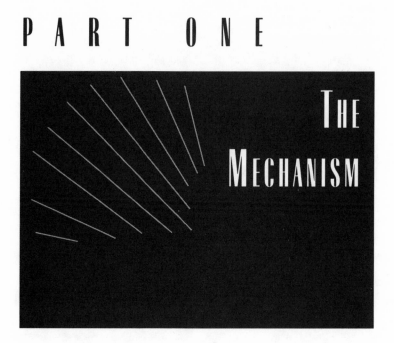

THE
MECHANISM

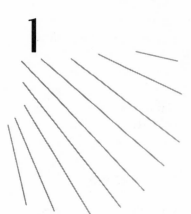

SOLZHENITSYN AND THE CREATION OF THE GULAG

THE moment of capture. The moment Volodin is seized. The moment time stands still and the world is unmade, the moment of arrest and disappearance, the moment of the rabbit hole, falling through space into the land beyond the mirror; that turning point, that pivotal electronic second. After which nothing is ever the same: after it everything is backwards, alien, hateful, futile.

And there is no going back. The moment one falls from grace. Grace being ordinary life, the humdrum of everyday. Mere citizenship. Life being so uncertain now, so without the guarantees we have grown accustomed to, the banal everyday civil conditions we have enjoyed over centuries. Forms of life which in retrospect now appear miraculous. Everything one took for granted, was bored with, content with, had always known. The familiar selfhood and security one had been enveloped by since childhood and still found the most authentic state of mind even after certain contradictions had entered one's life, a sense of another identity, a new consciousness at variance with things as they are, which in itself constitutes a certain risk. Of course there are those who are seized in their perfect innocence, their absolute ignorance of deviation like a fresh and naked skin about them perfecting their vulnerability. But Volodin had made a phone call.

Just that. One phone call. He'd even botched it, been so annoyed when he couldn't reach his party, was so frustrated by the woman who answered the phone that he forgot to continue to disguise his voice, spoke loudly and clearly. State Counselor Second Rank Innokenty Volodin, whose position within the diplomatic service was equivalent to a lieutenant colonel in the army, a privileged young man, even a glamorous one: "tall and narrowly built," as Solzhenitsyn describes him in *The First Circle*,* entitled to wear a gorgeous uniform with gold braid and shoulder boards. This evening, Volodin is dressed like the cosmopolitan bourgeoisie he aspires to be. Looking forward to his next assignment in Paris, he wears a well-cut worsted suit and looks "more like a young gentleman of leisure than an executive in the ministry of Foreign Affairs."

Unfortunately, there is one unpleasant thing on his mind, an obligation that is ruining his peace. He has just heard something disturbing about the eminent physician Professor Dobroumov—Dobroumov, who attended Volodin's mother during his childhood and was invariably kind to him during his visits: "On his way out he never passed the boy without asking him a question and he would stop to listen to the reply as if he seriously expected to hear something intelligent." Now Dobroumov is under suspicion for an act of generosity in promising to share his discovery of a new medicine with colleagues in France. "How, indeed, could anyone condemn what Dobroumov had promised? It showed the generosity of a talented man. Talent is always conscious of its own abundance and

---

*The extracts that follow are taken from Aleksandr I. Solzhenitsyn, *The First Circle*, translated by Thomas P. Whitney (New York: Bantam Books, 1976).

does not object to sharing." Volodin understands the man's motives, appreciates his goodness. But in his position such understanding is aside from the point. There are papers on Volodin's desk that indict Dobroumov as an enemy of the state: Volodin is its functionary.

"If all this had involved some other professor of medicine whom he didn't know personally, Innokenty would never have thought twice about trying to warn him. But Dobroumov!" All the impulses of family, good nature, old times. Volodin is an easygoing young man, his wife is the daughter of a general; in an age of bureaucrats and apparatchiks, he has somehow retained the character, possibly even the virtues of an aristocrat. One does not advance one's career by agonizing alone in an office over the fate of an old man about to be put on trial. Should Volodin telephone or not? "He leaned against the safe; his head drooped, and he rested there with his eyes closed." How much better if he had never known, if he had never learned of it.

THEN Volodin makes the mistake of his life: "It was more logical to wait. It was more reasonable to wait"—to put it all off, to ignore what he has so unwillingly, so accidentally come to know—instead, he falls into the temptation of what may be the one noble act of his career. "In the past few moments Innokenty felt a calm descending on him; he clearly realized that he had no other choice. It might be dangerous, but if he didn't do it. . . . If one is forever cautious, can one remain a human being?" Without calling the garage for his car, without even closing his inkwell, he goes out into the street, into the vibrant early evening of the city: "The Arbat was already lit up. Lines of customers in front of the cinema were waiting to see *The Love of a Ballerina.* The red letter 'M' on the metro was almost hidden by the gray mist. A gypsy-like woman was selling sprigs of yellow mimosa."

In saving his soul, Volodin has sealed his fate. Yet he had every reason to believe he was safe. Of course Dobroumov's telephone might be, probably would be tapped now, but in calling from an anonymous phone booth, Volodin is sure he cannot be caught; technology has not gone this far. The state cannot locate a single voice speaking for a moment; that is beyond power, that is magic.

"Could there possibly be a way of identifying a person speaking over a public telephone—if one wasted no time and hung up and left quickly? Could they recognize a voice over the phone? Surely there was no technique for that." Everything will revolve around this proposition. For in another world such a device is hurriedly being invented. Innokenty the "innocent" cannot know this. Nor can he predict that after going to the trouble of leaving his office, taking a cab, finding that he has just the right change in his pocket (a good omen), and selecting a discreet phone box where his back will be to the wall and he can see all around him through the glass—he would be unable to speak to the professor.

All because of this meddlesome woman who has answered the phone. Is she Dobroumov's wife? She won't even answer this question; instead, she demands to know who he is. An answer he dare not give. Infuriating. She will not call Dobroumov to the phone. Volodin, standing in a phone booth, his elegant "French-style" shoes full of snow, begins to plead excitedly: "Listen to me! Listen! I have to warn him about a danger!" This only makes her more obdurate—how can she be sure he's telling the truth?

The floor was burning beneath Innokenty's feet, and the black receiver on its heavy steel chain was swimming in his hand. "Listen to me, listen!" he cried in desperation. "When the professor was in Paris on his recent trip, he promised his French colleagues he would give them something! Some kind of medicine. And he's supposed to give it to them in a few days. To foreigners! Do you understand! He must not do it! He must not give the foreigners anything! It could be used as a provoca—"

"But—" There was a dull click and then total silence, without the usual buzzing or ringing on the line.

Someone had broken the connection.

The First Circle is about the power and effect of state paranoia on human society, the accumulated effect of decades of fear and suspicion and denunciation. The book moves between two poles of cause and effect: Stalin, Abakumov, and all the functionaries, guards, and paraphernalia of "state security"— and its victims, the political prisoners throughout the vast area of secret prison labor camps which Solzhenitsyn calls the "archipelago" of Gulag (after the Russian acronym for Chief Administration of Corrective Labor Camps), an area in itself the size of France. Another country, paradoxically both secret and mysterious on the one hand, and an ever present warning on the other; something hidden which nevertheless haunts, controls, and pervades "ordinary" life elsewhere.

Mavrino, the camp where the technology of the voice print is being developed whereby Volodin will be convicted for his phone call, is of a particular type, known as a *Sharashka,* or fraud, since by ordinary Gulag standards its conditions are nearly human and therefore luxurious, its prisoners are engineers, and their forced labor is the creation of technical devices for state espionage. Such devices will entrap more citizens into the Gulag and continue the supply of forced labor, a circular production of supply and demand through which the state ensures the possibility of its vast building enterprises and maintains its absolute authority.

Technology is of the essence. It is what distinguishes modern from earlier despotic conditions. Technology completes, even perfects the powers assumed by government, brings them toward an omnipotence previously imagined only in connection with the deity. The state now aspires to the condition of divine power, as its citizens, every day more subject, are inspired to fear and accept it with the unquestioning awe they once felt for God.

Omnipresent, God hears everything. How can this be translated into technological surveillance? The telephone is not without possibilities—given the power inherent in the control of transportation, information, and communications. Telephone records can be made available to the state that list all numbers called in or out, combined with the capacity to tap or listen in and record telephone conversations. If one were to add to this a means of identifying voices scientifically, as is the case with fingerprints, then powers of surveillance and therefore power itself would be much increased.

The idea has a fictive quality at first: I remember experiencing an uneasy doubt about the feasibility of such a device when I first read the book twenty years ago, but voice prints are commonplace now.

THE telephone is central to Volodin's undoing. He is very deliberately recorded over it a second time, and then a third, in order that the full range of his voice pattern be established for comparison with the original forbidden phone call. His superior calls him at home, finds him just about to leave for an operetta with his charming wife Dotnara, and assures him that all is arranged for his trip to Paris, ordering him to come at once to receive his diplomatic instructions. It does spoil the early part of the evening, it does mean changing quickly into full uniform, but Volodin's appearance at the ministry should not take long; he promises to give Dotnara a ring from there and meet her at the theatre for the second act. And it is such good news altogether that Volodin is overjoyed. In particular, the general's benevolence, his genial manner on the telephone is assurance that Volodin has not been discovered; the tension and fear which have enveloped him ever since that moment two days ago when the connection was broken dissipate into euphoria.

The phone call, like all that follows about the car and driver sent for him, has the character of playful sadism. The general's manner reassures Volodin and prevents him from suspecting himself in danger. Just as the delightfully witty character of this new driver, someone who has never driven him before, disarms him entirely.

The weekend has been hell for him, he has lived in a fever of anxiety over discovery. Now he is so happy that he scarcely pays attention, is slow to understand the driver's pleasantries; everything is all right now, his assignment is approved. When the car stops to pick up a stranger whom the driver claims is a mechanic from his own car pool who needs a lift—"He's my boss. I'm in a spot"—Volodin is magnanimous and opens his own door for him (the front door across from the driver seems to be stuck), his mind rushing toward Paris, the operetta's second act. Only the "mechanic's" cigarette offends Volodin; only the fact that the fellow has so little regard for his rank and presence as to blow smoke right in his face—only that might have tipped him off. But it fails. The ruse by which Volodin is trapped is so perfect in its deceit that only when the "mechanic" turns on a flashlight and presents a warrant for the arrest of one Volodin, Innokenty Artemyevich, "only then was he pierced by a single long needle the entire length of his body."

It has not occurred to Volodin to flee: "The idea of living under a false name, of running from hiding place to hiding place all over the country was unthinkable. It would not occur to him to try to avoid arrest, if his arrest was ordered." Different as he is from Ruska—a young man who in a few hours will be transported from the Sharashka to the labor camp at Vorkuta, where he will die of the cold even though he has managed to exist by forged passports and papers since he was sixteen and survived for two years on the All Union wanted list— Volodin is nevertheless like most of us.

He is different as well; he is a participant in the system about to crush him, and as a functionary of the regime he knows what he is in for, knows he will not be lucky enough even to see camp. As the car circles Lubyanka Square, it is to give Volodin one last glimpse "not only of the world he was leaving but also of the Old and New Lubyankas, five stories high, where he was to end his life." Though Stalin has officially abolished capital punishment, Volodin will be shot in secret somewhere in this great and terrible prison. Reading Epicurus in preparation, he has already discovered there are deaths for which philosophy does not prepare one, realizing what he fears is "not just death, but that they would torture him."

TORTURE makes all the difference. To be arrested knowing you will be tortured is to know absolute helplessness before absolute power. That situation is our subject. This is government through fear, even terror: state terrorism, which is to say the activity of respected and recognized authority. Not the activities of a few desperate individuals, but the collective force of the state, with all its attendant powers of police, army, weaponry, prisons; its resources in personnel and machinery, its control over roads, airports, borders, its technology in surveillance, its functionaries trained in deception and cruelty and indemnified in their functions. Vast, fearsome power.

Even before his arrest, Volodin knew there was much to fear. But fear has so many layers, level upon level from the conceptual to the physical; as knowing is so many kinds of knowing, as contemplation differs from experience. The mind may discern at a distance; the bowels react in proximity. To be the one captured, that cornered animal. To hear the door close, to understand in final and perfect understanding, that one is enclosed in a "box," the famous Lubyanka box, too small to lie down in, lighted for all its diminutiveness by an enormous 200-watt bulb, the box itself like an over-illuminated casket, compelling claustrophobia and the knowledge—physical, material knowledge—that you will never be released from this box, unless "they" release you. Together with this, the realization that you could be there forever. If such were their pleasure. That of your own effort you can do nothing whatsoever, that you are helpless in a way that you have never been helpless before. Caged like an animal, reduced to a condition humanity imposes at will upon the animal world; you had never noticed it before, never objected, rarely pitied even. And now you are this.

And the animal within you, the final self, the basic kernel at the center of being, panics. Its faultless perception comprehends that this could be eternal. All objective conditions make it so: the steel door, the stone walls, the cement floor, all substances too obdurate for the human body's petty strength, the flesh unarmed, naked against these forces, fingers, teeth— you have no claws, nor would they be of use. You have entered the animal condition, or, more precisely, one lower down, you have become an object, a thing in a box. Inanimate except for the terrible whir of consciousness, itself nothing but suffering.

The great weapon of the mind is betrayed by the mechanism of the lock, conceived by another mind, executed by other hands, produced by machinery which is the function of both. A lock is a riddle solved only by a key. Which can operate only from the other side of the steel door, not your side. A key in other hands, not yours. Theirs.

Volition is gone entirely, will is useless. You are a creature now, their creature. And they are free to torment you. Any way they wish. They can now inflict any pain or deprivation upon you, and for any reason: amusement, boredom, habit, even simple routine, the routine by which you will be broken, piece by piece.

You will do exactly as they say; not only will you have no option to do otherwise, you will do it willingly, trembling, hoping to appease, propitiate, avoid further hurt and humiliation. Cowed animal that you are, you appreciate that defiance is useless, pride something you must save for yourself, conscious of it leaking away before the reality of your predicament as your comprehension of it builds moment to moment. You will hold up your finger just at the instant the eye appears in the judas glass, signalling your mortified need to urinate, defecate. But even the hope of not befouling your box with your own filth, even that possibility is their decision, not yours, a "privilege" granted at their whim.

SURELY arrest and confinement itself, capture, can be a form of torture. For torture is so many things, psychic as well as physical. Strictly speaking, even the most benign and "civilized" conditions of incarceration—for example, a toilet in one's cell and privacy to use it—do not offset that cancellation of the will which incarceration represents: the freedom to come and go, to enter into nature, to see whom one pleases. Many circumstances, even many occupations, limit us thus; unfreedom too has layers, levels.

But Volodin's captivity is absolute. The conditions of the box, concrete as they are, are also symbolic, metaphorical, prophetic. His instruction comes to him by degrees, beginning with the trip to the toilet, the guard clicking his tongue in the traditional Lubyanka code that a prisoner is being escorted who must not see or have any contact with any other prisoner. Across Moscow at the Butyrki Prison, the guards snap their fingers. What is imperative is that the one newly detained be isolated and alone before the powers of the state, feel himself the only victim, smaller with each second of his new pariah condition. Then back to the box, to this utter impotence, enclosure: to know all this in the flesh, Volodin learning, knowledge descending moment by moment. His education continues through the procedure of the searches, the ceremonial inspection of his body cavities, nostrils, ears, the planned mortification of anal examination, the absurd dissection of the lasts and heels of his shoes. The cruel comedy of being without shoelaces, suspenders. The gold buttons of his jacket, the few that are left to him as his shoulder boards and insignia are torn away (honors, after all: service, nation, culture, profession), are finally just buttons. And he needs them.

As he needs sleep. Which is forbidden. The eye in the judas sees him curled upon the little floor and the jailer is quick to demand he rise. Time after time through the night. Sleep deprivation is in fact the favorite method of torture in this regime; Volodin will come to know it well enough during his interrogation. If they let him last that long. Many in the Sharashka have undergone six months of interrogation, some even two years. Three days of sleep deprivation is standard procedure; beginning in the Gulag, it has spread around the world. Though it is enormous suffering, depletes the body and can be a contributing cause to death, it leaves no marks, an ancient qualification for efficiency and secrecy in torture. Electric light functions this way too, merciless lights which incapacitate the eyes, prevent sleep, and dwarf the will of the frightened face before them, the patient interrogator merely waiting until the body betrays the will.

THE body in pain, in fear, in torment. Helpless, unable to sustain the demands of the mind, the loves or convictions of the heart, the certainty of the soul before all that it opposes, despises, has often spent a lifetime struggling against. And now slowly accedes to, surrenders before. Conquered. Because finally, ultimately, and at last it is simply overwhelmed. And those who never surrender—and for all its invincibility, there are some who endure torture—may die. Death or capitulation. It is only a matter of time. Determined victims produce still more determined torturers; a battle of wills between absolute power and absolute powerlessness is a foregone conclusion. One might argue sensibly that resistance is unnecessary suffering, even folly. In recent years the general practice in organized dissent and opposition groups has rejected the heroism of martyrdom; trained individuals try to hold out only a specified time, twenty-four hours perhaps, time enough for comrades to be warned and take cover.

We all die, of course, but it is a matter of how we die. Torture changes all this, makes dignity virtually impossible. Very much in the same way it distorts truth in testimony, it deprives the victim of his own truth, undoes the self, coerces it toward its own betrayal. Innokenty Volodin understood this even before his arrest. Consulting his favorite philosopher, Volodin foresees torture and shudders—if he only had that strength: "But he did not find it in himself." It is very rare indeed, scarcely to be expected of humanity: Epicurus' claim that one can overcome torture seems fatuous today, superhuman. Many captives die in captivity, but few persevere long enough to die of torture itself. A pyrrhic victory, but it does hold out the triumph of release, even transcendence. Rare, a miracle of courage.

The authorities generally win; it is not a game, after all, nor can it be mistaken for a contest, where one party has every resource in force and numbers and time and the other party has nothing but willpower. In contemporary procedure captives are routinely threatened with death, the revolver put to the head theatrically, the noose arranged in the usual plausible farce; but death itself, if it comes, is customarily only the execution of a husk already broken, exulted over, defiled.

This, after all, is the intention; it would be unusual that the party with every resource should fail in the end or with frequency. Torture is conquest through irresistible force. It is to destroy opposition through causing it to destroy itself: in despair, in self-hatred for its own vulnerability, impotence. It is to defile, degrade, overwhelm with shame, to ravage. In this it resembles rape. And the tortured come to experience not only the condition of the animal caged by man, but the predicament of woman before man as well. A thing male prisoners discover, a thing female prisoners rediscover. Torture is based upon traditional ideas of domination: patriarchal order and masculine rank. The sexual is invoked to emphasize the power of the tormenter, the vulnerability of the victim; sexuality itself is confined inside an ancient apprehension and repression: shame, sin, weakness. The victim tortured sexually is tortured twice as it were, first by being deliberately harmed, second by being harmed in a way regarded as the most humiliating of all humiliations.

TORTURE is all hierarchy intensified, magnified, brought back to its archetypal and most brutal level, the archaic pairing of master and slave. Anachronistic, oversimplified, all gradation, nuance, and shade proscribed. It is to create categories essentially artificial and fraudulent; ahistorical in this time, even if created through the medium of technology, bureaucracy, up-to-the-minute gadgetry. Not only atavistic and throwback but the product of costumerie. Cheap dramatization, sordid enaction, posturing; the torturer permitted to release and enact the most ephemeral fantasy, to do the unthinkable. Things imagined, dreamed of, joked about, acts that exist only in language or fantasy. All that does not, must not, cannot take place. The putative world, the shadow place, acts merely contemplated, notions so insubstantial as to be dismissed, pictures that float through the mind, glimpses of rage or evil only guessed at, intuited; the spectral and illusionary.

Grounded only in the scream of his victim, for whom it is all real. Only this reaction could convince the one who commits the cruelty that it is actual, does not exist merely in the realm of the anticipated, but is in fact material, is taking place. And as that unheard-of permission is granted by the state—enjoined in fact, indoctrinated, commissioned—the sensibility of the torturer is unleashed. Whatever it be, whether subtle or simple viciousness. Refined, educated, sensual, ascetic, angry, satisfied. Or gross, ignorant, repressed, vulgar, gleeful or furious. Nourished by the culture which sends him forth, primed on violence, steeped in hatreds, spurred on by extra pay, further privilege and prerequisites, additional indoctrination, specialized training.

Permission is crucial: to indulge fancy thus, without permission, is criminal and to be punished, a merely individual act, without meaning, self-indulgent, aberrant, and forbidden. But with permission it is patriotism, service, laudable activity, salaried, professionalized. Practiced upon "one's own," it would be insanity, treason, inhumanity. Everything depends upon permission. Which is the state. The torturer himself but an instrument, whether imagining he enjoys his work or is bored, even if disturbed or made uneasy by it. Yet what uses are made of his proclivity, ingenuity, gullibility, fidelity. Even his humor makes him of use, his own alienation gaily enlisting slang and euphemism: for example, "Yellow Submarine" as a term for shoving a prisoner's head into a toilet full of urine and feces to sicken or asphyxiate. The boyishness, the metaphoric wit, the childish fascination with excrement, the naughtiness, the transformation of activity into harmless language, the allusion to popular music, the Beatles, technicolor animation, the familiar and enjoyable.

Even art is enlisted, incorporated, like every other detail of quotidian existence. The South African writer Molefe Pheto, whose account of his own torture, *And Night Fell,** describes interrogation where he is forced to stand day after day, beaten savagely by the police every few moments, in an office where a reproduction of Van Gogh's *Sunflowers* hangs upon the wall before him, the painting itself finally assuming a part in his torment. The art of music is now routinely conscripted into the process; recorded music on tape or radio is played full blast as a cover to prevent discovery in suburban places of detention, to drown out cries, supplications, its volume operating simul-

*Molefe Pheto *And Night Fell. Memoirs of Political Imprisonment in South Africa* (London: William Heinemann, 1983).

taneously to galvanize the tormentors, to heighten their experience.

An Argentinean painter, a woman, abducted to a cottage in the countryside, blindfolded, told me how she recognized the sounds of a summer evening in the pauses between the sets of rock music as she was raped and beaten repeatedly by a houseful of men. She remembered the smell of barbecued meat all through the evening, the sound of the ice in their highball glasses, the odor of rum.

It is this inclusion of things from one's former world— friendly, recognizable things like rum or food cooked out of doors—which heightens brutality, gives it a further surreal quality. The plausible and familiar, appearing under these circumstances, introduce a discord of values which brings everything into question. What was malign seems also to be lunatic; cruelty has now yet another dimension of disorder. The purpose and intended use of music or painting has been subverted, traduced, appropriated.

Yet certain objects by their very frailty and triviality seem to resist this metamorphosis: when Volodin panics inside his box, pounds on the door, and begs for water, he is handed a green enamel cup with a curious decoration on it: "a cat wearing glasses pretended to be reading a book, but out of the corner of its eye it was watching a little bird hopping boldly near it." The cup is an unlikely choice for a purchasing officer to make on behalf of the inner prison of the M.G.B. of the USSR. Nor is it an accident, some guard's own private coffee cup; there is another such cup in the next cell that Volodin is given. "The decoration had, of course, not been chosen intentionally for the Lubyanka. But how appropriate! The little book was the written law, and the tiny swaggering sparrow was Innokenty—yesterday." The notion causes Volodin to smile, "and suddenly his own wry smile made him realize the whole abysmal catastrophe. Yet his smile also held a strange kind of joy—the joy of feeling a throb of life inside himself. He would never have believed that anyone could smile during his first half-hour in the Lubyanka."

As one procedure follows another, transforming the individual at liberty into the creature under absolute control, Volodin is fingerprinted; successful technology put in the service of state control. What progress has been made in recordkeeping since the time when Louis XIV could declare his absolute authority, "L'Etat, c'est moi," while not even knowing the names or the numbers of his subjects. Technology, particularly the technology of photography, has changed all that: the Polaroid facial photograph of identity cards, numeration and copying processes, even the tiny whorls on human fingertips, each little photographed line in the pattern declaring the ownership of the state over the being owned. At the top of the card of prints, in heavy black type, Volodin sees the words KEEP FOREVER: "crushing, cosmic words"; there is "something mystical about them, something superhuman, supernatural."

Each new piece of recordkeeping re-contributes to state control: birth certificates, driver's licenses, Social Security numbers—presumably reasonable and necessary innovations, harmless in their stated intentions, yet capable of other uses by the state, over time tolerated and habitual, but so unprotected as information that their subversion is finally unquestioned. Add to this informational reach the plethora of available civilian documentation of school, service, work, credit, bank, and hospital files, each item augmenting the power of locating, knowing about, and ultimately controlling persons. Then connect this network together with the electronic speed and memory capacity of recent computer recall and an internal surveillance is at command over vast populations, as well as the suspected few for whom more deliberate internal surveillance dossiers are kept.

Finally Volodin has been processed and can be moved from the induction section of the prison fortress to the main body of cells. It is then that he notices the steps of the Lubyanka: "He had seen nothing like it in his life. They were worn in oval hollows half a step deep, from the sides to the center. He shuddered. In thirty years how many feet must have shuffled here to wear down stone that way! And of every two people who passes, one was a guard and the other a prisoner."

THE worn steps of the Lubyanka. Crossed by a file of millions, this long, desolate procession since the beginning. In chronicling the Gulag from 1918 to 1956, Solzhenitsyn puts the total of those affected, including the kulak "resettlements," in the range of 10 million persons. The revolution took place in October; by November, the Cadets or Constitutional Democrats were already being rounded up. By December, there was a secret police (NKVD) in place; malingerers and intellectual saboteurs were being denounced. Extra-judicial reprisals were being carried out by the secret police, renamed the Cheka, combining arrest, interrogation, prosecution, verdict, and execution all within their own ranks and in secrecy. Through 1918 and 1919 the Right Socialist Revolutionary Party, the Social Democrats, the Mensheviks, and the Popular Socialists and all other political opposition, rivalry, and dissent were eliminated. Where actual resistance appeared, it was quashed: the Tambov peasants' rebellion, the Kronstadt sailors' uprising. Concealment of former social origins was cause for arrest among the middle and upper classes, the concept of preventative detention introduced as a kind of social prophylaxis. Then came the invention of plots, whereby other sectors of the population (the church, the military, the intellectuals) were brought into line through the persecution of scapegoats under the Central Committee's 1920 Decree Against Subversive Activity in the Rear. It was discovered in 1927 that the entire sector of engineers were actually "wreckers" plotting destruction; the trial of the Promparty and the pattern of large public trials and confessions produced by terror and torture followed.

By the late twenties, Stalin inherited this system of state terror only to improve and enlarge it. His first operation on a great scale was against the kulak or "well-off" peasant population, uprooting some 6 million, confiscating their land, transporting them in cattle cars, sending them to concentration camps to swell the ranks of slave labor achieving his vast building projects and canal systems. Or simply murdering them, setting a precedent of genocide for Germany to follow later with more elaborate system. All along, dissent or nonconformity of any kind was funneled into the Gulag, together with any individual who refused when asked to become an informer.

The result was a strange new ideological society living under fear and coercion, manipulated into policing itself, all modern constitutional safeguards long abandoned and the judicial process thoroughly suborned. Control established, it could only be improved upon and assured with exemplary purges: Leningrad was purged in 1937, the purge affecting every layer of the population and producing mass executions, one mass grave alone holding 46,000 bodies. Stalinist consolidation was crowned with the Moscow purge trials of 1937 and 1938. Interrogation rose to great heights then, theatrical confessions in court, absolute mortification urged upon the once powerful and significant figures of the revolution itself—Bukharin and the others—as one by one they accused themselves of crimes they could not possibly have committed.

The revolution had now become counterrevolution; it remained only to police the system and continue to supply it, even with fantasy, with paranoia of the West, uncovering subversion everywhere, often with farcical effect. But the principle was now firmly established that any dissent or even disagreement was treason, that treason was any offense against state power, state power having replaced the ideology of revolution. Furthermore, there was to be no distinction between intention and act. All this could be codified into law under the infamous

Article 58 of the Soviet Criminal Code.* Section 6 regarding espionage then created an apartheid of official secrecy and public ignorance that would become a model in many other places under the same rubric of "national security." It also introduced a potent xenophobia whereby contact with or interest in any outside place was in effect criminal. The labels of "terrorist" and "terrorist interests" were given their first blanket use, terms of great convenience, now worldwide.

The primacy of state power was given awesome dimension. While Stalin's own personal obsession, it was nevertheless also an impersonal principle that any system might apply. Most of all, Article 58 triumphed through Section 10 on propaganda and agitation, directed against any activity that sought to question or challenge state power. This could include any literary material, published or private communications, even conversations; any free speech was annihilated by this portmanteau device. Pervasive and invasive, it empowered the state to practice an untiring domestic espionage against citizens, gave rise to eavesdropping, informing, and denunciations. It permitted no private life or opinion, could cover words spoken between friends, even husband and wife. It could also censor personal letters: Solzhenitsyn's arrest and eleven years of imprisonment and exile were in punishment for a few sarcastic references to Stalin, whom he and a college friend referred to discreetly as "the Ploughman" in an exchange of letters while they were serving on the Russian front.

VOLODIN has reasons for apprehension: by the time he is arrested, an apparatus has been put in place that will assure his doom. He understands how an innocent act will be interpreted as crime, that he will have no trial, no legal defender, no bail.

---

*This is Lenin's Criminal Code of 1923 and 1926, in force under Stalin and until its repeal in 1958.

That there is no presumption of innocence, that arrest is tantamount to conviction. That the sentence, should there even be one, would be outlandish, ten years of hard labor or, more likely, twenty followed by five more of interior exile in Siberia. He is aware that a sentence to hard labor under Gulag conditions would kill him. But he knows he will never see court, will see no face past his interrogator's, his executioner's. He knows that he will be helpless, find only injustice and despair, knows that he must endure now as one alone in terror. Not an Epicurean but a Stoic. He knows that he is powerless in the hands of a merciless power who has thought of everything.

He knows that before he dies, he will be tortured. All of the above depends on this, torture. The last and greatest abuse, the very heart of it. But before torture can create absolute power, there must be the precondition of torture, that concentration of state power which makes torture—however illegal or secretive—possible. And through torture a final and absolute power is arrived at. If solitary confinement and enclosure in a box where one cannot lie down, if sleeplessness for the customary number of days which accompany the beginning of interrogation do not remain as marks upon the body—they are torture nonetheless. So too is the presumption of guilt; so too is a sentence of twenty-five years for a phone call, an act of mercy interpreted as treason. Whether Volodin will have his hand broken in a vise, be threatened constantly by revolvers against his temples, or be tied neck and feet in an arc and left suspended for days—it is all torture of one kind or another. There is no clear distinction between physical, psychological, and judicial torment.

Each is its own expression of power, interrelated in the world behind the mirror of legality, the secret state mechanisms controlling individual life from the other side of society's official logic and order. The normal world at the surface, the world from which Volodin has fallen, is only a trick reflection finally, barely disguising the real state of affairs. For one in his position there were a great many such warnings, warnings which Volodin had ignored in his once carefree urge to live and enjoy, to find other correlatives in love or travel, even in another system of thought. Private life.

Now he has fallen through the glass, a hand has reached out and grabbed him, suddenly vulnerable through magnanimity, his single gesture of depositing a kopek and dialing a phone. The grip that holds him now is all-powerful by virtue of locks and bars, transport trains and camps, the interrogator who awaits him. Its clasp will wring from him his every accomplice, though he has none.

In fact, the authorities, Stalin and Abakumov, were far-seeing when they began the case of Professor Dobroumov. Thousands of doctors would be implicated, and Abakumov is furious that Volodin has defused this first accusation: it was intended that Dobroumov would not be arrested until his return from France helped to convict him. The old man's conviction would lead to that of others, many others; interrogation would see to that. They had a big haul in mind.

From doing good, Volodin and other victims will, through the power of torture—all the tortures that lie before them and fear of torture itself—come to do evil, to name names. Those of the innocent. Innocent of everything. Finally, in their torment, innocence will not matter to them, their own or that of anyone they are forced or enabled to implicate through lies. Truth itself will not matter, just as it has never mattered to the interrogator working for quotas, since lies are the product of torture. There will be more arrests because there must be more arrests. The system feeds on this and it is never full.

2

THE NAZI CAMP SYSTEM

SOLZHENITSYN ends *The First Circle* with a view of a panel truck carrying prisoners off to transport trains and on to their probable deaths in labor camp. One watches as this vehicle maneuvers through Moscow traffic: "tossing about its cargo of crowded bodies, the gay orange and blue van moved through the city streets, passed a railroad station and stopped at an intersection. A shiny maroon automobile was waiting for the same red light to change. In it rode the correspondent of the progressive French paper *Libération* who was on his way to a hockey match at the Dynamo Stadium."

On one side of the van the word "MEAT" is inscribed in four languages, on the other side the word "BREAD." Solzhenitsyn comments ironically on this trick of appearance: "After the war, the idea of building Black Maria's exactly like grocery vans had been born in some genius' mind, and they were painted the same orange and light blue." The correspondent recalls that he had seen a number of such vans around Moscow and makes a note: "On the streets of Moscow one often sees vans filled with foodstuffs, very neat and hygienically impeccable. One can only conclude that the provisioning of the capital is excellent."

To practice torture on a wide scale, the state must first create the preconditions of torture through achieving nearly absolute control. To control people, one first controls ideas and ideology. When these are mastered, one comes finally to the control of things: objects reflect that control, embody and facilitate it. It must be reflected in systems, for example, the entire network of mechanical transport, both rail and truck. Organization is developed, method, process. What one state apparatus develops, another inherits and builds upon.

The victims of Nazi genocide arrived at the scene of their death on special trains whose schedules are still available to us; they were not even labeled "secret" at the time. Operating as a separate entity, German railway delivered for the SS, according to group rate terms which rail practices made available for holiday or excursion trips—when possible. There was a special refinement of process and economy here. As the historian Raul Hilberg explains in the published text of Claude Lanzmann's documentary film *Shoah:** "You have to remember one basic principle. There was no budget for destruction. So that is the reason confiscated property had to be used in order to make the payments." Those about to die were made to finance their own one-way tickets at the lowest possible excursion fare.

Of course ordinary citizens travelling in groups on a holiday did not ride in cattle cars to their extermination. Still less did they finance their own deaths through the confiscation of their property. But the administrative procedure for routing trains and ticketing passengers billing was handled in the same manner and by the same official travel agency: "Mittel Europäisch Reisebüro would ship people to the gas chambers or they will ship vacationers to their favorite resort, and that was basically

---

*The extracts that follow are taken from Claude Lanzmann, *Shoah, An Oral History of the Holocaust and the Complete Text of the Film* (New York: Pantheon, 1985).

the same office and the same operation, the same procedure, the same billing." Hilberg is examining Fahrplananordnung 587, a historical "artifact," "something which the original bureaucrat held in his hand." The document tells a great deal. It is a rail schedule for fifty freight cars filled with people. It spends five hours unloading at Treblinka, returning empty to another neighboring small town where it picks up new victims, leaves for Treblinka again, repeats the run again, and so on until, conservatively estimated, it has delivered ten thousand Jews to the gas chambers between September 13 and September 29, 1942. There might be additional charges: trains had to be cleaned because transports for most runs took many days, during which prisoners were systematically deprived of water or food or warmth so that great numbers of them died en route. Those who did arrive still living would be weak, confused, and easy to kill.

Fahrplananordnung 587 is one of the few pieces of physical evidence left to verify an entire historical event. One appreciates how cagey the Nazi regime was in committing its "total solution" to writing: one is forced to reconstruct events through clerical detail. Apart from what minutes exist of the Wannsee Conference on January 20, 1942, when Reinhard Heydrich announced to the assembled civil servants his appointment as plenipotentiary for the preparation of the final solution of the European Jewish question, or Hermann Göring's letter to Heydrich at the end of the previous July, the "total undertaking" was generally a matter of inference, euphemism, and innuendo, where a bland, colorless tone is adopted to describe what is unspeakable both in horror and in magnitude. Historians rely upon the official record, known procedures:

> The Reichsbahn was ready to ship in principle any cargo in return for payment. And therefore, the basic key—price-controlled key—was that Jews were going to be shipped to Treblinka . . . Auschwitz, Sobibor or any other destination so long as the railroads were paid by the track kilometer, so many pfennigs per mile.

The rate was the same throughout the war. With children under ten going at half-fare and children under four going free. Payment had to be made for only one way . . . the minimum was four hundred, a kind of charter fare . . . so even if there were under four hundred, it would pay to say there were four hundred and in that way get the half-fare for adults as well.

Since there was "no budget for destruction," the operation was made self-financing, and confiscated property had to be used to make the payments to the travel agency and the railroad, so that the victims themselves could be made to pay to reach their own deaths. However, with the forty-six thousand Jews of Salonika transported in the spring of 1943 there were confiscations as usual but difficulties arose in the exchange of drachmas for marks. For once there was a default, "and the railroad shipped all of these Jews to Auschwitz without compensation."

Fahrplananordnung 587 is marked *"Nur für den Dienstgebrauch"* ("For Internal Use Only"), but nowhere is the word *geheim,* "secret," marked on it. This is clever in one way, since secret documents invite curiosity. But in another way it remains astonishing. Hilberg emphasizes the sheer confidence of this, the bureaucratic formality with which government had learned to disguise atrocity: "the key to the entire operation from the psychological standpoint was never to utter the words that would be appropriate to the action being taken. Say nothing; do these things; do not describe them." It assumes a level of control that can count upon silence from travel agencies and railroads alike, a level of acquiescence, even agreement, truly remarkable.

But the denial of reality enters further into language: In a document labeled *"Geheim Reichssache"* ("Secret Reich Business") datemarked Berlin, June 5, 1942, a report directed to Walter Rauff of the SS, signed ironically with nothing but the single word "Just," it is reported with some satisfaction that since December 1, ninety-seven thousand victims at Chelmno have been processed *(verarbeitet)* by the three Saurer vans in service there. During the first or Castle Period at Chelmno, the killing was done not with the high technology of Zyklon gas crystals but in a primitive way: people were herded into a van, the doors shut upon them, a hose was brought from the exhaust of the van's own engine and fitted into a hole in the floor; victims were asphyxiated with simple carbon monoxide. As there were as yet no crematoria, the bodies were then transported in the van to the open countryside, dumped into ditches, and buried.

A few minor changes now suggest themselves. If the interior of the van were a bit smaller, the vehicle's stability would be improved. It would fill with gas more quickly, particularly if it were packed and loaded full with the same number of victims, here referred to as "pieces." "Operating time can be considerably shortened." Nor, as the manufacturer has tried to argue, is there any real danger of imbalance by diminishing the size of the van while packing it just as full. "Just" has observed the process and knows the nature of his cargo; what does Saurer know? Packed full during asphyxiation, "Just" knows exactly what happens inside the van: "the merchandise aboard displays during the operation a natural tendency to rush to the rear doors, and is mainly found lying there at the end of the operation. So the front axle is not overloaded."

This transformation of humanity into "pieces" and "merchandise" does not come about without considerable effort. It is necessary to create an ideology which will transcend customary law altogether and substitute for it a higher cause and greater necessity. Edward Peters describes the reintroduction of torture through political expediency: "In a number of states during the early twentieth century, the traditional separation of law and politics was sometimes abolished in the interest of stronger and more ruthless regimes," and in the name of a "magnified" idea of the state. The result was the emergence in our era of what Peters calls a "dual system of jurisprudence," whereby "normal" offenses and routine litigation have operated in ways that remain traditional, "however modified in form by the new philosophical principles of justice," while "certain categories of crime"—and there are a great many of them, any activity in fact that is "perceived" by the revolutionaries, the creators of either Communist or Fascist regimes to be "particularly sensitive"—have been created and set apart to be handled by "special tribunals according to novel procedures." The judicial system is forced to accommodate to changes in the political system so drastic that constitutional safeguards built up over centuries are cast aside and no longer operate on behalf of the individual. The individual is now at the mercy of the state to a degree he or she has not been for centuries; a state more powerful than ever before in history.

The Soviet state had instituted just such "novel" procedures, as did the Nazis, who also called their methods revolutionary. Political crime now took on a new meaning since the state chose to view its recent post-revolutionary existence as extraordinarily fragile and vulnerable to resistance of any kind. "Revolutionary necessity" could invest the state with extraordinary powers, which set older legal restraints aside. By virtue of the very theoretical and immaterial, delicate and ephemeral nature of its new ideology, the state now made greater claims than ever before to the realities of power. As the state became the ultimate good, force grew to be more and more expedient.

Mussolini himself describes this rationale in the *New Italian Encyclopedia* of 1932: "Man is nothing. Fascism raises itself up against the individual abstraction which is based upon materialistic foundations and utopias. Beyond the state, nothing that is human or spiritual has any value whatsoever." Under Italian fascism the state and nation were merged, and the state now proclaimed itself the agent of a larger and greater force, the people. It remained only to merge the state with the law.

There was resistance to such claims by the judiciary, as well as objections to the changes in legal procedure which followed in their train. But once in power, Fascist Party functionaries wielded extraordinary authority; after 1929, Peters observes, "the secret political police used torture regularly upon suspected enemies of state, party and people."

In Germany after 1932 this notion was carried even further: the German state became simply the vehicle of the Nazi Party, whose leader, Adolf Hitler, "personified" according to party literature the will of the people or *Volk*, itself construed as a national historical community. The party itself was unique in Hitler's view since political parties are generally inclined to compromise whereas "philosophical doctrines," such his own, never do so. "Political parties," Hitler declared scornfully, "arrive at agreement even with their enemies, philosophical doctrines proclaim themselves infallible." The National Socialist Party was not a political party at all in the conventional sense, but instead the active embodiment of an infallible "philosophy" of a people, the *Volk*, to which state and law were themselves both necessarily subordinated. Just as Lenin or Stalin, the Cheka or the Soviet public prosecutor, could divine both counterrevolutionary activity and the revolutionary path, in defining the will of the *Volk*, Hitler too could arrive at a mystical and absolute power.

The rhapsodic and subjective qualities of folk will and wisdom (*Volksgenosse* or *Volksgemeinschaft*) are transcendent; outside them, an individual has neither identity nor worth. One man alone may interpret them. This is an even more cloudy and personal matter than the correct interpretation of Marxism. Courts were now conducted around such criteria as *Volksgewissen*, "racial conscience," which had been introduced into the criminal law through the elevation of concepts like the "welfare of the people" and "healthy national sentiment." Such terms became official normative standards.

Peters traces the effect of this subordination of law to political ideology: "the judicial consequences of National Socialist theory and practice included the creation of special tribunals, the widening definition of political crimes, and the intensification of methods of interrogation and punishment." After 1933, special courts or *Sondergerichte* were set up for matters which the party regarded as too important to be left to the surviving judicial system, whose judges could not be trusted to find a politically acceptable verdict. The next year, the *Volksgerichtshof* was instituted to deal with cases of treason: panels of professional jurists were now augmented by party members of no legal experience. From this court there was no appeal, and "only rarely was any favor shown to the accused."

In 1942, Himmler issued an order authorizing the use of what he specified as "the Third Degree" in interrogations, in Peters's view "clearly intending by that term to indicate torture." The Third Degree was used to extract confessions from prisoners. Himmler gave a blanket permission for its use without further authorization against "communists, Marxists, Jehovah's Witnesses, saboteurs, terrorists, members of resistance movements, antisocial elements, refractory elements," and a group of unfortunates referred to as Polish or Soviet "vagabonds."

In the methods of the Third Degree lie the essential elements of all torture technique. Edward Peters and his predecessor, the great French legalist Alec Mellors,* designate this system as the basis for the modern practice of torture. It is as follows: close confinement, starvation diet, hidden cells, extraordinary exercise or labor, sleep deprivation, and beatings. Moreover, physicians were to be at hand to prevent prisoners from being killed under torture, that is, to preserve them for further interrogation. In this way the Third Reich not only brought back a systematic torture but transformed it into a medical specialty, a transformation which was to have great consequences throughout the second half of the twentieth century.

The practice of torture is assisted always by certain legal and legislative preconditions. Historians of Nazism and the Holocaust describe the creation of a web of legislation which, piece by piece, sealed the fate of the various "enemies" of the

*Alec Mellors, *La Torture* (Paris, 1949).

Third Reich, most particularly of the Jews. In many ways, as Hilberg, Martin Gilbert, and Lucy Dawidowicz, among others, point out, German practice only restored and intensified prejudicial law and custom that reached far back in European history. Now a groundwork of enabling legislation was carefully laid through strictures against Jews practicing the professions. Then they were forbidden to engage in one form after another of employment or business. Then came extortionary taxation. Next the Nürnberg laws on citizenship and racial purity, the punishments for intermarriage. Finally the apartheid of ghettos, finishing a network of legislation and directive of an increasingly malign character like the parts of a cruel machine. So that when the projects for "resettlement" through confinement in camps were put into place, they were moves against groups of persons (beginning with political dissidents, gypsies, and homosexuals, and ending with Jews) who were no longer recognized as citizens or persons, beings without any civil protection whatsoever.

In many ways these mechanisms repeat the steps to the Gulag. Mass confinement, extermination, and torture require an entire series of special enabling legislation, the creation of special state powers, all of which nullify and usurp the entire historical development of the rule of law as well as that of constitutional democracy, thereby undoing centuries of libertarian effort. After a pattern is set, however, and precedents are created, the destruction of traditional guarantees can be put in place with one simple piece of legislation which suspends all that came before; an overall "Emergencies" or "Special Powers" act has become a standard practice repeated over the decades, invoked routinely in the Southern American hemisphere, for example, or by any state where the military has taken precedent over civilian legal agency.

THE road to the camps was laid down with legal method. And scientific as well, for German psychiatry delivered over the "mentally ill" as the first group to be exterminated, and the earliest experimentation in mass death process was performed by psychiatric medicine upon asylum inmates. The ideology of Nazi racial purification looked next to the gypsies and homosexuals: here repressive measures were already at hand and needed only resuscitation.

A great many strictures against the Jews were simply a return to earlier Christian practices; the barring of Jews from office, the tactic of restriction to ghettos. But while, as Hilberg muses, "one can compare a rather large number of German laws with their counterparts in the past and find complete parallels, even in detail, as if there were a memory which automatically extended backwards in time," what still impresses him is "the next step"—that sheer leap of imagination and ingenuity which the achievement of the Holocaust represents on the part of the bureaucracy that was ordered to achieve it. "This was something unprecedented," he insists. "One cannot even read Göring's famous letter to Heydrich at the end of July 1941, charging him in two paragraphs to proceed with the 'final solution,' and examining that document, consider that everything is clarified. Far from it. It was an authorization to invent." The scale alone daunts administrative capacity. "In every aspect of this operation, invention was necessary. Certainly at this point, because every problem was unprecedented."

How do you kill that many people and keep it a secret? Always it is the scale of things, the overwhelming numbers; millions are now involved. How do you even deal with their clothing? Their corpses? "That was their great invention," says Hilberg, "and that is what made the entire process different from all others that had preceded that event. In this respect, what transpired when the 'final solution' was adopted—or, to be more precise, bureaucracy moved into it—was a turning point in history." Once precedent is created, it can be referred to, even built upon; it is axiomatic that any experiment can be repeated.

/   /   /

"OUR fate is beyond human knowledge," Primo Levi thinks to himself in *Survival in Auschwitz*.* He is twenty-four. When his convoy of Italian Jews arrived, a series of freight cars holding six hundred and fifty "pieces," as the Germans continuously referred to their human cargo, counting and recounting at every stage, those who would be cremated at once were separated off. Levi was one of the ninety-six men spared immediate death in order to be used as slave labor. Such prisoners are organized into lagers named for the sheds where they are housed and guarded in turn by other prisoners called *Lagerkommandos;* they in turn are supervised by *Arbeitskommandos,* and finally by civilian employees in a train of rigid authority presided over by the SS on constant watch with guns and blows.

It is a system that permits no solidarity. Prisoners are pitted against each other, everyone is starving, everyone steals. The purpose is to reduce the captive to a slave, a brute, even a number; therefore the tattoo on the flesh. "Nothing belongs to us anymore; they have taken away our clothes, our shoes, even our hair; if we speak, they will not listen to us, and if they listen, they will not understand. They will even take away our name; and if we want to keep it, we will have to find in ourselves the strength to do so, to manage somehow so that behind the name something of us, of us as we were, still remains."

The intended result of this plan of organization should be despair. Life under such conditions is not worth living, one grows accustomed to death, longs for it, submits. "Marched a hundred times backwards and forwards to their silent labors," Levi foresees this end, already comprehending the process by

---

*The extracts that follow are taken from Primo Levi, *Survival in Auschwitz,* edited by Giulio Einaudi (New York: Collier Macmillan, 1985).

which he and those with him will be "killed in our spirit long before our anonymous death."

Rebellion in the Lublin region was put down through liquidation: machine guns were placed in the four corners of the compound, huts full of prisoners were set on fire. Every contingency has been covered, every loophole closed. Even the rampant corruption of the camp, its protection rackets, its cynicism, its bewildering trade in tobacco and spoons and good behavior coupons only tighten the noose. The infirmary does not invest in medical supplies such as rubber tubing for enemas; instead, it embezzles the prisoners' own food ration, then barters it for rubber tubing stolen by prisoners from other workshops. The system of the camps is a great machine to reduce humanity to the level of beast and then to bury the evidence through the technology of mass extermination.

For those who die at once, its image is the chimney at Birkenau; for those who will live a while before they die, another image is superimposed upon the chimney—the marching band. "The tunes are few, a dozen, the same ones every day, morning and evening: marches and popular songs dear to every German. They lie engraven on our minds and will be the last thing in Lager that we shall forget; they are the voice of the Lager, the perceptible expression of its geometrical madness, of the resolution of others to annihilate us first as men in order to kill us more slowly afterwards."

It has been arranged that the prisoners shall suffer to music, shall depart and return from hard labor on starvation diet, freezing and exhausted, to the sound of music, an art form vulgarized into an incentive, even a force. "When this music plays we know that our comrades, out in the fog, are marching like automatons, their souls are dead and the music drives them, like the wind drives dead leaves, and takes the place of their wills. There is no longer any will: every beat of the drum becomes a step, a reflected contraction of exhausted muscles. The Germans have succeeded in this."

Through the device of a marching band, the prisoners have been as it were mechanized: "They are ten thousand and they are a single grey machine; they are exactly determined; they do not think and they do not desire, they walk." This above all other indignities—a kind of hubris in conquest: "At the departure and the return march the SS are never lacking. Who would deny them the right to watch this choreography of their creation, the dance of dead men, squad after squad, leaving the fog to enter the fog? What more concrete proof of their victory?"

There is an eerie similarity between Primo Levi's *Survival in Auschwitz* and Alexandr I. Solzhenitsyn's descriptions of labor camps, not only in *A Day in the Life of Ivan Denisovitch* but in the myriad of camps Solzhenitsyn describes in the three volumes of *The Gulag Archipelago*. Even camps that go way back into the twenties, preceding Nazism altogether. There is even a similarity in the routine of regimentation and privation of the tsarist labor camp which Dostoevski describes in *Notes from the Underground*. One also finds similarities in more recent descriptions of Robben Island, the hard-labor prison for political dissidents within South Africa's apartheid regime where Nelson Mandela was imprisoned for twenty years.

It is as if this institution, whereby slave labor is recruited and held in concentration under torturous conditions until a portion of it dies off to be replaced by new arrivals, were in itself a generic rather than specific form. What gives Levi's description of Auschwitz its particular poignancy is the background of the funnel and the chimney: that policy and process of mass extermination which is the Nazi addition and completion of the idea. One finds the institution in its most primitive state under the Tsar, less rigorous, scarcely populated, but recognizable; one sees it grow to vast proportion, involving millions under Lenin and Stalin, seemingly a finished system, until one is confronted with the final and absolutely logical elaboration of the nazi version . . . labor in concentration whose product is the mass extermination of that labor itself. The death camp.

Here as in other labor camps, vast projects in building are undertaken. Many of Stalin's enormous public works were accomplished thus, an explosion of Soviet highways, city apartments, canals, and factories which were the work of prison labor. In the Buna section of Auschwitz where Levi was held, it was planned that synthetic rubber would be manufactured for the war effort. Though certain camps were in some measure productive, it is possible that the secrecy of the hidden and self-sufficient world of the Nazi concentration camp system militated finally against other forms of productivity. Despite the fact that each extermination camp and the very ovens of their own cremation were constructed by prison labor, the end product of death seems finally to have become all-absorbing.

As Levi describes it, the Buna Camp at Auschwitz is, even excluding the German technicians and managers, a city of forty thousand persons, its diverse slave population speaking twenty languages, its factory landscape so blighted that the Germans themselves experience it as "a curse—not transcendent and divine, but inherent and historical," hanging over the "insolent building based on the confusion of languages and erected in defiance of heaven like a stone oath." Buna is ultimately an industrial failure "on which the Germans were busy for four years and for which countless of us suffered and died," yet it "never produced a pound of synthetic rubber."

Even in spring this industrial wasteland is "desperately and essentially opaque and grey. This huge entanglement of iron, concrete, mud and smoke is the negation of beauty. Its roads and buildings are named like us, by numbers or letters, or by weird and sinister names. Within its bounds not a blade of grass grows, and the soil is impregnated with the poisonous saps of coal and petroleum, and the only things alive are machines and slaves." The Nazi concentration camps did invent: punishment gave way to utter eradication, just as the persecution of dissent gave way to absolute racial proscription. Ambition is greater now, more categorical, a theory has come to have filled the sky—like its image, the chimney at Birkenau, belching out destruction in a cloud of filthy smoke. Entire populations are reduced to ashes. Heydrich's original target figure was 11 million dead.

THE great inventiveness, the miracle of efficiency Hilberg speaks of with bemused irony, was not created at one blow; it was improvised, improved upon. Its authors themselves were later appalled at its early clumsiness. At Treblinka during its first phase, technical process was only slightly advanced over Chelmno: this time gas chambers were built, but the gas used was still only engine gas. Since there were as yet no crematoria, bodies were buried rather than burned. Methods were still very inadequate. Franz Suchomel, SS *Unterscharführer,* testifying unwillingly in *Shoah,* remembers the system at this time as "catastrophic." "That was the period of the old gas chambers. Because there were so many dead that couldn't be gotten rid of, the bodies piled up around the gas chambers and stayed there for days. Under this pile of bodies there was a cess pool three inches deep, full of blood, worms and shit. No one wanted to clean it out. The Jews preferred to be shot rather than work there." Technological means are as yet incapable of serving the demands put upon them by ideology: "More people kept coming, always more, whom we hadn't the facilities to kill. The brass was in a rush to clean out the Warsaw ghetto. The gas chambers couldn't handle the load. The small gas chambers."

Under such conditions victims are left waiting, beginning to understand their fate. Suchomel observed it all: "The Jews had to wait their turn for a day, two days, three days. They foresaw what was coming." This was very undesirable; some cheated their fate with suicide; there was the possibility of revolt. "Because of the delay, Eberl, the camp commandant, phoned

Lublin and said, "We can't go on this way. . . . Overnight, Wirth arrived. He inspected everything and then left. He returned with people from Belzec, experts."

The new gas chambers at Treblinka were built in September 1942. The victims themselves were enlisted to perform the labor. Wirth is given credit for having arrived at a successful design and for having built the death camp "by assigning a detail of Jewish workers to do it. The detail had a fixed number in it, around two hundred people, who worked only in the death camp." Prisoners laid the bricks, Ukrainian carpenters built the door frames, "the gas-chamber doors themselves were armored bunker doors," Suchomel reminisces, booty from the Eastern Front: "I think they were brought from Bialystok, from some Russian bunkers."

Now, at Treblinka, "a primitive but efficient production line of death" had been achieved, a fortified structure where two hundred could be killed at once, the room refilled over and over. Nothing like Auschwitz yet of course, "Auschwitz was a factory!"—Suchomel is ready to grant that. Nevertheless, he still respects and insists upon the efficacy of the earlier Treblinka model: "Primitive, yes. But it worked well, that production line of death."

There is through all this a stupid wonder at numbers, a boastfulness over scale and size, production figures, that obsession with quantity and methodology, with administrative and bureaucratic achievement which Hannah Arendt called the banality of evil.

However decomposed, bodies are traces; secrecy recommends cremation. Therefore, as the solution advances, it is directed toward the huge chimneys of Birkenau in Auschwitz, the *Himmelsweg* or road to heaven and the funnel leading toward it. But in addition to the death camps and their crematoria, there were other remains to dispose of: the conquering German Army had contained special mass murder forces, the *Einsatzkommando,* who had committed massacres all over Eastern Europe. Near the end of the war all such evidence had to be disposed of. Moke Zaidl and Itzhak Dugin were among the prisoners from Sobibor called upon to exhume and burn all traces of the Vilna massacres. In *Shoah* they testify how, at gunpoint, they were forced to dig with their hands: "The Germans even forbade us to use the words 'corpses' or 'victim.' " The dead were blocks of wood, shit, with absolutely no importance.

> The Germans made us refer to the bodies as Figuren, that is, as puppets, as dolls, or as Schmattes, which means "rags." . . . The head of the Vilna Gestapo told us there are ninety thousand people lying there, and absolutely no trace must be left of them.
> In the first grave there were twenty four thousand bodies. The deeper you dug, the flatter the bodies were. Each was almost a flat slab. When you tried to grasp a body, it crumbled, it was impossible to pick up. We had to open the graves, but without tools. They said: "Get used to working with your hands." When we first opened the graves, we couldn't help it, we all burst out sobbing. But the Germans almost beat us to death. We had to work at a killing pace for two days, beaten all the time, and with no tools.

There are other considerations, mere everyday things, like clothing. But when one is dealing in such numbers, details count. Even if the work is undertaken by slaves, it is a monumental task, to undress thousands of corpses, hundreds of thousands, finally millions. How much more efficient to have them undress themselves. Then nothing is wasted, for the clothing is product and the waste of clothing is uneconomical. Finally the smallest details become monstrous; four thousand pairs of shoes take on heroic proportions to be solved by further heroics of efficiency. There is no end to the profit and savings involved: gold filings on this scale are a great asset in wartime. Yet the mountains of spectacles filmed by the Nazi authorities themselves—footage used in the classic documentary which the French director Alain Resnais assembled from Nazi archives after the war and entitled *Night and Fog*—all the rooms full of shoes and stockings, the bins of buttons, were a treasure to bureaucracy. A sorting and filing never quite finished, an industry of recycled life. Death became its own end, the numbers more staggering, the process more exact, larger and always larger in scale, swifter, more mechanically realized.

Filip Muller was twenty in May 1942 when he arrived at Auschwitz, where he was locked in a secret underground cell before being taken to a place where he expected to be shot. In *Shoah* he testifies that "suddenly, before a door, under a lamp in the middle of this building, a young SS man told us: 'Inside, filthy swine!' We entered a corridor. They drove us along it. Right away, the stench, the smoke choked me. They kept on chasing us, and then I made out the shapes of the first two ovens. Between the ovens some Jewish prisoners were working. We were in the incineration chamber of the crematorium in Camp 1 at Auschwitz." First he was ordered to undress the corpses of the dead, then hurried off to "stir the bodies" as they burn. Muller failed to turn off the fan system fast enough and the firebrick exploded, blocking the pipes which connected the crematorium to the smokestack. "Cremation was interrupted. The ovens were out of action." That day bodies had to be buried in pits. Temporary setbacks in a still imperfect system.

Improvements came in stages; it was not until German engineering at last constructed the four great crematoria at Birkenau that the efficiency desired all along was finally achieved. Muller was forced to serve during that stage as well and still survived. Although members of these special details were regularly killed in the interests of secrecy, he weathered five such liquidations and lived to give this eyewitness account of the operation in its final perfected form:

> Before each gassing operation the SS took stern precautions. The crematorium was ringed with SS men. Many SS men patrolled the court with dogs and machine guns. To the right were the steps that led underground to the "undressing room" . . . a large "un-

dressing room" of about three thousand square feet, and a large gas chamber where one could gas up to three thousand people at a time. . . . As people reached the crematorium, they saw everything—this horribly violent scene. The whole area was ringed with SS. Dogs barked. Machine guns. They all, mainly the Polish Jews, had misgivings. They knew something was seriously amiss, but none of them had the faintest of notions that in three of four hours they'd be reduced to ashes.

Even though the newcomers "saw everything," "the whole violent scene" of dogs and guns, they were still innocent as to what would become of them. Lest they discover their fate, deception was necessary. Muller describes the technique by which victims were duped as they arrived:

A sudden silence fell over those gathered in the crematorium courtyard. All eyes converged on the flat roof of the crematorium. Who was standing there? Aumeyer, the SS man, Grabner, the head of the political section, and Hossler, the SS officer. Aumeyer addressed the crowd: "You're here to work for our soldiers fighting at the front. Those who can work will be all right." It was obvious that hope flared in those people. The executioners had gotten past the first obstacle . . . it was succeeding. Then Grabner spoke up: "We need masons, electricians, all the trades." Next Hossler took over. He pointed to a short man in the crowd. I can still see him. "What's your trade?" The man said: "Mr. Officer, I'm a tailor." "A tailor? What kind of a tailor?" "A man's . . . No, for both men and women." "Wonderful: We need people like you in our workshops." Then he questioned a woman: "What's your trade?" "Nurse," she replied. "Splendid! we need nurses in our hospitals, for our soldiers. We need all of you! But first, undress. You must be disinfected. We want you healthy." I could see the people were calmer, reassured by what they'd heard, and they began to undress. Even if they had their doubts, if you want to live, you must hope. Their clothing remained in the courtyard, scattered everywhere. Aumeyer was beaming, very proud of how he'd handled things. He turned to some of the SS men and told them: "You see? That's the way to do it!" By this device a great leap forward had been made! Now the clothing could be used.

The deception reached elaborate proportions as the method was perfected month after month:

When they reached the "undressing room," they saw that it looked like an International Information Center! On the walls were hooks, and each hook had a number. Beneath the hooks were wooden benches. So people could undress "more comfortably," it was said. And on the numerous pillars that held up this underground "undressing room," there were signs with slogans in several languages: "Clean is good!" "Lice can kill!" "Wash yourself!" "To the disinfection area." All those signs were only there to lure people into the gas chambers already undressed. And to the left, at a right angle, was the gas chamber with its massive door.

In Crematoriums 2 and 3, Zyklon gas crystals were poured in by the so-called disinfection squad through the ceiling, and in Crematoriums 4 and 5 through side openings. With five or six canisters of gas they could kill around two thousand people. This so-called disinfection squad arrived in a truck marked with a red cross and escorted people along to make them believe they were being led to take a bath. . . . The gas took about ten to fifteen minutes to kill. The most horrible thing was when the doors of the gas chambers were opened—the unbearable sight: people were packed together. . . .

You see, once the gas was poured in, it worked like this: it rose from the ground upwards. And in the terrible struggle that followed—because it was a struggle—the lights were switched off in the gas chambers. It was dark, no one could see, so the strongest people tried to climb higher. Because they probably realized that the higher they got, the more air there was. They could breathe better. That caused the struggle. Secondly, most people tried to push their way to the door. It was psychological: they knew where the door was; maybe they could force their way out. It was instinctive, a death struggle. Which is why children and weaker people, and the aged, always wound up at the bottom. The strongest were on top. . . . The people were battered. They struggled and fought in the darkness. They were covered in excrement, in blood, from ears and noses. One also sometimes saw that the people lying on the ground, because of the pressure of the others, were unrecognizable. Children had their skulls crushed.

It was felt that the old and infirm would slow down the deliberate speed with which victims were quick-marched into the gas chambers and imperil the deception that haste made possible, so there were different arrangements made for them, arrangements where even the surreal greed of saving the victims' hair (the Germans would eventually find uses for it) and the efficient thrift and convenience of saving victim clothing were relinquished. This solution was called the "Infirmary." Richard Glazer was in the special detail at Treblinka and recalls in *Shoah* what took place there:

> This execution site wasn't covered, just an open place with no roof, but screened by a fence so no one could see in. The way in was a narrow passage, very short . . . a sort of tiny labyrinth. In the middle of it was a pit, and to the left of it as one came in, there was a little booth with a kind of wooden plank in it, like a springboard. If people were too weak to stand on it, they'd have to sit on it, and then, as the saying went in Treblinka jargon, SS man Miete would "cure each one with a single pill": a shot in the neck. In the peak periods that happened daily. In those days the pit—and it was at least ten to twelve feet deep—was full of corpses.
>
> There were also cases of children who for some reason arrive alone or became separated from their parents. These children were led to the "infirmary" and shot there.

Glazer's survival, like Muller's, was accidental and never intended; members of the special brigades were deliberately and regularly executed so there would be no witnesses: "The 'infirmary' was also for us, the Treblinka slaves, the last stop. Not the gas chamber. We always ended up in the 'infirmary.' "

THERE is a certain cunning in these methods, a derisive deception, a loutish trickery—but ingenuity is the lesser part of its brutality; force is the real foundation of the process. The victims have been long in the trains, their numbers are diminished by deliberate starvation, exposure, and thirst; the corpses of those who have already expired from these causes are first removed by trucks; children and the infirm have been led away to be shot under the fraud of the "infirmary." It remains only to dispose of the majority who must be persuaded they are fortunate in being considered useful. The promise of work, even if it is only as slave labor, is a promise of survival. A haircut points toward the future, so does the prospect of cleanliness after a thousand indignities.

The heart of the lie is that once naked and cold, hungry and thirsty, one will finally, after all one's sufferings and patience, enjoy a shower of hot water—be clean, warm, welcomed and made at home even in hell. The induction ritual of all prisons, the moment when the regime washes you and hands back your clothes, stops making you wait and begins feeding you and giving you a place to commence even this dreadful new existence—just here there has been the cruelest of substitutions. It is gas that comes through the showerhead, death, not the water of life.

At Treblinka, too, everything was based on false conclusions and a bewildering haste. Beginning with the moment of arrival, the windows of the railroad cars covered with barbed wire, the barking of the dogs, the machine guns, the Ukrainian and Latvian kapos who mount the rooftops of the cars as they pull to a stop and are already screaming for haste, the SS with machine guns commanding with one terrible alien word, *Schnell, Schnell* (Hurry, hurry). One is surrounded by a bedlam of haste, the blue squads running along the ramp shouting: "Get out, get out. Hurry, hurry."

Franz Suchomel of the SS remembers it well; he saw it over

and over in the line of duty: "So that while five thousand Jews arrived in Treblinka, three thousand were dead in the cars. They had slashed their wrists, or just died. The ones we unloaded were half dead and half mad. . . . Thousands of people piled one on top of another on the ramp. Stacked like wood." The able are forced to undress and the red squad make off with their clothes; naked, one is hustled along with more shouts to hurry, *Schnell, Schnell*. The guns, the dogs.

All activity leads to a concealed point, the funnel. "Here stood two Ukrainian guards. Mainly for the men. If the men wouldn't go in, they were beaten with whips." There are no explanations. One is driven, herded, stampeded toward the inevitable funnel. But—and this is crucial to the plan—never understanding. Because the funnel is a secret, inscrutable as the steps in human sacrifice practiced by totally alien beings. This unlooked-for, impossibly bizarre scenario, the needle's eye, the point of no return. It is, in *Unterscharführer* Suchomel's feeble phrase, "camouflaged": a narrow opening only thirteen feet wide toward which the thousands, tens of thousands were rushed pellmell—to either side barbed wire; "Woven into the barbed wire were branches of pine trees. You understand?"

There is something staggering about this choice of material—evergreens with their associations in nature, the woods, the countryside. The ingenuity of winding them into barbed wire to screen a gas chamber is a comment on the minds of those in charge which may be pondered a long time: consider its economy, its realization of Teutonic pagan symbolism, its hubris. "There was a Camouflage Squad of twenty Jews. They brought in new branches every day from the woods. So everything was screened. People couldn't see anything to the left or right. Nothing. You couldn't see through it. Impossible."

But once past it, one sees: "At the top of the slope was the gas chamber. You had to climb up to it." Those who have penetrated its secret call it the *Himmelsweg*, "the way to heaven," also "the ascension," a grimly perverse allusion to Christian imagery, so grim it takes on the character of the religious mystery to which its brutal irony was intended to refer.

The funnel is the last trick of all: it is a baffle, a trompe l'oeil of layout, like the way to the infirmary—but with far greater need and sophistication. Tactically and strategically, it borrows from the power of the labyrinth, the ability to hide the truth and bewilder, to dominate and disarm through confusion—a device from which those in the know derive a geometric power to carry out their plan. There are no more than five SS in this operation; all the others who understand the arrangements are themselves prisoners, dependent for survival upon their ability to keep the secret, to refrain from warning the victims, yet capable of making common cause with them if the perfect timing of the operation fails even momentarily. The SS are armed with machine guns but they are only a handful against thousands. Their entire strategic power lies in the very staging of this mass execution, its "floor plan," the layout, the funnel.

But all deception, even strategy, is only an adjunct to force, and it is the very brutality of the plan that assures its success. And its speed: "Again the chase," as Suchomel explains the technique, "A hail of whiplashes. The SS man Kuttner's whip was this long. Women to the left, men to the right. And always more blows. No respite. Go in there, strip. Hurry, hurry! Always running." There is a deliberate confusion induced by this haste, it is the essence of the technique. "You must remember," Suchomel reiterates, it had to go fast." The men are sent up the funnel first—"whipped in first. You understand? They always went first."

Of course this is tactical as well, since the SS believe they have more to fear from their male victims; the women are perceived as harmless cattle. "The men were chased through," whereas "the women had to wait until a gas chamber was empty." The women waited in the open area before the funnel, perhaps hearing the motors of the gas chambers. Maybe they also heard the men screaming and imploring. As they waited, "death panic" overwhelmed them. "Death panic makes people let go. They empty themselves, from the front or the rear. So often, where the women stood, there were five or six rows of excrement." In the course of his duties, Suchomel observed this phenomenon with interest: "They could squat or do it standing. I didn't see them do it, I only saw the feces." So as "not to delay the flow of people to the gas chambers," the old and infirm and children were led off to the "infirmary." This too was a baffle in layout.

"It had a white flag with a red cross. A passage led to it. Until they reached the end, they saw nothing. Then they'd see the dead in the pit. They were forced to strip, to sit on a sandbank, and were killed with a shot in the neck. They fell into the pit. There was always a fire in the pit." Suchomel still sounds satisfied with the arrangements: "With rubbish, paper and gasoline, people burn very well."

ONE hears Suchomel as one hears a maniac. Then one listens again to the voices of the survivors of the world he helped to bring into being. There are two discourses. Each describes the infirmary, yet the descriptions are worlds apart: "people burn very well," Suchomel says, content with what he says. Even after Nuremberg, forty years after the event. Still in fear of reprisals, Suchomel insisted that he be interviewed without the use of his name or face. Imagining himself invisible and anonymous, he is carried away—so carried away that he begins to sing, happily demonstrating the song his prisoners were forced to sing in Treblinka, relishing its indignities:

> All that matters to us now is Treblinka.
> It is our destiny.
> That's why we've become one with Treblinka
> in no time at all.
> We know only the word of our Commander,
> we know only obedience and duty,

we want to serve, to go on serving
Until a little luck ends it all. Hurray!

Referring to the creatures burning in the "infirmary" pits,
Suchomel fails to register them as human beings at all. Though
he well remembers driving them naked into the gas chambers,
naked even in winter, he remembers even more clearly that "It
was cold as hell for us too. We didn't have suitable uniforms."
His victims were "undesirables"; they remains so, "the Jews,"
beings utterly remote from his own humanity, the permanent
achievement of racial ideology, ethnic indoctrination, the
trained habits of militaristic culture.

Alternating between such a voice and those of its victims as
one does in reading the text of Lanzmann's *Shoah*, or even
turning back and forth from academic historians to Primo
Levi's account of Auschwitz, is a very disturbing experience.
So radically different is the point of view between the torturer
and the tortured, or even between the tortured and the objective historian of that torture, that the reader can actually experience the gap in him- or herself, an insight we are generally
spared. While hearing the Nazi state narratives, even hearing
the Nazi voice, one participates unconsciously, perhaps even
necessarily, in its mentality, succumbing however slightly or
momentarily to its point of view, and then one is aghast:
experiencing revulsion with Suchomel one feels revulsion with
the self. Conversely, when hearing the accounts of Nazi victims, one's usual placid compassion for them changes, becoming anger. The violence done to them is now done against
oneself. In time the very futility of the prisoner's situation
brings on a certain despair in the reader.

Reading Levi, one has fallen into hell: no one would believe
you even if you could return and explain. Watching a freight
train go through the camp, Levi imagines escaping on it:

Oh, to climb into a corner, well-hidden under the coal, and to stay
there quiet and still in the dark, to listen endlessly to the rhythm

of the wheels, stronger than hunger or tiredness; until, at a certain moment, the train would stop and I would feel the warm air and the smell of hay and I would get out into the sun; then I would lie down on the ground to kiss the earth as you read in books, with my face in the grass. And a woman would pass, and she would ask me "Who are you?" in Italian, and I would tell her my story in Italian, and she would understand, and she would give me food and shelter. And she would not believe the things I tell her, and I would show her the number on my arm, and then she would believe. . . .

But the most terrible dream of all, a dream each prisoner has, a shared nightmare, is that were he to escape, no one would believe him: "It is an intense pleasure, physical, inexpressible, to be at home, among friendly people, and to have so many things to recount: but I cannot help noticing that my listeners do not follow me. In fact, they are completely indifferent: they speak confusedly of other things among themselves, as if I was not there. My sister looks at me, gets up and goes away without a word."

Can there be realities so terrible they are incredible?

My dream stands in front of me, still warm, and although awake I am still full of its anguish: and then I remember that it is not a haphazard dread, but that I have dreamed it not once but many times since I arrived here, with hardly any variations of environment or details. I am now quite awake and I remember that I have recounted it to Alberto and that he confided to me, to my amazement, that it is also his dream and the dream of many others, perhaps of everyone. Why does it happen? Why is the pain of every day translated so constantly into our dreams, in the ever-repeated scene of the unlistened-to story?

Levi's surroundings are pitiless, humanity hasn't a chance here; the darkness so palpable that the reader, like the prisoner, hears the Allied bombardment which may destroy even as it liberates, sharing the same wish to annihilate the fact of

Auschwitz even as one yearns to survive it in Levi. But what if Auschwitz had survived and not Levi? Indeed, the early passages of the text are just that, the triumph of evil, the perfection of a regime of death and cruelty. Until the distant bombing is heard in the second winter of his life in Auschwitz, Levi not only understands he will probably be in the next "selection" for death, or the one after that, but he also has no reason to imagine that anyone will ever live to tell the tale.

The Nazis will get by with it. They will win and keep on winning. The final death of resistance will occur, the last prisoner capable of defiance will be eradicated, and with him all hope of hope. One event occurs which seems to foretell this: at the end of the day's labor the prisoners are assembled for roll call, the band plays, then there is a speech in German which no one understands—but the gallows has been erected to make everything plain. The man who is to be executed there has rebelled, has probably taken part in the sabotage at Birkenau—one of the crematoria there has been blown up: "The fact remains that a few hundred men in Birkenau, helpless and exhausted slaves like ourselves, had found in themselves the strength to act . . . perhaps the Germans do not understand that this solitary death, this man's death which has been reserved for him, will bring him glory, not infamy." The man about to die shouts a last defiance: "It pierced through the old thick barriers of inertia and submissiveness, it struck the living core of man in each of us: *Kameraden, ich bin der Letzte!* ('Comrades, I am the last one!').

"I wish I could say that from the midst of us, an abject flock, a voice rose, a murmur, a sign of assent. But nothing happened." The man is hanged without any sign of protest from his fellow prisoners. "The trap door opened, the body wriggled horribly; the band began playing again, and we were once more lined up and filed past the quivering body of the dying man. At the foot of the gallows, the SS watch us pass with indifferent eyes: their work is finished and well finished. The Russians can come now: there are no longer any strong men among us, the last one is now hanging above our heads." That night, Levi and his friend Alberto eat the extra rations they have organized in shame and silence: "Because we also are broken, conquered; even if we know how to adapt ourselves."

In his last volume of essays,* Bruno Bettelheim spoke of the dangers the camps posed to the souls of those whom they intended not only murder but to dehumanize as well. Levi comes to the same realization during a short respite in the camp hospital: "One begins to consider what they have made us become, how much they have taken away from us, what this life is." Here in an "enclosure of relative peace we have learnt that our personality is fragile, that it is much more in danger than our life."

Because of this, it is crucial, even life-saving, to protect that personality and to assert it as one's humanity. Levi does it in a passage of great beauty, remembering Dante line for line, the canto of Ulysses, teaching it to Jean, a bright young Alsatian student, and Pikolo (clerk-messenger) of the chemical brigade who has asked for lessons in Italian while they share the momentary happiness of a long unsupervised walk to pick up lunch for their brigade. Strolling through Auschwitz, passing SS men and informers, the two young men engage in the most amazing discussion of towns and houses, books and studies, "the important thing is not to lose time, not to waste this hour. . . . Who is Dante? What is the *Comedy?* That curious sensation of novelty which one feels if one tries to explain briefly what is the *Divine Comedy.* How the Inferno is divided up, what are its punishments. Virgil is Reason, Beatrice is Theology."

Primo begins to recite the great canto, remembering whole passages, searching for a line and then coming up with it as

*Bruno Bettelheim, *Surviving and Other Essays* (New York: Vintage Books, Random House, 1980).

they walk along, two Jews condemned to death for their culture and religion, delighting in a pagan passage in a Christian epic, savoring its language between their own two languages; for example, the Italian phrase *"misi me"* whereby Ulysses puts to sea, how it is stronger than the French equivalent *"je me mis."* "Much stronger and more audacious, it is a chain which has been broken, it is throwing oneself on the other side of a barrier, we know the impulse well. The open sea: Pikolo has travelled by sea, and knows what it means; it is when the horizon closes in on itself, free, straight ahead and simple and there is nothing but the smell of the sea; sweet things, ferociously far away."

In the long history of literature built upon literature, this must be one of its most moving passages:

How many things there are to say, and the sun is already high, midday is near. I am in a hurry, a terrible hurry. Here, listen, Pikolo, open your ears and your mind, you have to understand, for my sake:

Think of your breed: for brutish ignorance
Your mettle was not made; you were made men,
To follow after knowledge and excellence.

As if I also was hearing it for the first time: like the blast of a trumpet, like the voice of God. For a moment I forget who I am and where I am.

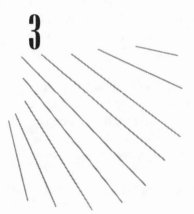

3

HENRI ALLEG AND
COLONIALISM IN
ALGERIA

THE resumption of torture under Hitler and Stalin had a decidedly ideological character. Under Lenin, the aggrandizement of state power that torture represents is presented as merely defensive, a necessary expedient to preserve the revolution from its enemies. "The remedy invented by Lenin and Trotsky, the general suppression of democracy, is worse than the evil it was supposed to cure," Rosa Luxemburg observed. Difference or dissent come to be seen as disloyalty: soon all opposition to the Party came to be seen as insult to the revolution as well, threats to a struggling new order surrounded by danger. The infant state, tragically vulnerable in a corrupt world order, is permitted any tactic for survival; the proscription of dissent is merely the first step in its self-preservation.

A thousand such steps result in the accumulation of a monumental power which Vasily Grossman could describe as "This fear that millions of people find insurmountable, this fear written up in crimson letters over the leaden sky of Moscow—

this terrible fear of the state."* Through this century that fear has spread and generalized; it is part of our age. It permeates society today, no matter what form of government is at issue as all government swells now and encroaches upon its citizens with increasing force. At this moment it is probably strongest in the authoritarian regimes of the Near East and South America, where state brutality has a new lack of shame and often does not even truck with ideological rationale or justification.

The terror of the individual before the state is a modern condition. A literature has come into being whose subject is this aspect of twentieth-century experience. Not only a rich and vital literary record, it constitutes a kind of history and psychology of our time as well. Kafka may be its greatest master, but there are many. Its two great themes are power and fear: the state's physical force put in the service of its own ideology carried now into dogma, and the attack this represents upon the citizen and individual. The great pitted against the small and isolated, the state omniscient, omnipotent; its victim, single and powerless.

Dizzy and overcome by a labyrinthine terror, the individual watches as official authority, not familiar community or even organized society, but a new creation responsible only to itself and its own continuation and consolidation in power, defines and codifies reality. At times it merely crushes all before it. At other times it first picks the meat from the bones of contention, cruel with an elaborate intellectualism. There are moments it is as blunt as a boot, as the pounding at the door. At other times it is as complex as Christian theology, as ponderous as scientific classification. Victims hold their breath as it creates vast intellectual structures, mythologies, rituals. The power to destroy plays games, splits hairs, toys with ideas, pauses before it strikes.

---

*Quoted in Robert Conquest, *The Great Terror: A Reassessment* (London and New York: Oxford University Press, 1990).

The state has usurped the role of its once divine predecessor; more powerful than God, more visible, it also covets as rich and complicated an intellectual system, as airy and elaborate a paradigm of good and evil, virtue and deviance, subordination and obedience, compliance and docility. Casuistical and subtle as the Inquisition at certain moments, moments like the Moscow Purges or those described in Koestler's *Darkness at Noon,* the elusive question of revolutionary correctitude, slippery as religious grace, stretches out to form a brilliant and distracting surface extended over the underlying brutality inherent in the unbridled use of state power.

As it advances, it creates fear: the vacuum preceding a dynamo. Like waves of pressure, like decibels of tension, this fear has an enormous range, but is also a spectrum full of variation, dense here, tenuous there. In one place it merely creates anxiety before pretense, intellectual dishonesty, false nomenclature. At other moments it is a naked terror before physical force, technological entrapment. The blow, the cell. Often it is a dread of impoverishment rather than arrest, the fear of being shunned, blackballed, forbidden employment or residence. There is a sea of hazards in papers and official forms, permits, licenses, the labyrinth of taxation, the maze and snare of regulation, accountability—always the penalties in wait, unforeseen, unexplained.

There is surveillance, harassment, the predicament of having an enemy, moreover one that is all-powerful, omnipresent, its agents everywhere, eyes that see everything but cannot be seen, hear and know everything but cannot be known. So great is the power of enforcement, so entire the allegiance it demands, that the individual assumes an air of defensiveness, even guilt. And the condition of the criminal becomes nearly a general condition, a sense of wrongdoing, the impression of being at fault and accused, suspected.

This modern relationship to state authority has come upon us so slowly we have not quite noticed. Yet it has been forming all along, has proliferated through the century, has increased with each decade, keeping pace with the speed of new inventions, their swiftness in communication and transport. Awareness is only partial and intermittent; most of us still maintain a certain illusion of safety, innocence.

But in certain other places fear of the state is a constant condition, the terror of the defenseless against the all-powerful. No other factor underlines this general uneasiness before the state so much as the restoration of torture. Torture was always possible, always materially if not culturally available— but there was a time when popular opinion would not, once it was discovered, accept the continued use of torture. We have now gone beyond that, we have become habituated, acquiesced. An acquiescence which brings with it fundamental political change: it is the nature of that change which this essay tries to explore, explain, even portray.

ONCE torture was back in its arsenal, state authority could assume different attitudes, act upon different assumptions. Once governmental force could lay hold of the body, violate its integrity again, some dam was broken, something archaic permitted again which summed up old and dearly held beliefs. Categories and groups reemerged—status and race, dominance and subordination, superior and inferior. Torture thrives upon role and type, definitions of the familiar and the alien. It gravitates toward confrontations where there is enmity and strangeness, us and them.

Reintroduced under two grand ideologies, torture weathered another general disavowal after World War II, yet made small progress except in outposts, remote colonial situations away from the public eye. At first as it reasserts itself it does so in situations where ordinary standards and behavior are not thought to apply, where they are suspended by circumstances, by dealings with beings very different. Race enters, color, occupying forces. Sex enters as well, the persecution of the homosexual caste, the universal denigration of women under patriarchy. Sex and gender simplify: bias here is generally acceptable because traditional, even applauded as moral and natural; custom excuses and extenuates such abuses of power. Domination is regarded as nature when men practice it upon women, whites upon blacks. It is simpler in the colonies. It might also be quieter, torture there might be marginal, possibly invisible, a phenomenon still off in the corner, unnoticed.

Given the widespread renunciation of torture at the beginning of this century and the general revulsion against it following the discovery of its use in World War II, the spread of torture throughout the world since the end of that war is somewhat of an anomaly. The Gulag was well hidden, and where known it was viewed either as a tyranny to which time would supply an end or as a domestic situation incapable of influence by outsiders. Even assuming that Stalin could act with impunity because his empire kept his secret, Hitler's crimes were plain to all and repudiated by all. Yet, finally, had he violated a taboo, which once broken was now possible to override, quietly at first, but then in bolder ways over time? Or had the very scale on which torture was practiced by these two dour regimes made it part of the modern world forever; "advanced," "scientific," "logical"? Was the possible now converted to the inevitable, an inescapable part of how things are run in the modern state?

Certainly not at the level of announced public policy. After the war Hitler's reintroduction of torture was formally put to an end in the Nuremberg Trials, an innovative series of inquests where the prewar prohibition against torture was reiterated with such force and majesty that the circle of nations might feel a certain confidence it would not return again. Over and above the effect of the Nuremberg Trials, the United Nations gave a great impetus to the impression that torture was now a thing of the past among human governments as charter and protocol were elaborated to forbid and censure its use anywhere in the world.

It was still not possible to see torture as the future; certainly not as a continuous present. Not till Algiers. The discovery of torture in the French colony of Algiers, torture carried out by French troops, and the public scrutiny and debate which was inaugurated by such a discovery—still more its virtual admission by government and the effect of that admission upon policy, even upon history—had a profound, if unfortunately not a lasting effect. France finally relinquished Algeria behind the shame of having practiced torture there. It is disheartening to realize that such a thing might no longer happen, that nations now are less capable of such shame: dishonor has less effect, the collective conscience far harder to mobilize than was French opinion when Jean-Paul Sartre and Henri Alleg assailed it for the behavior of its forces abroad, forces operating out of the crudest racism and colonial hatred. Here was a brutality which once exposed could no longer be endorsed, endured or kept quiet.

When Henri Alleg's *The Question* was published in 1958, there was also a special circumstance, the still recent memory of Nazi occupation and torture in the infamous Gestapo Headquarters on the rue Lauriston in Paris. And there was the postwar prestige of the French Resistance, whose members had frequently been tortured, even the prestige of Sartre, Malraux, Mauriac, and other French intellectuals who championed the book and objected to its being suppressed on political grounds by the government. Finally there was the fact that an astounding number of copies were sold in the first two weeks after publication and before the book was banned and confiscated—the first such act by the French authorities since the eighteenth century. Copies were smuggled back into France across the Swiss border and the text was translated and published throughout the world; there was no getting away from what was being said.

Nor could one refuse to listen once Alleg was able to make himself be heard: here was the tortured speaking in his own voice, a Frenchman and a journalist, one of their own, a being completely credible. For five years Alleg had been the editor of

Alger Républicain, the only daily paper in Algeria which printed all sides of democratic and national opinion until suppressed in September 1955, an interdiction he was able to challenge and even to have acknowledged as illegal by the administrative tribunal of Algiers. Nonetheless, Alleg was still unable to restore publication; members of his staff were detained, Alleg himself was informed of an order for his arrest. He went into hiding.

On June 12, 1957, Henri Alleg was ambushed and captured by members of the tenth division of French parachutists: "On the previous day my friend Maurice Audin, an assistant at the Faculty of Science of Algiers, had been arrested at his house and the police had left a detective behind. It was this man who opened the door to me when I fell into the trap. I tried, without success, to escape, but the detective, revolver in hand, caught me on the first floor and forced me into the apartment."* The detective telephones headquarters for reinforcements. The game is up.

There is something of déjà vu in it all.

From the moment when the lieutenant entered the room I knew what to expect.
    "Where have you been hiding?"
    "That I won't tell you!"
    He smiled, raised his head and then, very sure of himself, said: "We will prepare a little questionnaire for you later on which will change your mind. You'll answer, I promise you." And then to the others: "Handcuff him."

It is as if the roles are already known, the lines, like dialogue from movies, the thing nearly rehearsed between them. Alleg has been in hiding since November. It is now June 12: he has been through five months of underground existence, awaiting this lieutenant for something like a hundred and fifty days. He

*The account that follows is taken from Henri Alleg, *The Question.* Introduction by Jean-Paul Sartre; translated by John Calder (New York: George Braziller, 1958).

has also known about his opponents' methods. As a journalist he has considerable information, even the names of men and women who have been tortured; he has guessed the fate of Ali Boumendjel, for example, barrister of the Algerian Court of Appeals, said to have committed suicide in detention. As he is led away Alleg knows what to expect: "You've even written articles about it," his captors jeer.

In Alleg's account every detail has clarity, simplicity, immediacy: the make and model of the car waiting outside, the paratrooper who sits next to him holding a Sten gun against his ribs. The place he is taken to is strange, even slightly improbable at first—the construction site of an apartment house, a place of disorder and concrete dust and reinforcing bars sticking out of masonry; overhead are the wires of an unfinished electrical installation. It is industrial, masculine, unfinished and secret; the archetypal clandestine prison of the future, a place particularly suited to the secret and unaccountable practice of torture.

Interrogations take place in what is "apparently the living room of a future apartment." In this place of impermanence there are collapsible tables, blurred photos of suspects, a field telephone, and stairways full of paratroopers ascending and descending in noisy boots, laughing and trading obscenities as they haul along Arab prisoners dressed in rags with several days of beard. There is something informal and unreported about the setting, something unplanned and spur of the moment; one comes to appreciate the methodical formality of legitimate state buildings, their public character, their known location. Arrested into such places one is accounted for, relatives will be informed, records are kept, attorneys have access. One is somewhere. Here, one is nowhere.

The character of clandestine detention, the practice of bringing victims to undisclosed locations, is central to torture—both to its secret and illegal character and to its terror and force. One is in limbo, one disappears. Reappearance now requires something like a miracle. One is surprised to realize the actual safety of conventional state custody. It crosses the mind as one vanishes that one is now utterly vulnerable: no assistance can be given by associates; all the succor of the law is withheld. Under these circumstances, one is not so much arrested as kidnapped. You are not in the hands of the law, but in the power of persons who have put themselves above the law while still using its authority. The state itself has become a criminal force; the sky's the limit.

BUT first there will be a routine appeal through ordinary means. Paper and pencil are put before Alleg, his handcuffs are removed: "You're going to tell us where you live, who has been sheltering you since you went into hiding, who are the persons you've met, what your activities have been." Alleg replies that he has been looking out for the interests of his newspaper, has been to Paris, names the persons he met there.

> "I have nothing else to say to you. I shall write nothing and don't count on me to betray those who have had the courage to hide me."
> Still smiling and very sure of themselves, the two lieutenants exchanged glances: "I think there's no point in wasting our time."
> ... At heart I, too, agreed with them; if I was going to be tortured, it didn't matter very much if it was earlier or later. And rather than being kept in suspense, it was better to face the worst right away.

A young officer appears. "Ah! So you're the customer?" he addresses Alleg as if he were a client. "Come with me." Alleg dutifully follows directions, just as Volodin did. They do not lie down and kick and scream, they do not go limp and refuse to cooperate, they realize the inevitable and they maintain a manly demeanor. One cooperates, one obeys the inevitable, one hopes for the best. One does not yet realize the full extent of one's helplessness; one has not yet been tortured. On the floor below they enter what will someday be a kitchen and there, amidst an earthenware cooking stove, a sink, and some unfinished shelving, Alleg is forced to undress—"If you don't we'll make you"—and then to lie down on a black plank. It is a repellent object, "sweating with humidity, polluted and sticky with vomit."

The plank is simple but to the point. Leather straps have been fixed to the wood, so that once the victim has been made to lie down on it, he can be strapped in. The torturer stands over him, his feet astride his victim, his hands on his hips, "in the attitude of a victor." "Everybody talks—You'll have to tell us everything—not only a little bit of the truth, but everything!" Alleg is naked on the damp plank, there is cold air blowing in on him from a window. " 'Are you afraid? Do you want to talk?' 'No, I'm not afraid. I'm cold.' "

Alleg maintains his dignity. Four paratroopers pick him up, still bound to the plank, take him into the next room, and put him down on the cement floor. The officers sit down around him on boxes brought in by their men, he is a spectator sport. The electric magneto is presented for his inspection: "the machine that had already been described to me a hundred times by its victims," and Alleg makes a brave speech, "If you have any charge to bring against me, hand me over to the appropriate authorities." He will not be intimidated, objects to his torturers addressing him contemptuously in the familiar *tu* form, a Frenchman standing upon the rights of man and the citizen, undaunted by the laughter around him.

A paratrooper sits on his chest. Alleg describes him as very sunburnt, "with the broad smile of a boy who is going to play a good trick." The officers are ranged in a circle on their boxes, the non-commissioned paratroopers on the floor; there are also "several others with no particular function," who are in the room "just to watch the fun." The electrodes are attached to Alleg's right earlobe and to a finger on his right hand.

> Suddenly I leapt in my bonds and shouted with all my might
> . . . a flash of lightning exploded next to my ear and I felt my heart

racing. I struggled, screaming, and stiffened myself until the straps cut into my flesh. All the while the shocks controlled by C——, magneto in hand, followed each other without interruption. Rhythmically, C——repeated a single question, hammering out the syllables: "Where have you been hiding?"

Between spasms Alleg reminds his tormentors, "You are wrong to do this. You will regret it!" They turn up the electrical charge of the magneto and stuff a gag into his mouth— "My God, he's noisy." Smiling down into his victim's face as he does it, a paratrooper attaches the electrode to Alleg's penis: "Suddenly, I felt as if a savage beast had torn the flesh from my body." The shocks going through him are strong enough to loosen the straps holding him to the board.

"They stopped to tie them again and we continued"—the phrase "we continued," rather than "they continued," is curious. A duality has been established, a relationship of force and resistance: Alleg is defying his tormentors.

Now the lieutenant takes over and stretches the wire over the entire width of Alleg's chest: "The whole of my body was shaking with nervous shocks, getting ever stronger in intensity, and the session went on interminably. They had thrown cold water over me in order to increase the intensity of the current, and between each spasm I trembled with cold. All around me, sitting on the packing cases, C—— and his friends emptied bottles of beer." One is forced to recall the audience on their packing cases; that they drink beer while they watch is like the kitchen sink and the future apartment itself, an indecent occurrence of the ordinary in the midst of the extraordinary.

"At last they stopped. 'All right, untie him!' The first session was over." Not really, and not yet. Alleg's necktie is placed around his neck again and used as a leash, a paratrooper dragging him along behind "as he would have dragged a dog" into the office next door. He is ordered to get down on his knees, then slapped repeatedly until he cannot stand, cannot even stay on all fours. "You're finished, do you understand?

You're a dead man living on borrowed time!"

"Bring in Audin," one torturer says, as the other goes on slapping Alleg with all his might. "I saw the pale and haggard face of my friend Audin looking at me while I wavered on my knees." It is a terrible meeting. Audin too has been tortured, probably longer and more savagely. " 'It's hard, Henri,' Audin said to me. And they took him away." We never hear from Audin again. He will disappear forever, tortured to death or executed, his only guilt his association with Alleg; he will die for it. "It's hard, Henri' "—what an amazing economy in its bitter simplicity, even an echo of the antique; the French word for "hard," *dur,* is the old phrase for torture, *la peine, forte et dure:* pain, strong and hard.

The paratroopers begin to boast in a demented way that they are the Gestapo, a treasonous statement but indicative: torturers tend to have a particular admiration for the Nazi regime, recall it respectfully in many corners of the world. Especially in South America, where many Nazis fled and took refuge in military establishments perpetuating a politics of cruelty. An impression takes form that fascism was by no means put to rest with Hitler's death but is a living idea, a political vision still striven for and only temporarily eclipsed.

Alleg is determined and will not give in, so he is dragged back into the first room in time to see a naked Muslim being kicked and shoved out into the corridor. A bigger magneto is now attached: "Instead of the sharp and rapid spasms that seemed to tear my body in two, a greater pain now stretched all my muscles and racked them for a longer time. I was taut in my bonds. I tightened my teeth on the gag with all my might and kept my eyes closed. They stopped, but I continued to shake with nervous convulsions."

Alleg's torturers then ask him if he "knows how to swim"; they offer to "teach" him through water torture. "The kitchen was lit only by a weak light from the corridor. In the gloom I could just make out the faces of S——, and C——, and Captain D." They attach one end of a rubber tube to the tap and shove the other end of it into his mouth and down his throat: "With a rag already over my face, L—— held my nose. He tried to jam a piece of wood between my lips in such a way that I could not close my mouth or spit out the tube." The water is turned on.

> For a while I could still breathe in some small gulps of air. I tried, by contracting my throat, to take in as little water as possible and to resist suffocation by keeping air in my lungs for as long as I could. But I couldn't hold on for more than a few moments. I had the impression of drowning, and a terrible agony, that of death itself, took possession of me. In spite of myself, all the muscles of my body struggled uselessly to save me from suffocation.

Alleg has now ceased to defy: "It was better to die of asphyxiation right away. I feared to undergo again the terrible moment when I had felt myself losing consciousness, while at the same time I was fighting with all my might not to die. I did not move my hands [the sign he will surrender, will talk] but three times I again experienced this insupportable agony. In extremis, they let me get my breath back while I threw up the water." Alleg's tormentors have now broken his physical resistance: "The last time, I lost consciousness."

But they will not stop there; they have not yet broken his will:

> Then, altogether, they lifted me up in order to hang me head downward from the iron bar of the shelf above the sink. Only my fingers touched the ground. They amused themselves for a while, swinging me from one to the other like a sack of sand. I could see L——, who slowly lit a paper-torch at the level of my eyes. He stood up and all of a sudden I felt the flame on my penis and on my legs, the hairs crackling as they caught fire. I straightened myself with such a violent jerk that I bumped L——. He scorched me again, once or twice, then he started to burn me on the nipple of my breast.

They step on his hands with their boots; he cannot rise and when taken away falls down an entire staircase, but he does not talk. Delivered finally into a cell, Alleg discovers that the mattress he has crawled to is full of barbed wire. A soldier's voice laughs at him behind the door, but another soldier comments that "all the same, he has gained a night to give his friends a chance to get away." Of course, that's what it's all about: this contest of wills is a question of time, a series of moves between two sides; advantage lies in surprise, a quick move or capture. Traditionally the captive buys time with a terrible resolve against appalling pain during that first day when the state's resolve to break a new victim is at its keenest. Alleg is a member of the Communist Party, as were many Resistance fighters: there is a code, an expectation. After many more days of torture, he hears himself being discussed by an experienced senior officer: "For ten, fifteen years they've all had the same idea, that if captured they must say nothing: and there is no way to change them."

TIME becomes endless in torture, one day bleeds into the next, sessions are blurred eternities. The victim can no longer stand, handcuffs can be dispensed with, even a gag is unnecessary when you are three stories underground. "All the same," one paratrooper complains, "It's disagreeable." Calmly the victim's trousers are unbuttoned, his underpants taken down and the electrodes attached to each side of his groin. He can no longer shout very loud when shocked, it is not considered necessary to tie him to the plank.

"While the torture was going on I could hear a loud-speaker blaring out popular songs of the day." Alleg's voice comes back to us, his person now so dazed and passive, so much the victim of sadism, the studied detail of sexual assault, a distancing familiar and banal to us through the conventions of pornography, that one is surprised to hear the victim speak again,

reminding us that his selfhood resides in his voice: the alienation is achieved by the others, their dehumanizing torment.

The whole power of Alleg's account is that it is in the first
person, the testimony of the tortured himself. Accusing his
tormentors before the ears of the world, publicly and out loud.
Breaking the silence, the secrecy, the smut and inhumanity
inherent in traditional and distanced third-party accounts
where a creature is observed and tormented and observed
again. One thinks of de Sade and the *Histoire d'O*, the cruelty
that can be carried along in such oblique narratives. There are
always elements of the playful in them, the coy, the hypocriti-
cal; also the fantastic, humorous, exaggerated, the witty, the
naughty, the forbidden; most of all, the adventitious and unreal, which appear to excuse everything. The reader is rendered insensitive, merely curious, invited to share in the elation
of the bully.

Here one is never permitted to approach that view: "One of
the two lieutenants detached one of the clasps and fastened it
to my face until I jerked upright. 'My word,' said C——, 'he
likes it.' " Here is the usual invitation to scorn and derision;
the victim is written off as a fool now, deserving his fate, one
torturer encouraging the others into a position of absolute
contempt. But the reader remains with Alleg: "They went
away leaving the clasps still sticking into my flesh."

It is our flesh too. Yet Alleg has taken a great risk. *The
Question* is based on a desperate faith in human compassion,
Alleg's faith in its saving power increased, paradoxically, in
proportion to his experience of its denial by his torturers.
Because torture exists and because there are torturers there is
a greater need for the counter force of sympathy and outrage.
Otherwise the world is mad and it is hopeless, an attitude that
Levi failed to maintain even in Auschwitz.

Alleg has lost all sense of time, lives in the dark, is never fed,
has no routine but the twelve-hour beatings; he is more and
more incapable, a sack bashed about, shocked, kicked—but
still proof against his enemies: "I felt my resistance was mak-

ing them more and more brutish and irritated." "We'll give it to him in the mouth," they say to each other, incensed. We do not see Alleg's stubbornness, only his patience. His courage, his determination and stoicism, his ability to last. We do not see what they see; we see what Alleg sees, the wire soldered to his jaws by the huge current they have thrown into his throat:

> . . . it was impossible for me to unlock my teeth, no matter how hard I tried. My eyes, under their wrinkled lids, were crossed with images of fire, and geometrical luminous patterns flashed in front of them. I thought I could feel them being torn from their sockets by the shocks . . . the current had reached its limit and so had my sufferings. . . . I thought that there was no greater harm they could do me. But I heard S—— say . . . "Do it by little shocks: first you slow down then you start again . . ."

In order to control his pain, to frustrate these "sudden easings and sharp increases," in order to have pain of his own making, some autonomy, and independence even in his suffering, since existence now is only suffering, Alleg begins to bang his head on the floor. Earlier he tried to make his fingers bleed by scratching his fingertips over cement: as a diversion, as an alternative to the searing pain of electric shock.

Curious twentieth-century apparatuses: the army interrogator's electrode, the psychiatrist's electroconvulsive machine, such similar and simple devices, military and civilian, lay and clerical, both of them discreet engines of the state. How the use of something "modern" and "technical" like electricity increases the prestige of the one who inflicts pain, just as it increases the terror of its victims, making suffering quantifiable on a dial for the one who inflicts it but potentially endless for the one who experiences it, an invisible and incomprehensible force.

One may see in the faces of patients condemned to electroconvulsive therapy an expectation that they are scheduled for torture; the casual order—"No breakfast for you, you're getting shock this morning"—can produce hysteria and panic. Even were it beneficial, which it is not, the patient's conviction that he or she is subjected to torture makes the procedure such. As arms and legs are held down and the body thrashes under the force of the electrical charge, one is observing torture under the guise of "treatment."

The victim in this case has, like an enemy, been assigned to some category of "other" for whom such treatment is possible, even justified. Unlike the enemy, however, he is alone, a creature of absolute solitude and singularity, isolated from his fellow sufferers with whom he has contracted no bond of group identity or shared experience. The inhabitants of the camps saw themselves as Jews or gypsies, socialists or even homosexuals—part of a whole body subject to persecution. Alleg is a member of the Party and of the opposition; he will never be as alone as someone alleged to be mad. There is a difference in kind in this experience; between the group member's experience and that of the isolated scapegoat. When, by mistake, an Arab is put in Alleg's cell for a few hours, the newcomer comforts him, calls him brother, and accepts Alleg as his comrade in the struggle. Alleg can pass on his fate to this man, identifying himself and his journal: "Tell them outside, if you can, that I died here."

A little while later, the door opens and Alleg, immune and passive by now, waits for the blows. But instead a flashlight is trained on his bruised face and he is looked at sympathetically by two new recruits, who are appalled at what is happening within their own corps "Horrible, isn't it?" one young voice asks. "Yes, it's terrible," replies the other. There is recognition here that what is being practiced is unfair, against the rules of war for the general treatment of prisoners, the whole body of civilized and humane behavior.

THIS is never true of those said to be mad. When they are tormented, there is no agreed-upon general disapproval, just as there are no allies or constituencies. The Nazis began with those said to be mad. There was a logic in it. Here was a group who were utterly unprotected, a group who were arguably not even human. It is the issue of our humanity which Sartre addresses in his Introduction to *The Question:* the inhumanity of imposing days of thirst upon Alleg, giving him salty water, the paratrooper who thinks he will break Alleg's silence by burning his nipple, another who will break him with the threat of execution and plays with his revolver during interrogations. Alleg himself is terrified that his fingernails may be torn out: ". . . there was not much more they could do to me. Memories of old tags kept coming to my mind: 'The body cannot go on forever, a time comes when the heart gives up.' " He is subject to fever and delusions. He begins to think of his young friend Djegri, who died of torture two months before, hidden in a basement. "It was in this way" that Djegri had died; he begins to experience and undergo the despair of that death.

"There is nothing left for you to do but to kill yourself," a high-ranking officer informs him after threatening him with the sight of his wife and children undergoing torture, trying to bribe him with safe conduct to France if he talks. "In a week you will be in France with your wife. You have our word. If not, you will disappear." Both of these invitations to die are part of the process of dehumanization, the attempt to break the prisoner, deprive him of all hope, all self-respect, to bring him to the point of suicide through self-hatred or one of many available despairs: the despair of ever living through his torment, coming out alive or coming out with his lips still sealed. Death would save him this dishonor, or despair before further and finally annihilating torture, or simply despair before an eternity of captivity. Or the last despair, that of someone who has given in, broken down, betrayed everything, and now despairs on the grounds of his unworthiness, not only before his captors and enemies but his allies and former friends. Imagine the loneliness of one who has been "turned" by torture, the worst fate among all these.

The practice of torture is an imposition of the body upon the mind. So that the mind (self, idea, will) is put at the mercy of the body's capacity to withstand pain. Physical torture implies all that we imply by psychological torture, plus a great deal more. For one suffers here the frustration of insult and ill will, the hurt of being hurt on purpose, the realization that one is deliberately made to suffer physical pain—the body's pain compounded by the injury of injustice and contempt; psychic wounds.

If insult is the psychological equivalent of a blow, torture aims at the organization of insult so general and overwhelming as to destroy: through helplessness, the shame of helplessness, an exhaustion and impotence directed toward a final surrender of the self. Its ideal outcome is not only its own injunction to execute oneself, but an injunction assented to, welcomed. This is to be conquered utterly. Such pressure is constant. In the cells around Alleg's, torture goes on all night:

> Through the partition, I could hear shouts and cries, muffled by the gag, and curses and blows. I soon knew that this was in no way exceptional, but just the routine order of the day. The cries of suffering were part of the familiar noises . . . none of the Paras [paratroopers] paid any attention to it, but I don't believe that there was a single prisoner who did not, like myself, weep with hatred and humiliation on hearing the screams of the tortured for the first time.

There is the impression of two sides performing before history; the fact of present power pitted against the long run and one side's final victory. " 'We have time,' said the major. 'They're all like that at the beginning. We'll take a month, two months, or three months, but he'll talk.' " A civilian official present at the torture session compares Alleg to Elyette Loup and Akkache, heroes of the Algerian uprising, meaning to deprecate and not to praise: " 'What he wants is to be a hero, and have a little plaque on the wall in a few hundred years." Alleg is informed his children will arrive by plane tonight from

France, then that "They will have an accident." Alleg, who has
spent several nights fearing that the woman being tortured in
the next cell is really his wife, Gilberte, still refuses to go for
the bait. "Don't you care what happens to your children?" The
lieutenant pauses a moment and then concludes—"Good!
Then you will die."

"Everybody will know how I died."

"No, nobody will know anything."

"Everything is always known."

Everyone is bluffing, everything is not always known, not
for a long time. In many cases, never. Perhaps it is not really
a lie, it is hope becoming conviction, as a life lived on principle
is hope, as integrity is also necessity, at certain times and in
some cases. Torture and imprisonment were almost invented
to discover these truths. To test them, to place assertion upon
the rack. There is something very terrible about this examination, something exaggerated and unfair: our intentions and
protestations should never be so tried and savaged. Yet those
who endure are admired and their nobility acknowledged. "A
little plaque on the wall in a few hundred years" is nothing to
the civilian employee of the Department of Security; or rather,
it is contemptible and absurd in comparison to the fact of his
side's power at this moment. The moment when he and his
companions, the brotherhood of soldiers and officers, stand
before their victim.

But as one reads the book, the fact that the book is there to
read (its author alive and his manuscript printed, distributed)
evens the contest and changes the balance. What the book
achieved is its own victory; the dishonorable regime this nameless state functionary further dishonors has fallen decades ago,
fallen in good measure because of this book, written in a time
where, if the truth could come out, it would triumph.

Alleg's account of torture is elemental, archetypal, a scenario followed by history; he also introduces us to a character who is to become part of our time, the torturer-physician. The Nazis made this a medical specialty, though few who met Dr. Mengele lived to tell of it and he is always a distant figure. Alleg's physician is so near he hovers above him administering drugs. Because they bypass the will, drugs are a great weapon in torture. While they can cause great anguish, they deprive the sadist of the pleasure as well as the exertion of administering torment blow after blow and measuring the effect. Drugs are easy and convenient, they offer quick access and great opportunities for conquest; technology can develop them further.

Alleg is administered sodium pentothal, a drug he is able to withstand at least this time and in this dosage. "I shall not beat you and I promise not do you any harm," the torture doctor assures him, a curious perversion of the Hippocratic Oath. The drug makes Alleg very voluble and he goes on at great length about newspaper production. But he has been forewarned that if the willpower of the patient is strong enough he cannot be forced to say what he does not want to, so he is also forearmed when the doctor begins his blandishments and pretends to be his friend Marcel, nearly getting him to give his address in hiding. At the end of a session, "I had succeeded in not answering his questions, but how would I evade him the next time? I knew that I was delirious . . . but every time I returned to reality, I was unable to allay the fears that the drug raised in me."

By now one is aware that Alleg's escape is sheer luck, and that drugs can be far harder to withstand than simple physical pain, that if certain persons can resist blows and physical torment even to death, there is still a good possibility drugs exist or will exist which cannot be withstood at all. Yet even against drugs the mind struggles—how long, how hard depending upon the body's condition and the mind's. Drugs are a new dimension both in the physical and mental suffering they impose and the manner in which they transcend the will. There is the factor of time as well, for with little trouble to one's tormentors one can be tortured with drugs over long periods of time. Analogous physical torture would require great commitments in the expenditure of personnel time and effort: beating prisoners is hard work. By a mere injection or a pill, days of torment can be imposed, which bring about a physical as well as a psychological and spiritual capitulation. The victim's will is vitiated by nightmares, hallucinations, delusions, fears for his own sanity, hideous repetitions, optical blurring, double sight, muscle fatigue or spasm, dry mouth—an army of torments.

Alleg is deeply shaken before the power of the drug: "I asked myself if I was not going mad. If they continued to drug me would I still be able to resist as I had done the first time? And if the pentothal made me say what I didn't want to, my agony under torture would have served no purpose." With prolyxin, a common neuroleptic or anti-psychotic drug which has been used upon Irish political prisoners, the effects of an intravenous dosage can last for weeks. Drugs have been tested upon persons incarcerated as political prisoners for later use upon "mental patients": understood in the first case as control and punishment, excused in the second as medicine and healing, and perceived differently for that reason. In fact, experience and effect are similar. However, the acknowledged prisoner resists them out of an organized and coherent self-image: they are invasions of his body, invasions condemned not only by his comrades and allies but by international law. He must withstand them over a period of time until his status as a political prisoner is respected and acknowledged. Until help comes, for he has a side and there are others on his side; whether they arrive in time to save him or not, they exist in any case. This is not true for "patients" forced to consume the same drugs.

For the one called mad, there is no system of support nor any guarantee of temporality; this difference is made particularly glaring when one reads the accounts of Soviet dissidents labeled "schizophrenic" and confined as psychiatric cases. The injustice of their position is very clear to them; to be treated as the mad, drugged and confined, is hell. For the mad, it is presumably something else: hospitalization, care, and medication. The existence of a double standard of imprisonment and invasion is made abundantly clear; just as clear is the greater jeopardy of the alleged mad, their utter and unprotected loneliness before the conditions they face. The effort needed to maintain sanity under such conditions—while drugged over a long period of time and without any redeeming self-image or social reinforcement—is indeed an enormous one. Wonderful as the mind is, powerful as its will and determination, the limits of endurance are finite.

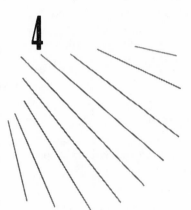

4

THE BRITISH IN
IRELAND

As the mad are to the sane, so are colonials to imperialists. Historically, it is important that Henri Alleg is a Frenchman, deeply involved with French sensibility and patriotism; he began his book with the words of Jean-Christophe: "In attacking a corrupt France, it is France that I defend." He ends on this conciliatory note: "All this, I have had to say for those Frenchmen who will read me. I want them to know that the Algerians do not confuse their torturers with the great people of France, from whom they have learnt so much and whose friendship is so dear to them. But they must know what is done IN THEIR NAME."

In Jean-Paul Sartre's dynamic and influential Introduction, Alleg's French identity is a source of satisfaction:

Alleg has saved us from despair and shame because he is the victim himself and because he has conquered torture. This reversal is not without a certain sinister humor; it is in our name that he was victimized and because of him we regain a little of our pride: we are proud that he is French. The reader identifies himself with him passionately, he accompanies him to the extremity of his suffering; with him, alone and naked, he does not give way. Could the reader, could we, *if it happened to us,* do the same? That is another matter. What is important, however, is that the victim saves us in making us discover, as he discovered himself, that we have the ability and the duty to undergo anything.

Given its context, this celebration of national pride seems excessive, even granted the desire to save face before the infamy of French conduct in Algeria: one good Frenchman put to torture and brave enough to withstand the ordeal hardly balances accounts. Would an Arab's recital elicit the same sympathy? Would an Arab ever have been heard? It is likely that Alleg was the only Frenchman tortured by the paratroopers. Thousands of Arabs were tortured, but it is Alleg's torture, or rather his testimony of its occurrence, that can shake the French government in Algiers.

There is protocol in torture. Roman law established this formally: until the late empire, barbarians could be tortured but not Roman citizens. Indeed, it was a sign of late imperial corruption when persons protected by the sacred name of Roman citizenship could finally be subject to torture as well: by then freeman and slave were the same under imperial yoke. In the opinion of Edward Peters in his *Torture,* Roman law remains important in understanding the concept of torture since it "constituted the greatest body of learned jurisprudence known to western tradition," and "its doctrine of torture influenced strongly the two revivals of torture that the western world has experienced—those of the thirteenth and twentieth centuries."

Under Roman law, slaveowners were permitted the absolute right to punish and torture their own slaves when suspected of offense, a right preserved until A.D. 240. Such practices led the historian Theodor Mommsen to argue that Roman domestic discipline was the basis of later Roman penal procedure in civil and criminal law. This paradigm of patriarchal authority, the configuration of the *pater potentes* over wife, child, and chattel, still underlies modern family law.

Of course the revival of torture in the Inquisition was a revival of Roman permissions and practices of torture as Peters describes them, "precise, limited, and highly regulated in law and legal theory," even "the subject of an enormous legislation and an even vaster body of technical legal scholarship." After more than a millennium of Christian proscription, the Inquisition restored Roman practice into canon law, permitting and regulating the practice of torture from the time Pope Innocent IV issued his decretal *Ad extirpanda* in 1252 until the Holy Office was at last foregone in Spain in the nineteenth century after long and determined campaigning by Enlightenment forces. When torture reappears in the twentieth century, it no longer has any express legal foundation. Instead, it follows obliquely upon a body of peripheral legislation—special powers acts, suspensions of constitutional rights under emergency provisions, martial law, extraordinary detention statutes, none of which literally permit, sanction, or regulate torture as did Roman law. Yet each creates a series of circumstances whereby torture can be practiced in secret.

The distinction between the citizen of Rome in the period of his immunity to torture and a mere barbarian is one still felt by members of empire versus colonials, a distinction Sartre and Alleg oppose wholeheartedly, a legalist version of racism. Both of them understand that the French imperial reaction to Algerian independence is a fury not merely imperial but racist, since the imperial/colonial nexus is built on racism and notions of race, ruling and subject races. An entire historical rationale, even an elaborate emotional practice, is built around this conjunction. Within it much is possible. The concept of the "other" is important: upon this, other unthinkable things can be practiced. One may experiment, try out ideas, test theories of behavior. The study of psychology can be brought to bear, concepts such as sensory deprivation can be developed.

Methods can be simple once principles are understood and applied. The psychologist Robert Storr in his *Solitude, a Return to the Self,** examines British practices upon Irish colonials in the light of sensory deprivation theory:

> The heads of the detainees were covered with a thick black hood, except when they were being interrogated. They were subjected to a continuous, monotonous noise of such volume that communication with other detainees was impossible. They were required to stand facing a wall with legs apart, leaning on their fingertips. In addition, they were deprived of sleep during the early days of the operation, and given no food or drink other than one round of bread and one pint of water at six-hourly intervals. If they sought rest by propping their heads against the wall they were prevented from doing so. If they collapsed, they were picked up and compelled to resume the required posture.

The type of soundproof and lightproof chamber used in sensory deprivation research is extremely expensive; here the British have achieved the same results with scarcely any outlay. The hood prevents a victim from receiving any visual information: one is blind and worse than blind because balance itself is affected as well. The machine ensures that one receives no auditory intake other than a loud, exasperating noise. Kinesthetic information from skin or muscles is reduced by the position of leaning against the wall: each detainee is isolated from virtually all ordinary stimulus, even though there may be many prisoners in a room.

"The effects were devastating," Storr reports;

> partial starvation, which causes rapid loss of weight, combined with deprivation of sleep and an uncomfortable posture are themselves enough to cause extreme stress and some disruption of brain function, even without additional deprivation of auditory

*The extracts that follow are taken from Robert Storr, *Solitude, a Return to the Self* (New York: Free Press, 1988).

and visual information. Subject to breaks for bread and water and visits to the lavatory, some men were kept against the wall continuously for fifteen or sixteen hours. Many experienced hallucinations and believed they were going mad. Afterwards, some said that they would prefer to die rather than face further interrogation.

The damage done is of a lasting character: "Examined after their release, these men were found to have persistent physical and psychological symptoms of stress and tension, headaches and ulcers; some at least would never recover." Most of this is achieved with a simple piece of black cloth, the hood. Add to this crucial device the trouble of forcing people to stand in physically untenable positions for long hours, and the standard practice of sleep deprivation, and one has arrived at a perfect regimen of psychological torture.

Britain has long depended on extraordinary powers and emergency legislation over Ireland; habeas corpus itself was suspended for all but twelve years of the nineteenth century. From the 1920s onward Special Powers acts were in force which made internment without trial fairly common; in 1971, the Special Powers Act was reintroduced on a large scale to detain and intimidate at will; in 1973, there was the Emergency Provisions Act; in 1975, the Prevention of Terrorism Act. Under the rubric of dealing with "terrorism," the state had amassed enormous powers and set a precedent. These controls—together with the Special or Diplock Courts ratified in 1972 by the Diplock Commission, which validated detention and abolished jury trial in favor of a single magistrate liable to convict—created a situation where sentences of twenty years were routinely given and routinely served for "scheduled" offenses, confirmed again in the 1978 Emergency Provisions: namely, any type of offense connected with the political situation. Interrogation centers were set up and civil liberties suspended; confessions were frequently the result of tortures like those described above.

The British were first discovered to be using torture in Aden in 1966. In that same year, Amnesty International filed its Rastgeldi Report accusing Britain of violating the UN Declaration of Human Rights. There was scandal, but no reform. By the next decade, when torture was adapted for use against dissident Irish colonials, it had become routine. Britain was repeatedly accused of torture in Ireland by Amnesty International and tried before the European Court. In 1958 Henri Alleg's accusation devastated France, but by the seventies Britain could face down shame with a new sophistication. At first it weathered accusations through bureaucratic studies and semantic evasions. Later it exerted enormous energy in saving face before the European Community and world opinion, and succeeded at last in having the court's first decision that Britain itself was guilty of torture in Ireland reduced, on appeal, to a judgment that cruel and unusual treatment toward Irish political prisoners was used—but not actual torture. A significant victory in public relations.

Evidence was accumulating that states could get by with torture now. Particularly if it were against a colonial subject, if the issues could be made muddy or "complex" enough, if the situation had "two sides" to it, if it were old and complicated and presented as virtually insoluble, if the "story" could be controlled, if you could keep television out. If there was no footage of British tanks, then there was no invasion, therefore no war and no prisoners of war. The issue of war and a British invasion are crucial; they explain the great importance which the British placed on criminalizing those who resisted, and the equally great importance that Irish resistance placed upon recognition of the political status of those people while imprisoned.

In 1976, the political status of Irish dissidents as prisoners of war was withdrawn; they reacted by "going on the blanket," refusing to do prison work or wear prison clothing, naked except for the blankets from their prison cots. This was met with twenty-four-hour solitary confinement and a denial of mail, radio and television, books, and all reading material. Protesting prisoners were fed little, their cells were barely heated in winter, they were frequently and systematically beaten. In final protest to these conditions, Irish political prisoners have staged hunger strikes to the death: in the last one, that of 1981, ten men died a long and terrible death.

The British never relented. One of those who died was Bobby Sands. At the time of his death, Sands was a Member of Parliament, elected while in prison. When he was arrested in 1977, Sands was tortured with repeated beatings, and though the hood was not in use, he was forced to spend long hours leaning against the wall, a position meant to exhaust him and break his spirit. It was also one where his captors could assault him comfortably: "I was spreadeagled against the wall with my finger tips only, high up against the wall and my feet spread apart and back as far as I could manage. The detective who was reeking with alcohol was punching me in the kidneys, sides, back, neck, in fact everywhere. The other detective was holding me by the hair and flinging questions into my face." Sands is testifying in *The H Blocks,* a collection of statements by Irish political prisoners incarcerated at Long Kesh, near Belfast, County Antrim, compiled by the Catholic chaplains Father Denis Faul and Father Raymond Murray, and printed in 1979. (There is no publisher listed since the book was proscribed in Ireland as an illicit publication.)

I was threatened that my wife would be brought in to where I was and that she would also get what I got even though she was pregnant. . . . I was once again hauled up on my feet, beat about and made to take my boots off . . . the detective who was still reeking with alcohol was standing at one side of me and he was leaning into my face screaming abuse . . . I was still spread eagled. When he sat to the front of me, on my left hand side, he was swinging his foot between my legs and kicking me in the privates. He hit me about four or six times like this which sickened me and took the breath from me. I fell twice, only to be hauled to my feet in the same position again . . . I don't even remember falling, but I must have because I was being hauled off the floor and put on a chair when I regained my senses. . . . I had been interrogated and beaten for about seven hours or so with only a break for the doctor to examine me.

The H Blocks is a collection of first-person accounts of human rights abuses against Northern Irish, and like any book about torture, it is a book about fear, about falling into catastrophe. Sands continues his account: "I was put back into the cell exhausted and in pain. The bright light still shone and the four walls depressed me. I got off the bed and walked up and down the cell, four paces each way. I was, as I said, exhausted, pained, depressed and demoralized, but I knew that if I didn't keep walking and keep my mind going that I would break down and sign my name to a lot of things I knew nothing about. I had been asked to put my signature on a blank sheet which I refused."

THAT personal sense of catastrophe which is the very stuff of the prisoner's experience is, through a reader's participation in the event, generalized, shared, transformed into a collective catastrophe. One victim after another tells his story; the effect is cumulative. The prisoner's fear is something we begin to experience too as we read. His mistreatment is something we share emotionally through the literary and psychological experience of empathy. Eventually we become immersed in it logically, politically; gradually we are introduced to political consequence and possibility: If such treatment is meted out to any citizen, then perhaps no citizen is entirely safe from it.

The prisoner's own sense of the catastrophic is always at odds with what goes on around him: "I remember an interrogation at approximately 10:00 to 10:30 P.M. . . . I remember the time as one of the detectives who I knew by name said he wanted to get home to see the Match of the Day on TV." The reader is as removed from the detective as is Bobby Sands; we are on Sands's side of a glass wall constructed by attitude that separates him from his tormentors. Now it separates us as well—something unusual since most readers generally identify with police and government rather than prisoners and persons accused of crimes.

The fact of political crime changes this, puts our habitual friendly relationship to the state in grave question, but it does something even more radical, even more tonic: it puts us in contact and sympathy with those behind bars, the outlawed, the condemned. We know their long days, we suffer through the nights of their abuse and terror. A literature of this kind does something basically seditious, something ethically radical: it not only questions authority but the very grounds of social cohesion which it has been the historical role of most literature to uphold and defend.

The prisoner-as-witness turns the world upside down for us, humbling us with his courage, since we know we couldn't endure what he endures. But his integrity humbles us, too. It is all he has. It is his only possession. Naked, cold, full of bruises, destitute, his property confiscated, having lost his family and friends, his profession and education useless, reduced to a criminal, afraid of what will befall him in the next hour, close to death and afraid of it, he still manages to live on principle alone.

There is also something remarkable about the victim's habit of refraining from naming names: Alleg refers to his tormentors by their initials; Sands, even after telling us he knows his interrogator's name, withholds it. Fear of reprisal, one wonders, or a refusal to take revenge? There is a vulnerability about the prisoner so overwhelming that, paradoxically, it constitutes in itself a form of safety. In peril from all those around him, the witness is at ease only with the reader: he has put himself in our hands and is safe there as nowhere else.

Do we read these books taking comfort in the fact that their circumstances are so much more terrible than our own? Does the witness's predicament present a temptation to fantasy for the reader, imaginative refuge and escape from his (or her) own realities? Do we enjoy what will never happen to us—a world where the worst has already come to pass? One remembers Alleg's knowledge that there is not much more that they can do, thrown into his cell the first night to realize in a wonderful moment that he could endure this far and might prevail. And if over time he cannot prevail, then at the worst he can welcome death as release.

Death—which we fear much of the time—becomes, under these circumstances, something wished for, an escape. And if we all fear death, we all fear torture more, have dreaded it from childhood, have dreamed and imagined it since then, our first brush with it in beatings, "corporal" punishment, physical intimidation and vulnerability. The child's terror becomes the adult's. The state, assuming paternal, sometimes even divine, power, administers torture as its final prerogative, the last and most awesome of its powers. Having relinquished such powers, having renounced them for the social contract in the age of reason, it has now on the sly retracted its oaths, assumed the ultimate force again, ready to violate and invade our bodies beyond all possibility of our endurance. The state grown into a total force, surpassing or deposing religion, becoming its own religion. Dogmatic, pitiless, cruel. A hideous god, the last and worst of all.

The victims of such power are heroes fighting against the last remnants of tyranny or, with beautiful futility, against the first triumphs of a new totalitarian order. Admirable even if they lose, they represent us in our last moments of rebellion. Do we therefore read this literature as hagiography, satisfying the same needs for heroism and example that the lives the saints and martyrs once fulfilled, a civil and secular hagiography, inoculation against the lay religion of patriotism? Reading in empathy with the resister, we resist without unpleasant consequences, sin as it were against the state, while keeping faith with an unofficial and by now quasi-heretical creed of freedom. The martyr exercises a virtue we increasingly fear to profess, experiences a grace we shall not experience. Because we don't want to be arrested. Or because the occasion to be apprehended is not part of our immediate landscape. A vicarious defiance is all we shall ever experience.

But the voice we hear is also our own conscience. If heard and supported in large numbers, we are as safe and ultimately as effective as the Amnesty letterwriters who shake governments and annoy ministers, even open prison doors. The prisoner makes a reader uneasy, represents the dangerous, the terrible consequences of risk. But he also stands for direction and action, forlorn, isolated, and extreme as he may seem. The detainee carries the onus of these damned by the full force of victimization under power, yet, paradoxically, in resistance he prefigures the possibilities of salvation from it as well.

Krishnamurti tells us that our worst fear, in fact fear itself, is merely fear of the unknown. To disappear into political imprisonment is to undergo just such a fate: here is the worst it gets. Reading these accounts, we experience terror and despair in the person of another. We are with Artur London, the Czech diplomat, awaiting trial during a Communist Party purge: through him we come to know the anxiety, the suspense, the gun put to our temple, the rope around our neck in mock hangings that we believe are real. We wear London's blindfold with him in *The Confession.** He lived to tell it; we live to hear it.

Of course, few survived the purges; most died alone and in sickening fear, in perfect and entire despair. Does literature lie or tell the truth? Sometimes? All the time? Any of the time?

MAINTAINING secrecy and distance, torturers are traditionally masked. The executioner's mask is sign that he *is* his

---

*Artur London, *The Confession,* translated from the French by Alistair Hamilton (New York: Ballantine Books, 1970).

function, its dignified cruelty, and no mere individual who, were it not for his office, might be committing a crime. His office, a public and acknowledged identity, has subsumed his own personal identity and absolved him of responsibility. The torturer, the modern interrogator, is usually under orders either to blindfold his prisoner or to hide his identity behind a mask. Officers go slack, however, grow arrogant like Alleg's paratroopers abroad, smug among persons they regard as inferior. The British and their collaborators in the Royal Ulster Constabulary do not aspire to the French paratroopers' swagger or their self-conscious Nazi evil. There is no glamour here; they have long ago ceased to find this exciting. They are beating lesser beings whose retaliation they have no cause to fear and whose complaint has time and again failed to harm them as it fails over and over to get a hearing. They operate with a kind of impunity, a bored brutality that would like to get home in time for the Match of the Week.

They are also confident that they have the support of their own superior officers and even, by and large, of the public. With the British public, they can depend on a long history of attitude which on examination is distinctly racist. Though both groups are Caucasian, even Christian, British contempt for the Irish is ancient and entire, a racial hatred, in fact. The English poet Edmund Spenser, serving as secretary to the Lord Lieutenant of Ireland under the first Elizabeth, was an early member of the colonial administration; he fell in love with the beauty of the Irish landscape but spoke frankly of annihilating the native population. Hundreds of years later, Northern Ireland, "settled" by conquest with a large British population— the parallel of what in Algeria were called *colons,* whose wealth, prestige, and superiority depend upon the original colonial power's presence and support—also believe they have much to fear on its departure.

Torture is introduced into this situation through a long habit of malice. As Sartre observes: "The purpose of torture is not only to make a person talk, but to make him betray others.

The victim must turn himself by his screams and by his submission into a lower animal in the eyes of all and in his own eyes. His betrayal must destroy him and take away his human dignity. He who gives way under questioning is not only constrained from talking again, but given a new status, that of sub-man," Sartre points out, analyzing the conjunction of brutality and colonial status; ". . . colonialism ends by the annihilation of the colonized. They own nothing, they are nothing . . . under the constant pressure of their masters, their standard of living has been reduced year by year. When despair drove them to rebellion, these sub-men had the choice of starvation or of re-affirming their manhood against ours . . . this rebellion is not merely challenging the power of the settlers but their very being. For most . . . colonists are backed by divine right, the natives are sub-human."

Founded upon a solid ground of economic exploitation, the racist construct of overman and subman is "a mythical interpretation of a reality, since the riches of the one are built on the poverty of the other." Sartre's summary of Algeria is equally apposite to Ireland, the longest colonization in history, a case study in methods of exploitation and repression. The factors of racial and colonial attitude are important because later torturers will follow the same lines; Americans following the French in Southeast Asia—Vietnam and Cambodia—and finally operating on their own throughout South America.

For the colonial, Sartre goes on, "it is not only the economic question of the emancipation of the 'wogs' that appalls him, but the implied threat to his own status as a human being. In his rage he may dream romantically of genocide. But this is pure fantasy. Rationally he is aware of his need for the native proletariat to provide surplus labor, and chronic unemployment to allow him to fix his own wage rates." And if he has accepted the "others" as human beings, Sartre argues, there is then "no sense in killing them." Instead, "the need is rather to humiliate them, to crush their pride and drag them down to animal level. The body may live, but the spirit must be killed.

To train, discipline and chastise; these are the words which obsess them." Sartre is not arguing that the colonizer himself is responsible for inventing or even for introducing torture into this confrontation; given the circumstances, its appearance is natural, inevitable: "it was the order of the day before we even noticed it. Torture was simply the expression of racial hatred." Because in a sense colonialism demands a more robust humanity for one party and a lesser one for the other: "It is the man himself that they want to destroy, with all his human qualities, his courage, his will, his intelligence, his loyalty, the very qualities that the colonizer claims for himself." And if the colonizer ever comes "to hate his own face," it will be from seeing it reflected in that of the Other—Sartre predicts—the Arab, the Oriental.

Or the female, one thinks to add, as Simone de Beauvoir did. For perhaps Sartre, in saying "man," means only men: "It is a bitter and tragic fact that, for the Europeans in Algeria, being a man means first and foremost superiority to the Moslems. But what if the Moslem finds in his turn that his manhood depends on equality with the settler? It is then that the European begins to feel his very existence diminished and cheapened." And in considering "these two indissoluble partnerships, the colonizer and the colonized, the executioner and his victim, we can see that the second is only an aspect of the first." The literal executioner, however, is not the colonial settler, but a young soldier from the imperial power, a young Frenchman or Englishman, American, whatever; young men "who have lived twenty years of their life without ever having troubled themselves" about the Algerian, Irish, or whatever problem. "But hate is a magnetic field: it has crossed over to them, corroded them and enslaved them." Algeria, as Alleg put it, was a "school of perversion for young Frenchmen." Sartre carries the description still further: "Among these little cads, proud of their youth, their strength, their numbers, Alleg is the only really tough one, the only one who is really strong."

There is, however, a series of assumptions in Sartre's Introduction which gives one pause. First, the presumption that real
men, shall we say, do not talk. "A tough one," the one who,
in the end, "made the archangels of anger afraid": for "when
the victim wins, then it is goodbye to their absolute power,
their lordship. Their archangels wings droop and they become
just brutish men, asking themselves, 'And will I be able to take
it too, when I am tortured?' Because in the moment of victory,
one system of values is substituted for another; all it needs is
that the torturers should become dizzy in their turn. But no,
their heads are empty and their work keeps them too busy and
then they only half-believe in what they are doing."

The assumption throughout Sartre's essay is the conventional one that the victim and the executioner are paired, like
the colonial and the colonizer; that mankind has always struggled for its "collective or individual interests," so much so, in
fact, that it is even "normal" for us to kill each other. Torture,
Sartre argues, is different: "in the case of torture, this strange
contest of will, the ends seem to me to be radically different:
the torturer pits himself against the tortured for his 'manhood'
and the duel is fought as if it were not possible for both sides
to belong to the human race."

At a stroke one sees the limitation of equating manhood
with humanity, a philosophic difference one had imagined was
simply linguistic. Somehow this struggle over "manhood" fails
to apply to the courage of the Irish hunger strikers, women as
well as men, who have chosen the ultimate pacifist tactic of
conquest through self-sacrifice, even self-immolation. And
what Sartre means by "manhood" is intended to be something
masculine, active, a combat (whether physical, mental, or
moral) that is exclusive to the male ego. The hunger strikers
are heroic with a different heroism. There are in fact types and
kinds of courage, diverse notions of chivalry, different codes.

It is also possible for the oppressed to be only the mirror
image of the oppressor, the tortured to the torturer, the victim

to the victimizer—permanent pairings such as female submission and male dominance, black and white under racism, colonial and colonizer. It is possible then that change from this condition consists only in reversing it, the tortured becoming free to torture. Are we to imagine that this potentiality must be attained before torture is renounced?

For torture will merely be repeated and perpetuated if the pairing is not broken, the chain of opposites, the duality, the positive and negative electrical energies. Sartre himself is aware of how these forces produce an explosion which, when carried to extremes, creates a tedium of "craziness." "Torture is senseless violence, born in fear. The purpose of it is to force from one tongue, amid its screams and its vomiting up of blood, the secret of *everything*. Senseless violence: whether the victim talks or whether he dies under his agony, the secret that he cannot tell is always somewhere else and out of reach. It is the executioner who becomes Sisyphus. If he puts the *question* at all, he will have to continue forever."

Sartre has glimpsed the echo, the repetition, the endless quest of interrogation, the mad scramble for a power never satisfied and becoming a drug: "But this silence, this fear, these always invisible and always present dangers, cannot fully explain the obsession of the torturers, their desire to reduce their victims to abjection and in its final stages the hatred of mankind which takes possession of them without their knowing it." Perhaps it is out of such reflexes that people, women as well as men, torment children to death.

It is finally about power, as the rapist knows too, it is about a reflex Sartre is wise to call anger. This is rage—where all the remembered frustrations of life are given expression, permission. Permission one simply does not encounter in ordinary life, where we are fairly matched, where there is every possibility of the victims' refusal; where one can simply get up and leave.

Here is where the state is crucial. And capture. State authority and state incarceration: if state permission is added, one has a recipe for torture. The remedy is as simple: state prohibition of torture. When one considers torture, one comes to under-stand how crucial a precondition is capture; how great an invasion of the human condition is imprisonment itself. How any confinement erodes humanity, and how broadly it is ex-tended in the case of political imprisonment where there is no criminal offense to extenuate the arbitrary cruelty of human incarceration. Still more irrational to extend this detention in legal commitment under state psychiatric power and deten-tion.

Detention without trial or charge is responsible for torture to a greater extent than any other modern factor. In *Amnesty International, the Human Rights Story,** Jonathan Power re-ports that in more than 50 nations one could then be detained without trial or charge; of the 154 member nations of the United Nations, there had been allegations of the practice of torture by governments in 60. In the 1984 report *Torture in the Eighties* (Amnesty, USA), the number had risen to sixty-six. Psychiatric torture is not consistently recognized or recorded as such; political dissidents in the Eastern bloc experience it, but not the "mentally ill." It is difficult to differentiate be-tween a process which is a crime against humanity in one instance, but merely an example of care, science, and concern in another.

It is also difficult to see a body whipped and bleeding in one instance as a being tortured and abused, and to differentiate the same fact in another instance as the free exercise of erotic imagination. The ground of distinction generally made is one of volition. Even that fails to be present in psychiatric impris-onment; those committed voluntarily, once exposed to treat-ment, are not permitted to retract their voluntary status and thus become involuntary. Shocked or drugged repeatedly against their wills, they are still on paper volunteers.

It is understood, however, that captivity of the sadist and

*(New York: McGraw-Hill, 1981).

masochist is not only voluntary but a form of play and acting, whereas capture and incarceration by the state are reality. Perhaps our increasingly easy acceptance of state authority hastens our danger before it; our trust in permitting its constant extension. The ability to detain and hold the citizen against his will, even for his own good or the good of all, is the beginning of our undoing.

For captivity is an absolute state. Once captive, one can be treated in any manner the captor chooses: this is the physical fact of capture. There are no guarantees in captivity: power need not concede anything at all. One is physically at the mercy of a captor; every potentiality is on one side, none on the other. There may be mercy or there may be none. It is beyond the captive's power to make or unmake any aspect of his captivity. Captivity is an entire state; entire helplessness before entire power. This, like all absolutes, is wise to avoid: capture is physical fact.

In sadomasochistic play-acting, even here, this becomes the case. One who even voluntarily submits to bondage can find it absolute as well. Once handcuffed, one cannot extricate oneself, is unable to defend oneself. If circumstances are conducive, the would-be experimenter, once bound, could be actually imprisoned, a clandestine imprisonment with all the drawbacks that secrecy and isolation entail. Access and assistance disappear. Murder itself can take place under the rubric of sadomasochism, though it rarely does.

The facts, namely, the physical circumstances of such personal theatre, resemble those which the state employs, so that one is "playing with" dangers that could become actualized; the premise in such thrill-seeking is that one trusts the lover not to betray a trust. Given how frequently trust is betrayed in love, sadomasochistic ritual has a commendable reliability.

Nevertheless, it is cause for unease that torture and capture, the very area staked out by the state for an invasion of human rights in modern times, should in the same historical moment become a source of widespread and erotic play-acting, now public and open. Or perhaps it is entirely logical that what overshadows imagination in our time—the might and cruelty of the state—enacted in real incarceration for one population should become a form of entertainment for another. Faddish, incoherent, a form of mimicry. Individuals who identify with state power share the power they admire, share through fantasy. The colonial victim twists in the wind; the citizen of empire visits a shop for sexual devices, finger chains, and selects a whip or manacle, novelties which only gather meaning when dramatized. *Mutandis mutandi.*

Strange new circumstance, when relics the race once assumed it had put behind it and remembered only in harmless if corny Hollywood artifact (Roman slavery, the knout, the rack), when articles and circumstances of power recalled only in costume pieces and historical melodrama become again reality through the reintroduction of torture as state policy. Surely the great evil of our time, and a far greater threat than erotic fashion.

Yet now when torture is real and present, there is something offensive in a sensibility that has come to mime it for sport, to make it a game, a ritual, an aesthetic. One might argue a congruence between a society's crimes and its nightmares, its excesses and its amusements. Assumptions of state power reflect and are reflected back in personal expressions and obsessions with power; this is the purpose of jingoism. What collective desires does the state satisfy? Still more, what desires are inspired through the example of state immanence?

Consider electrodes applied to the genitals viewed in this light: how sexy, at what voltage? Questions of style. Sadomasochistic enthusiasm might detumesce here, fingering chain and whip, prefering older paraphernalia. Contemporary technology may be too actual and therefore less romantic; antique forms are more attractive, represent power fallen into a certain agreeable desuetude. The oldest, most basic forms of authority still have force and attraction, the required veil of fantasy. But the lines of prohibition and power differ only in detail. There is still the principle of obedience and submission, dominance and subordination, an appropriation and acceptance of force.

One might argue finally that state religion is puritanical, that it habitually disguises or sublimates sexual excitement while counting on sexual shame. It counts on history, too, and upon individual lifetimes of repression, the identification of sex with sin, with pain, with punishment; all profoundly conventional notions. And in the explosive acts of its cruelties, its wars and police violence, the state can draw upon these conditioned responses for allegiance and obedience. We have been punished all our lives, have accepted penalty and repression, been habitually forced to substitute violence for sensuality.

The sadomasochist aspires to stand apart as a sexual rebel, a last romantic, an enemy of the state, a true believer in passion. But it is only more of the same thing: repetition, mirror image. Tired hierarchy, ancient paradigm, threadbare patriarchy, the old roles, the old rules of domination. The true lover is enjoined to bear the whip even to bleeding; if the ethic of suffering is maintained somewhere, is it not perpetuated everywhere? Where is the way out of this?

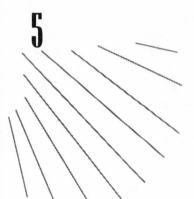

5

THE APARTHEID
SYSTEM IN SOUTH
AFRICA

THERE are some places where control is total. South Africa. If you are black. Here the power of the state and the power of a dominant race have reached a crisis point, a web of restraint unmatched in history. Even as it crumbles, the omnipotence of this system is awesome. One sees it best through the eyes of the black youth of the townships, its greatest victims and over the last decade, its most determined enemies. Like that of their parents', these children's very presence was illegal under apartheid. Nearly everywhere black existence itself was against the law of the invader: white South Africans, who comprise only 5 percent of the population, had appropriated 87 percent of the landmass to themselves, including all major cities, permitting South African blacks, who comprise 95 percent of the total population, only small parcels of arid soil for black "homelands," compulsory reservations.

Under the apartheid system, a series of laws made it technically illegal for blacks to appear anywhere else at all, since their presence outside the slender reserves of land allotted to them might be a criminal offense. However, this land could not support them, and the only opportunities for survival and employment lay in the white districts where their labor was needed and counted upon by the white economy. So, while on the one hand their presence anywhere outside the reserves was forbidden, on the other hand the very operation of white society depended upon exploiting them as its work force. Blacks were forced to lurk in shantytowns outside white population centers in supposedly clandestine if not invisible settlements in order to serve the white population. Hence the townships. And the pass system.

Passes were complex and difficult to get—you needed a job to get one, you couldn't get a job without one, as a result, few residents of the townships actually had a pass. A valid passbook involved a strict correctitude of job description and hours, it had to be current and regularly renewed. The bureaucratic regulations, details, and updates of passes were very arcane. To satisfy them required days of waiting in line, days one missed work. Therefore, very few of the hundreds of thousands of blacks crouched near white cities in the only hope of subsistence employment were there legally. The great mass were subject to arrest and imprisonment at any time.

All township residents, legal or illegal, were subject to search and seizure at any moment. Life under such surveillance and the danger of imminent and violent attack was a nightmare. Especially so after dark. And for children living in abject poverty and housed in conditions that resemble those of domestic animals, sleeping in shacks without clothes or beds or sanitary facilities, it was a nightmare of enormous proportion.

Waking upon another police raid, the five-year-old Mark Mathabane stirs on the floor beneath the kitchen table. There is a torn blanket thrown over the table; under it, he and his little sister Florah sleep on a piece of cardboard laid over the dirt floor with a few newspapers to cover them. It's six in the morning, his father left for work at five-thirty, his mother has gone outside to the privy in her underwear and found a raid in progress. Mark sees her by the light of their only candle, crouched in a corner like "an animal cowering in fear."*

The invasion is still a block away, but the alarm—"people leaping over fences in a mad dash to escape the police"—and a collective terror have already formed: there will be beatings with whips made of animal hide (shamboks), people will be dragged naked from bed and arrested, there will be gunshots and chases, households will be ransacked and destroyed, and when it's over, abandoned children will cry alone among the ruins.

Mathabane's mother is going to make a run for it. The candle flickers in the wind but does not go out; the child's fear overcomes him: "I felt something warm soak my groin and trickle down my legs. I tried to stem the flow of urine by pressing my thighs together, but I was too late; a puddle had formed about my feet, and I scattered it with my toes." The last time the police were here they had beaten up the boy; the last time his parents had been arrested. Frantic until she finds her passbook, his mother takes it and goes outside again into hiding.

He is alone now, to face whatever comes: screams from outside as "more doors and windows were busted by the police; the vicious barking of dogs escalated, as did the thudding of running feet. Shouts of 'Mbambe! Mbambe! (Grab him! Catch him!)' followed by the screams of police whistles." A shaft of very bright light penetrates the uncurtained kitchen window for an instant; the boy drops the candle in fright and is then in darkness. As he gropes about, this abnormally strong light shines again into the kitchen: "This time it stayed. It seemed daylight." The boy's little brother awakes and begins to cry; he must be silenced or the police will hear.

*The extracts that follow are taken from Mark Mathabane, *Kaffir Boy* (New York: New American Library, 1986).

"Let him suck thumb," the mother had whispered before she left; there was no other comfort. The boy bolts the door and then barricades it, a five-year-old

dragging things from all over the kitchen and piling them up against the door—a barrel half filled with drinking water, a scuttle half-filled with coal and several tin chairs. Satisfied that the door was now impregnable I then scuttled back to the bedroom and there leaped upon the bed by the latticed window. "Shut up you fool!" I yelled at my brother, but he did not quiet. I then uttered the phrase "There's a white man outside," which to small black children had the same effect as "There's a bogeyman outside," but still he would not stop. I then stuck my thumb into his wide-open mouth, as my mother had told me. But George had other plans for my thumb, he sunk his teeth into it. Howling with pain, I grabbed him by the feet and tossed him over and spanked him on the buttocks. "Don't ever do that!"

He became hysterical and went into a seizure of screams. His body writhed and his mouth frothed. Again I grabbed his tiny feet and shook him violently, begged him to stop screaming, but still he would not quiet. I screamed at him some more; that made him worse. In desperation I wrenched his ears, punched him black and blue, but still he continued hollering. In despair, I gave up, for the time being, attempts to quiet him. My head spun and did not know what to do.

I glanced at the window; it was getting light outside. I saw two black policemen breaking down a door at the far end of the yard. A half-naked, near-hysterical, jet-black woman was being led out of an outhouse by a fat laughing black policeman who from time to time prodded her private parts with a truncheon. The storm of noises had now subsided somewhat, but I could still hear doors and windows being smashed, and dogs barking and children screaming. I jerked George and pinned him against the window, hoping that he should somehow understand why I needed him to shut up; but that did not help, for his eyes were shut, and he continued to scream and writhe. My eyes roved frantically about the semidark room and came to rest on a heavy black blanket hanging limply from the side of the bed. Aha! I quickly grabbed it and pulled it over George's head to muffle his screams. I pinned it tightly with both hands over his small head as he lay writhing. It worked! For though he continued screaming, I could hardly hear him. He struggled and struggled and I pinned the blanket tighter and tighter. It never crossed my mind that my brother might suffocate. As he no longer screamed, I waited, from time to time glancing nervously at the window.

Suddenly I heard the bedroom door open and shut. Startled, I let go of my hold on the blanket and turned my head toward the door only to see Florah, her eyes wild with fear, come rushing in, screaming, her hands over her head. She came over to the bedside and began tugging frantically at the blanket.

"Where's Mama! I want Mama! Where's Mama!"

"Shut up!" I raged. "Go back to sleep before I hit you!"

She did not leave.

"I'm scared," she whispered. "I want Mama."

"Shut up you fool!" I screamed at her again. "The white man is outside and he's going to get you and eat you!" I should not have said that; my sister became hysterical. She flung herself at the bed and tried to claw her way up. Enraged, I slapped her hard across the mouth; she staggered but did not fall. She promptly returned to the bedside and resumed her tugging of the blanket more determinedly. My brother too was now screaming. My head felt hot with confusion and desperation; I did not know what to do; I wished my mother were present; I wished the police were blotted off the surface of the earth.

I could still hear footsteps pounding, children screaming and dogs barking, so I quickly hauled my sister onto the bed, seeing that she was resolved not to return to the kitchen. We coiled together on the narrow bed, the three of us . . . but the din outside after a temporary lull surged and made its way through the bolted door, through the barricade, through the kitchen, through the blanket, through the blackness and into my finger-plugged ears, as if the bed were perched in the midst of all the pandemonium.

Finally Mark creeps toward the kitchen door: "a piece of sackcloth covered the bottom half of the window where several panes were missing, the result of a rock hurled from the street one night long ago. My father hadn't replaced the window but used the flap as a watchpost whenever police raided the neighborhood." The boy spies two black policemen coming out of the shack across the street to join a white man "with a holstered gun slung low about his waist, as in the movies," pacing about and "shouting orders and pointing in all different directions." Further off, another white man, "also with a gun was supervising a group of about ten black policemen as they rounded half-naked black men and women from the shacks.

The sight had me spellbound. Suddenly the white man by the entrance gate pointed in the direction of our house. Two black policemen jumped and started across the street toward me. They were quickly joined by a third. I gasped with fear. A new terror gripped me and froze me by the window, my head still sticking halfway out. My mind went blank; I shut my eyes; my heart thumped somewhere in my throat. . . .

Suddenly my sister came screaming out of the bedroom, her hands over her head . . . I stared at her . . . not wanting to move.

"It's G-george," she stammered with horror; "B-blood, d-dead, b-blood, d-dead!" her voice trailed into sobs. She rushed over to where I stood and began pulling my hand, imploring me to go see my brother who, she said dramatically, was bleeding to death. My mouth contorted into frantic, inaudible "Go aways" and "Shut ups" but she did not leave. I heard someone pounding at the door. In the confusion that followed angry voices said:

"There's no point in going in. I've had enough of hollering infants."

"Me too."

They left. It turned out that George had accidentally fallen off the bed and smashed his head against a pile of bricks at the foot of the bed, sustaining a deep cut across the forehead. The gash swelled and bled badly, stopping only after I had swathed his forehead with pieces of rags. The three of us cowered together in silence another three hours until my mother returned from the ditch where she had been hiding.

Without ever having knocked on the door during this particular raid, the police have been responsible for the near death of an infant first by asphyxiation and next by head injury. Mathabane's description of the endemic brutality in his childhood environment demonstrates how effortlessly a force initially social and exterior rebounds into the psyche, reaching even the domestic sphere of children, macro- and microcosm one terrible whole.

THERE is something amazing in the way that children have become the rebellion in black South Africa, its troops, its soul. It is a new turn in history for youth to take such a leading role. But the struggle has been a long one. In *Amandla*, Miriam Tlali's novel of the student protests in Soweto, outside Johannesburg, a character outlines the course of events which led to apartheid: "With the discovery of gold and diamonds, the inevitable was on the way. For the Africans, the die was cast. It was only a matter of time and they would be robbed of all their land. These same raw materials, the mineral resources which have to be tapped by the use of African cheap labor (the main prop of this Apartheid system) are now the trump card."* White control was consolidated in one piece of legislation after another: the Land Act of 1936; the Color Bar Act of 1926; the Native Administration Act of 1927, maintaining tribalism with chiefs to act as agents of white rule; the Conciliatory Act of 1924, whereby whites were allowed trade unions excluding blacks, who were not permitted to strike. Then came the legislation creating the "homelands" and, finally, influx control and the pass laws.

The system of apartheid was an extension of Nazi racial method and, like its predecessor, did not neglect education; legal categories and legislation were set up: "Colored Educa-

*(Soweto, S. Africa: Raven Press, 1986).

1 2 3

tion," "Indian Education," and finally "Bantu Education," all of which promoted racial myth and ensured a deliberately inferior education to create a servant class.

It was over the issue of education—specifically the issue of the language of instruction—that the system broke into pieces in 1976, when the Department of Bantu Education suddenly decreed that all black schools had to teach Afrikaans instead of English, depriving black youth of a world language and imprisoning them in the language of their oppressors. Mark Mathabane was there:

> The first spontaneous explosion took place in Soweto on the afternoon of Wednesday, June 16, 1976, where about ten thousand students marched through the dirt streets of Soweto protesting the Afrikaans decree. The immense crowd was orderly and peaceful, and included six- and seven-year-olds, chanting along with older students, who waved placards reading: "To Hell with Afrikaans, We Don't Want to Learn the Language of our Oppressors, Stop Feeding Us a Poisonous Education, and We Want Equal Education Not Slave Education."
>
> Unknown to the marchers, along one of the streets leading to the Phefini High School, where a protest rally was to be held, hundreds of policemen, armed with tear gas canisters, rifles, shotguns and sjamboks, had formed a barricade across the street. When they reached the barricaded street the marchers stopped, but continued waving placards and chanting. . . .
>
> While student leaders argued about what to do to diffuse the situation, the police suddenly opened fire. Momentarily the crowd stood dazed, thinking that the bullets were plastic and had been fired into the air. But when several small children began dropping down like swatted flies, their white uniforms soaked in red blood, pandemonium broke out.

Mathabane's description has an air of bemusement about it. He was there, he saw it, yet still cannot quite believe what he saw. Miriam Tlali's *Amandla* has the same astonishment in describing the same demonstration, the same massacre. The carnage is symbolized in a famous photograph, later a poster, of a boy carrying the lifeless body of another child in his arms.

The next day, Mark is there again and there are more students: "We painted placards that condemned Bantu Education, Afrikaans and apartheid. We demanded an equal education with whites. We urged the government to stop the killings in Soweto. Student leaders were chosen to lead the march to other schools in the area, where we planned to pick up more students for a rally at a nearby stadium. Within an hour we had filled the street and formed columns."

The rebellion had begun in Alexandria, outside Johannesburg, but in a few days it had spread to the other black ghettos of Pretoria, Durban, Port Elizabeth, Cape Town. There is no school, there is widespread looting, riot. Then a boycott, enforced by youngsters, which has devastating effects upon the white economy. Strange forces are now engaged. A war has been declared upon the young. It will go on for a long time. Still more curious, the children will triumph stage by stage, the attempt to impose Afrikaans will fail, and the example of courage and determination of its young people will inspire Soweto and finally a whole nation to resist and in time to resist successfully against the enormous machinery of their oppression.

But the costs were staggering even from the first; thousands of children are imprisoned under the laws permitting detention without trial. There is mass arrest and incarceration of the young. Detention without charges or trial have proven everywhere to create the circumstances of torture. South Africa is the first place this abuse of law has given rise to the widespread torture of children. As apartheid reasserts its control, the arrests begin; the army raids classrooms searching for "ringleaders," soldiers invading homes to pit child against child by bringing youngsters they have arrested and terrorized along with them, knocking on doors and pushing the small hooded figure into the room. The hood has slits so the child can see but not be seen and is given orders to identify his or her friends.

The child inside this hood has been interrogated, beaten, put through solitary confinement and electric shock torture. A prisoner may be returned to these conditions whatever he does: but what if the hood disguised and protected him, what if pointing out another student could free him?

Children are hunted down and arrested merely for attending each other's funerals; expressions of collective grief are forbidden and taken as resistance. Tlali describes how two girls who have been pursued from Doornkop cemetery into a private house are caught hiding in a bedroom by security police: "They dragged them both out, hitting them, and pushed them into a van full of other sobbing kids, and drove them to Protea Police Station. . . . They locked them—about forty of them—into a small room with black-painted walls. They kept them there, confined in that small place, for hours and hours on end. It would become so hot, sweat was just running all over their bodies . . . like being baked in an oven."

In Sipho Sepamla's novel of revolutionary youth, *A Ride on the Whirlwind,* a number of student dissidents undergo detention, but the most compelling of the group is the middle-aged woman who has harbored them.* When arrested, she brings her purse along. Sis Ida sells cosmetics and has her own matchbox house in Soweto; now she faces the indignity of prison. She's been kept up most of the night and is very hungry. Stripped of the freedom of her house ("at home she could scrape something together but here there was no way"), she spends her first night in a place as foreign for its institutional masculinity as for its filth and confinement, and finds herself reading the graffiti scrawled all around her cell: "rough, vulgar and with figures distorted." "It was a new thing to see the

---

*The extracts that follow are taken from Sipho Sepamla, *A Ride on the Whirlwind* (London: William Heinemann, 1981).

mind articulated on the walls like this." There are bedbugs, the blanket is reprehensible:

> Every bit of it felt coarse and spikey. She unfolded it to spread it on the mats. The stench of vomit and the white streak of a dried substance on the blanket made her recoil with disgust and horror. She let the blanket drop out of her hands, folding it a bit. She didn't know what overcame her: but she was aware of a dizziness around her. She went to lean on the water basin, stood there for a while; arms across her breast, she shut her eyes as if the act would make the present experience disappear.

Sis Ida spends her first night in a state of desperation, listening to the keys turn in the locks of cells nearby: "That grating sound reminded her of her own loss of freedom. She tried to forget the sound, but its recurrence made it impossible. It became a fact of life." Panic builds up in her: "The stuffiness in the air caused her mind to be in turmoil. She wondered if she would survive life in a cell for any length of time."

At her first interrogation, the nature of South African detention is explained to her by one of her captors: "The law allows me to keep you in custody as long as I feel your answers are not satisfactory." He stares at her and Ida feels the contempt in the man's eyes. "I don't care if you grow grey in jail. Know that!" Hearing him, realizing his absolute power, "she became acutely aware that she had lost her life somewhere outside the prison." Conducted back to her cell after interrogation, "the strange thing was the relief she felt as her cell door was locked outside," as if it were a refuge: she is still alive and for a few hours will be free of her interrogators.

But one session follows another. "At this point she couldn't remember the number of interrogations involving her nor was she able to focus on the various faces of her interrogators. The experience alone was enough to be a torture: a harrowing of her spirits. At this juncture she seemed to have no care of what to expect of these sessions: they could kill her if they wished."

One morning, her interrogator greets her with the words "Ida, today you are going to die." He forms a noose with his hands: "An eye for an eye! Your buddies have killed one of us." "Ida remained silent, but the news of another policeman killed settled badly with her. She sat with her hands on her lap, sad." (One loves her for this humanity, maturity.) "She sat in solemn silence, numb from the realization that she was now at the mercy of the policeman."

> The man acted swiftly, aware of his advantages. He swung the towel into Ida's face, catching her flush on her broad features: her eyes cried, her nostrils tingled and her mouth tasted the wetness of the towel. She was still dazed by the blow when she felt its chilly coldness wrapped around her neck and a strangulating pull closing her throat. The force of it made her struggle on her feet as she tried to free herself from the threat of death. For the first time since her detention, Sis Ida saw herself staring into the wall facing her as one stares at death.
>
> Her effort to free her encircled neck seemed to be futile, as indeed it was, because every time she turned and twisted the otherwise soft towel dug painfully into the flesh in the neck.

The interrogator stops just short of killing her. He takes a piece of wire from a drawer: "This and the towel can finish you off immediately without any trace of evidence." "Sis Ida cleared her throat because suddenly she experienced a constriction of the throat. She was at that point in time resigned to death as her fate. There was no hope of rescue, not at that late hour within the confining walls of the interrogation room and in the presence of a man who looked as if he was happy to laugh at her fears."

Suddenly the interrogator crumbles; "she never saw the signs of transformation except that he seemed to sag on his feet." He lays the towel and the wire on the table. The interrogator has lost. Ida is willing to die to protect those she protects with her silence; maybe she doesn't even know where the fugitive is hiding—but she will never talk. "She watched the man agonized by what he couldn't verbalize in her presence." She knows that she has won and feels a momentary triumph at his pain. "Then she felt sorry for the cop." The statement surprises one, but the author insists on it: "It was a natural feeling of human compassion." It is also characteristic of Sis Ida: "Once more her large-heartedness was revealed for the law to see, but no-one seemed to see her as a human being."

The boy and girl to whom Sis Ida had given refuge are also in detention. Things go worse for them: the girl is sexually tormented, the police using a pliers on her nipples; the boy is made to stand on bricks for hours and then days, the standing torture much in use in South Africa. Roy stands on two bricks, hands raised above his head, still holding fast, not betraying his comrades. He fights for his mind, for concentration. The cops come and go in the room. He stands on his bricks. No one even questions him any more. They beat him whenever anyone notices him. He hears another prisoner being lashed and screaming. Days go by, he is never fed, voices seem far away. He is ignored except for the frequent beatings. Roy continues standing on his bricks, wishing he'd rehearsed his detention: "But how does one rehearse torture?"

He passes out. He comes to and is beaten again. Then he is nearly strangled. At the last second, he struggles free and in doing so hits a policeman. The pack of them attack: "It wasn't long before the inert body of Roy lay still on the floor, dead. The office became smelly, sweat churned in the air as if it had been sprayed. The men felt hot on this winter day, they were heaving and panting." An officer's voice says "the only thing to be spoken under the charged atmosphere"; all are enjoined to silence, their superiors will of course cooperate in the cover-up: "We cannot have a man of the law assaulted the way this boy did before all of us."

ROBBEN ISLAND is eleven kilometers off Cape Town. The road to the quarry where prisoners perform slave labor lies along the sea; they see it and smell it. Just over there is the city of Cape Town, glaring at them with its tall skyscrapers and shining lights. Table Mountain looms above, a white mist and clouds. This is a scene of great beauty; looking out at it, Moses Dlamini is standing in hell: he is a political prisoner on Robben Island, betrayed by an informer to Special Branch, the political police. "A cold wind blows and the waves splash over the seashore. The tide is rising and five kilometers away, two passenger liners ply slowly toward Cape Town Harbour. They carry many tourists from the Western countries who are going to tour 'sunny South Africa' . . . these tourists will return back to their countries, some with disgust but others with pleasant memories," Dlamini says, watching the other world go by.*

Prison is another world, as the Afrikaans writer Breyten Breytenbach observes in *End Papers*.† A white anti-apartheid activist, he has been imprisoned several times. In exile, still visualizing the familiar landscape, he detects beneath it the secret places of the South African police state:

Who will send up a little grey thought as he comes breasting the neck of the Old Cape Way in his motorcar on his way down to the beaches of Muizenberg, when he sees the labyrinth of Pollsmoor prisons spread out at his feet? If he were to pass by there on a winter's morning before daybreak he might notice the searchlights and hear the snarling dogs; he would not get close enough to see the men waiting crouched down, hip against hip, behind the wires in a circle of light . . . waiting to be counted.

The land itself is affected, nature coerced, borders are sown with mines along the thousands of miles where South Africa shares a frontier with Mozambique, Zimbabwe, and Bot-

---

*The extracts that follow are taken from Moses Dlamini, *Hell-Hole Robben Island* (Trenton, NJ: Africa World Press, 1984).
†(New York: McGraw-Hill, 1986).

swana: electric fencing, blade wire, electronic sensing equipment, miles of lighting along a militarized buffer zone. "In that 'other world,' " as Breytenbach calls it, "the decisive factor, the idol" is "the state"—seeing in the regime not only its racism but the outlines of totalitarian power itself, a structure "feeding on 'informing' and betrayal . . . the mind is shown its blanks. It leads to immobility. It is death."

On Robben Island it has become a kind of insanity. Emaciated prisoners wheel impossibly heavy barrows full of stones, beaten mercilessly and continuously. Far away from the new state technology, Dlamini's fellow prisoners are actually breaking stones in a quarry, working under the most primitive conditions: "The wheelbarrow stops. . . . Look at how the man struggles to take it out of the sand. See his tongue coming out. See the muscles of his arms and legs, how taut they are. He pushes. The wheelbarrow does not move." There are blows; an old man puts a hand to his head and sees blood on it. A man who used to be a radio announcer broadcasting revolutionary songs during the Pass Strike shovels lime as fast as he can, an eleven-year sentence before him; the prison guard shouts orders. It is the work of Sisyphus, it is the Gulag. Here too there is a population of professional criminals whose role is to rob, intimidate, humiliate, and if possible kill the political resisters deliberately placed at their mercy. There are the same gangs and gangsterism that dominate civilian black life in the townships, the Big Fives and Big Sixes, thugs who have swastika tattoos and use the Nazi salute. Apartheid has produced demoralization and brutalized its victims. Henchmen of their white Afrikaans guards, gangsters truckle before them, curtseying as they hand them their coffee, one of them removing a rag from his pocket and polishing a guard's shoes as he drinks, "looking around his kingdom, to see whether everything was going according to plan."

Dlamini's Robben Island is barbarous, sadistic, but it is only an intensification of general circumstances: an overblown white supremacy, a demoralized black servility, and a concentrated campaign to break black resistance. It has all the same assumptions as the great world around it; in carrying them to their logical conclusion, it only perfects them. When the Big Sixes lose a battle to the Big Fives, the losers experience the worst fate in prison: they become "wyfies," females. From now on they would "have a taste of domination which would make them submissive and dependent and never again to dare fight against the Boer warders and the Big Fives. From now on they would be infused with feminine ideas and play the role of women in prison society. They would be taught to walk like women, smile like women and to sit like women." Sex, like race, is class, rank, servitude. The new wyfies will prepare food for their masters, wash and press their clothes, and be their sexual slaves. The prison authorities depend on rape as a means of keeping order among prisoners, the same order they themselves maintain between races.

Buried in this awful place, Moses Dlamini must stay alive, maintain his political consciousness. Looking at the other prisoners, covered with sweat and dust, breaking rock in the sun, he already wonders "how I look." Can he last? "I could imagine leaving prison like a vegetable, unable to speak coherently—stuttering or with a slur and fearing any White man I come across. And when someone tells of the struggle for freedom—looking at him in shock and just shaking my head."

Dlamini is a member of the Pan African Congress, his leader Robert Sobukwe is at Robben Island too, a force, an inspiration. So is Mandela. After two years there, in June 1966, Dlamini is told he will be released: that afternoon he sees Nelson Mandela and Walter Sisulu coming back from another day's work in the quarry, "They looked tired. Their faces and clothes were covered with lime which they had been digging the whole day at the old Landbouspan site—the site of many tortures." Dlamini is a part of history, a generation whose grandfathers began in the passive resistance campaigns. "We are the tools of history and when we are gone history will find other tools," Sobukwe has taught him.

When he leaves the island, it is not even into freedom: "The struggle," an old comrade reminds him, "is not like a coat which you can put on when it is cold and remove when it is hot. You must continue with the work outside from where you left off." It has gone on so long now, decades; become a faith, a way of life, the conscious dedication of entire lifetimes. "I noticed Sisulu's hair was fast greying but Mandela still looked robust and had a proud bearing." There are only these things: suffering and faith, the slavery and torture of prison, the hope of freedom someday.

PART TWO

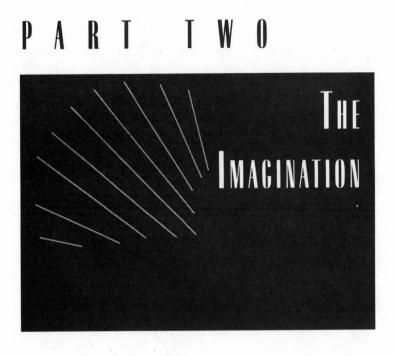

THE
IMAGINATION

6

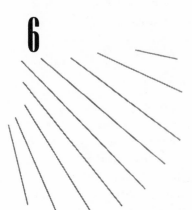

PHOTOGRAPHY: THE
EXPERIENCE OF SHOCK

TORTURE, even conveyed from "inside" the experience, the point of view of the victim, might still remain an impersonal political and historic event taking place in the past or far away. Yet it impinges on all of us. If not in fact then in potentiality, since the practice is expanding and may reach those presently immune. If those unaffected cannot be stirred to empathy, it will expand still further; hence the importance of Amnesty International reports, the accounts of witnesses. Through this literature, torture enters our imagination.

But it has always been there, since childhood, perhaps even because of it; the fear of pain and helplessness before pain and cruelty has occupied a corner of our minds, lain in wait for us, motivating or preventing understanding or action. In torture itself, the most personal terror is politicized: the inward and outward join in an awesome conjunction. But in thinking of torture, what happens, what is called up?

In writing this, I could not avoid examining my own reactions, my own fear of the state of cruelty itself, the history of this fear, its location in my own particular and individual past experiences as well as its location in the elements of the culture around me. Since I have not undergone torture, my responses are limited and limiting, yet all I have when I turn inward and away from the testimonies of victims. My own personal reactions are what I bring to them, even what I bring to that contact with cruelty which is instantly registered upon us in pictures, photographs, the documentation of torture that constitutes its proof. Photographs of Palestinians tortured in Israel confirm the fact, establish it. A Latino policeman is set upon by white policemen in New York: we see his swollen face in the paper and know that it happened, believe, empathize.

But at one point or another one faces a photograph which does more than that—it nearly annihilates one with its power, it becomes an epiphany. My relationship to this subject was formed by a series of such epiphanies that became milestones on a journey. I have first experienced them as trauma, then obstacle, and finally as goads forcing me to face what I feared and hated but was compelled to confront.

As I summon these images and examine them, I retrace the steps that have brought me to this subject—moments of what seems to be abjectly personal emotion, powerful, perhaps embarrassing, feeling that overwhelms and overmasters one, devastates. I call this reaction "shock," attempting to analyze it, to discover its source, describe it, deal with it, control it, transcend it. My attempts, located in my own identity, are circumscribed by it as well: class, nationality, and sex. I have found this last category probably the most formative of all, odd and circular as its effects may be in that instant when one is assailed by evidence which one resists, even in a photograph.

Catherine Alport has photographed the struggle for South African freedom and exhibited these pictures extensively. I saw them first in a relatively private circumstance, a small screening of slides at a friend's studio in New York. One of them deeply upset me: a photograph of a man burning alive. An amazing circumstance in itself, still more so when witnessed and preserved in a photograph. A stunned silence greeted this image. One felt a sudden tension among those in the room, till now a pleased and unified community enjoying the good news of black protest in solidarity against apartheid. Catherine explained the image with a certain *sang-froid;* for her it no longer had the power it carried for the rest of us. The creature in the fire was no longer an astonishment of human suffering but a political event, for the victim was actually a native policeman upon whom the crowd had taken vengeance. He was a black man set on fire by other blacks who, because of his office, viewed him as a traitor and stood about watching him die, surrounded by a crowd of men, women, and children. Catherine photographed the event.

Without this explanation, one might have interpreted it differently: given the locale, one nearly automatically imagines any black the victim of whites. The figure on fire, who could be any profession at all, is merely a pillar of flame with a face in it, isolated from the crowd around it—who could be for or against him, one has no way of telling without verbal explanation. The picture explained now, one interprets the crowd to be persecutors rather than sympathizers unable to help; indeed, one now perceives that the figure on fire is encircled by his very tormentors. One looks at their faces for signs of doubt or pity or remorse, but sees amusement instead, or hatred. One imagines seeing these things.

Were I to see such a photograph in a "neutral" setting—a book or newspaper, the work of a photojournalist, a stranger—it would never occur to me to take issue with it. But Alport is a friend, however professional her work on this occasion—the exhibitions are proof of it, so is the clarity and precision of the images—there is a personal element in how I respond, how I even question, am able to question the photographer, inquire after her motives.

Catherine continued to explain, a certain defensiveness entering then surpassing the patience in her voice as I, by my very tone, put myself at odds with this phenomenon: How did it feel to photograph such a thing? A foolish question, but I want her to face the fact in the image, appalled as I always am that people take pictures of things one wishes they could stop: one wants the photographer to intervene on behalf of the starving child, give it something to eat rather than photograph the moment it expires of hunger. But of course they do not; will not or, sometimes, cannot.

Clearly Catherine could do nothing, a white permitted to observe only because her commitment had earned her connections among the most trusted white activists. Helen Josephson herself had taken Catherine under her wing and extended the privilege of entering Soweto to observe and take part in the funeral processions, record them, and serve the cause with these pictures.

It is my cause, too, and I have loved each photograph and admired her courage and opportunity; but through exposure to this particular photograph, I feel suddenly alienated—as much by my friend's attitude to the event as by the event itself—my head spins in confusion, I experience a moral disorientation. Yes, of course, I know about traitors. More blacks died in Kenya than whites; the Mau-Mau executed more blacks for collusion than they terrorized lonely white settlers; in fact, there were very few such victims. Many groups have to deal with collusion: becoming free is sometimes a matter of cutting off dead wood; I know the logic.

Catherine goes on explaining, but we are at odds. I also realize that my feeling of being at odds is stronger against Catherine than against the hostile figures in her photograph; the motivations of black South Africans are easy to understand, would be difficult not to share were one to live their lives. However dangerous to political morality, the emotional temptation to vengeance would be enormous. Catherine's apparently calm acceptance of what is, despite extenuating circumstances, actually an atrocity, strikes me as thoughtless and partisan, uncharacteristic of the feminism and pacifism we share; it smacks of leftist orthodoxy, a response quite unlike her. I try to put it down to the depth of her identification with the struggle, the strength and freshness of her experience. But I am still uneasy, profoundly disturbed. With a disturbance I do not entirely understand and can hardly control.

I call it shock: I am trying to understand it. Convinced that it is very important to understand; it is now controlling me, has taken over, operates upon me like anger or passion, confuses, consumes. I even suspect that understanding it would be to comprehend something deeply important politically as well as personally. This response of shock is something I have never seen investigated or explained. Instead, it seems that this is an emotion we experience but do not examine. As if it were too obvious to merit explanation: we are appalled by cruelty; what else is there to say?

But surely there is more. The shock we undergo is an emotion of great force, we are overcome and overwhelmed by it. Beyond moral outrage, one may experience something more puzzling and deeply painful. We may be personally affected, as I believed I was while responding to this photograph; we confront horror and feel a certain despair. Shock is probably always an individual response, rooted in one's own personal history. There are also collective responses: the outrage over atrocity that powers armies, factions, hatreds, myths, allegiances, and memories. We react through them, but we do not break down and examine these mechanisms.

Meanwhile Catherine's adoption of the colloquial term for this execution, the "necklace," with its mocking folk humor, repels and angers me, disappoints me in a cause I have championed all my adult life and now must take issue with. One excess, be reasonable; consider what these people have endured. And yet the emotional response one feels is not reason, but pain: the victim's. Even one's own. Assailed by these emotions, I ask again, what is the nature of this response? Why is there an element of surprise in this pain, of betrayal?

If you had not put her on the defensive, Catherine would no more endorse this act of execution than you, I remind myself.

Were you to defend a parallel act via some abstruse political theory, she would deplore it just as you do now; she is simply maintaining solidarity with the oppressed, with their outrage over decades of suffering. But she watched the man die too, watched him burn and scream. And had the self-possession before this sight to photograph it. Surely quite unable to help, make a move, object, turn away, even frown. Or fail to get the shot?

However comprehensible the political event, emotion refuses to accept it and continues to suffer. Odd details haunt one: how does the tire stay on the victim, why doesn't he remove the burning ring, is it only around his neck or around his arms too? Does it bind him; surely he could free himself by pushing it over his head or down below his waist and step out of it, save himself? Are his hands tied, broken? A South African friend told me later they are sometimes chopped off. The horror of the case bears in as one considers it. It becomes real to you. You become him.

Merely hearing of this, what is the quality of this assault one experiences: what is shock like? That rush of blood to the head, that feeling of asphyxiation, that pounding in the ears, that increase of pulse and heartbeat? As to the victim, one shares a little, so very little, in his suffering. One watches the spectacle in horror. One participates in his helplessness, paralyzed by the absolute judgment against him, experiencing his isolation—all on such a minimal scale compared with his screams and anguish; even the greatest empathy is nothing to this.

And I approach him first from the side of his enemies, hearing their rationale first, which is not only the accusation against him but his sentence as well: a policeman, a collaborator. Only with difficulty and imagination do I take sides with his life against their dismissal of it: his poverty, the necessity which drives such a man to take work with his oppressors, feed himself or his children this way. But, carrying it further, one can guess at the thrill of identification he experiences with power, the begrudging praise of his superiors, his sense of righteousness in police work, the uniform, the car. On the other hand, the growing hatred in the settlements, the detestation finally summarized in the crowd around him, no more than a mob, the usual cast of tormentors around the unfortunate. Who might also be innocent—this is any policeman, after all—they simply caught a cop.

Don't you remember how Catherine explained it? Two police cars came barreling out to the funeral procession, in itself a political demonstration, an angry protest held against police orders. The body has been interred by now, they are coming home. They are hungry and tired and angry, it is late, they are feeling mean. The three policemen, realizing that there are thousands of demonstrators, panic at being so outnumbered. The two white cops take off in their car. The black cop, abandoned, his car surrounded and overturned, is necklaced. Betrayed on every side. A stranger executed by strangers simply because he wore a uniform. Without it he could be one of the crowd of mourners, mourners at a funeral—driven by their rage, or perhaps ultimately their self-indulgence, to commit a murder. A puzzle, a comment on the circular quality of torment, oppression, injustice.

One tries again to examine one's own dismay, the pain which the contemplation of this man's pain causes. What is it? Pity? Terror? Betrayal as well: one's own disappointment before human cruelty excusing itself through history or politics or getting even or settling a score, but alas only starting the next round of injustices. If you come to power behind acts like this, individually or as a regime . . .

But of course this is scarcely fair. The cause of South African freedom, inaugurated first by Gandhi and stamped with his likeness through a thousand moods and changes, has practiced non-violence longer and better than any parallel cause. The Spear of the Nation *(Umkhonto we Sizwe)* was very slow to be taken up by the African National Congress, and it is not reached for here; this is mob violence, folly, officially denounced if not always abhorred in practice. And surely if one builds consensus through punishment, there are consequences which follow inevitably upon the original taint of injustice, the first revolutionary crime, familiar as its defense by the fervent.

But this is not the politics of revolutionary movement, this is an act of the people, which even if it were incited, is genuine, authentic, horribly so. Probably even fun, funny or fashionable to persons who have seen it more than once, participated in it a number of times, joked about it, grown excited by the act, by the memory of the act. An act of war in one sense: what difference if execution were with a bullet, summary and without trial, but instant? One difference: to die this way is not only to die horribly and in great pain but to be seen to do so. An *exemplary* death therefore, a warning. Publicly given, publicly received. It is the deliberate cruelty one perceives in torture.

And the emotion one experiences upon seeing it is fear. If one refuses to feel fear, one denies the meaning of the spectacle. And if one is unable to feel such fear, one has lost a connection with other beings in time and place, history and locale. When that is the case, one cannot be roused easily on behalf of others, perhaps cannot be roused at all, has lost thereby a vital kind of imagination upon which our humanity depends.

What if this "spontaneous" mob act is revolutionary terror? How long before it is "organized" and assumes political significance, becomes an arm of faction or state? Historical uses of terror come running to mind, the Cheka campaign, the Brownshirts; parallels of many times and places orchestrated by political parties coming to power, or in power perpetuating ritual vengeance: the *sans-culottes* institutionalized as Saint-Just's Directorate, the Chinese village People's Council, Castro's football stadium executions. Even a lynch mob: it is difficult to separate the group revenge from its social origins and its official practices. In this way, custom or state brings about a general obedience and diminishes the humanity of those brought into participation. One recalls the custom of stoning to death and remembers it is no longer a thing of the past but as contemporary as Islamic *sharia'a.*

PHOTOGRAPHS have great power. A photograph brought me to write this book: the image of a boy crucified in Cambodia, seen by chance as I was walking along a street in Paris once with my editor André Bay, intent upon nothing more than a Pernod and a good lunch. Unexpectedly, I was assaulted by a photograph on the cover of a new book in a bookstore window. A crucified figure, perhaps a child, certainly someone very young. Across the top of the book in large type, *La Torture,* and below it a subtitle, *La Nouvelle Inquisition*—a view of the present in view of the past, written by two members of French Amnesty International, Michel Ternisien and Daniel Bacry. A book in a window that changed my life in an instant.

I was that very day back in the store, reading it, hypnotized, struck down, given sight. Because it was the photograph, this boy on the cross. The title, the word *"Torture,"* without the picture, might have repelled as much as interested, threatened more than attracted curiosity; it would never have brought me in from the street. But fifteen feet away and through a window the photo could not be denied; it said all . . . and by a curious double take. Because this is a new crucifixion, crucifixion seen for the first time. As for the usual silhouette of a crucified being, you have seen it a million times, to nausea—a whole culture and religion has been built around this necrophilial image. The fact of the crucifix as means of torture and execution has disappeared beneath the larger fact of organized religion, bureaucracy, Christian money, prestige, hypocrisy. The crucifix has not really been persuasive, an actual crucifix, an emblem of literal suffering since one's childhood.

But this is a photograph. This, you realize, is taking place right now. The photographic finish, the quality of the black and white, technical clues make you aware that the event it records is a present event. Impossible, but surely everything in this crucifixion is contemporary: the boy's shorts, the uniforms of the soldiers, those distant figures who appear to be in charge standing further back on the endless silent plane which stretches on forever immobile behind the young figure in torment, hardly more than a child, skinny, exhausted. Tied at the wrists for eternity to his cross. There is a terrible dryness and silence, a heat and quietude in this photograph—the world behind the figure is depleted and dead even as he may yet be violently, painfully still alive.

Or perhaps he is already dead. Only his face could tell us, and it is in shadow, its mouth contorted, open to scream. The photograph is as silent as it is still: arrested, motionless. His mouth may be only slack and already unconscious. He may be stunned by the heat, somnolent as his now-silent screams and straining young arms tied in the long impossible pain of the crossbars.

It is dusty with real dust . . . one is looking at a photograph, not an illustration. One registers the visual image instantly; it takes much longer to explore its consequences. The currency and authenticity take a moment to sink in. This is happening now. This is photographed fact. Not a painting, drawing, graphic; not an enactment or performance, but that record of fact we know as photographic: reality not appearance. A real crucifixion taking place in the world, taking place now.

Moreover, it is not a man on the cross, but a boy. A boy's chest, starved as it is, the rib cage stripped of flesh but bloated as starving persons tend to be. The posture unnatural, his small arms are tied hard by rope to the crossbars, so that the body droops from its own weight, the toes may even touch the ground and yet fail to give real support because the heels are not there as well. So the whole body must hang from its arms and pull them out of their sockets, or the toes and balls of the feet must support all the weight to save the arms from dislocation. The figure is being torn apart; the arms will leave the sockets soon; this is a position of infinite suffering. He may actually even be dead already.

Or perhaps it is ordained that he will hang this way in anguish for whatever eternity may satisfy his tormentors. Who presently ignore him. He is therefore completely alone. And completely in the present: his jacket is fetched up behind him on an ingenious peg attached to the vertical member of the cross upon which he is stretched, the shorts he wears are the very clothing of the present, of youth, warm climates, summertime. His cross is skinned wood, rough poles, not milled lumber, a makeshift thing. His hands have not been nailed, nor his feet either, the toes uncertainly touching earth but the feet unable to stretch far enough to stand and relieve his arms.

This is not necessarily crucifixion unto death; perhaps it is merely "punishment": he may not be dying but only hung a while in torment, a Khmer Rouge example to others, his fate customary in this hell. If he is to die, it may take him days, hundreds of hours without food or water, the muscles stiffening, the suffering long, unendurable, unimaginable. And he cannot be more than thirteen, even given his evident malnutrition.

I was married for ten years to a Japanese; this boy is part of him, as was every dead Vietnamese ever seen on American television. And because of Fumio, this boy's humanity is not only real but dear to me. I absorb the arms and chest, the tired legs of this young Cambodian, another among the people my own compatriots were content to call "gooks." Because of Fumio, all racial distance is impossible for me: manhood was this shape, this smooth boyish skin was masculinity as I knew it most intimately, longer and closer and with greater tenderness and identification than the bodies of black or white men. Was it this, some chance if not irrelevant similarity to a lover or a husband, which made me accessible to that photograph, that book, that cause and phenomenon?

I had already begun to be haunted by the fact of modern

torture through political work with Iranian dissidents under the Shah's regime, but starting with the shock and power of its cover photograph, Ternisien and Bacry's text gave greater dimension and threat to the issue and drew me in. Yet the initial experience was emotional, was that sense of shock I am trying to analyze, to understand. For it penetrated all defenses, this photograph of a young man upon a crucifix; here and now and in the present, even if halfway around the world. I could see him because of Fumio, I felt, whereas I might otherwise never have seen him at all; my own race, even my sex, might have made him invisible to me.

Personal experience crossed a boundary and gave larger and more general meanings. The boy was close, was Everyman, was man crucified again. Suspended in the neglected isolation of his empty plain, one laconic soldier in the background, ignoring him, this boy inhabits a world so savage that executions are no longer even the subject of ritual or interest; there is everywhere a quality of silence and inattention that resembles routine, tedium, habit. One is shocked, then one is furious.

The killing fields came alive, the very contemporary and immediate quality of torture, its confident and secure return within the modern world, its confidence as a method of rule—a new Inquisition, as the authors had subtitled their text. Impossible that the term "Inquisition" should not ring a bell in a feminist with a Catholic heritage: the circularity of history, its repetition, no evil ever left behind, no liberty maintained without constant vigilance. But that one would ever have to consider crucifixion again . . . it made one reel, the full horror of Cambodia in this age, this century of torture and mass death.

In responding to the photographic image one is responding also to photography, that visual language series of black and white or even colored spots which we have come to accept as actuality. The thing represented becoming the thing itself; not art but science. A record of fact virtually interchangeable with fact. The substitute for reality which evokes it with certainty, is its historic evidence and trace, its documentation. We are now inured to certain photographs: the famous photographs of Dachau, Bergen-Belsen, the emaciated corpses of hundreds and thousands, the dead in piles like stacked wood, the living mere stick figures on the brink of death, the fact of their continued erectitude a miracle; like the miracle of their eyes, eyes that have seen horrors they can scarcely describe for us, though they have survived to tell us. I do not only mean the immediate horrors of executions and torture, outright gestures of cruelty, nor even the innumerable bodies first made naked and then dead, as one by one the chimney swallowed the lives of millions, leaving only these the last survivors. I mean instead that these eyes have known not only the one-by-one of selections for murder, they have also known time, the hour by hour, day by day, of starvation and cold, the moment by moment of a suffering prolonged over years—entire years of torture, of humiliation and pain and despair—and these eyes are open still.

One saw them first in childhood. I was born in 1934, and was eleven years old when these pictures were released in *Life* magazine. I was staggered at the encounter, but after nearly fifty years they are familiar now, their taboo nature has evaporated, the nudity of the victims was never sexually exciting— this was remarkable in itself since every form of nakedness had a sexual impact on an eleven-year-old then, even if it was merely informative, as one had seen so few unclothed bodies in life or in representation: Greek statues, a few buxom females painted in oils. The many bodies, living and dead, were informational only of the essential humanity of their naked forked shape of starvation and abuse. Even as a child you saw them as merely sexed, the male victim, the female victim, their genitals representing nothing but their human identity. How reassuring that the very emaciation of these bodies did not become confused with the chaos of sexual curiosity, desire, or repugnance.

This was not true of the first image of cruelty I encountered in childhood, oddly enough in the "funny papers," in that curious offshoot of the comic-strip pages called "Believe It Or Nor by Ripley." That day's offering was a peculiar one for a Sunday paper in a small Catholic town—but perhaps not, perhaps it was the very essence of predictable social information, even conditioning. And my response was already carefully prepared for, though it terrified and confused me. The item itself, which I remember badly and in a blur, was a terse and brutal account of the martyrdom of a female saint, her name like mine Catherine—a detail which made her a patron and myself particularly susceptible: according to Ripley, she was stripped of her clothing, dragged through the streets behind a chariot, the crowd screaming out for her death. Rudimentary as it was, this was an account situated outside the victim and by no means oriented to her point of view. Perhaps it was just that, the distanced character of it, the objectification of such a death for a woman.

Of the hundreds of martyrdoms I had absorbed from the nuns in religion classes—pamphlets of saints' lives were our chief diet during occasions like "retreat," thoroughly comfortable and familiar reading and entirely without threat—I had never experienced the slightest humiliation. Lovely pity and rapturous identification with the great, since saints are like stars in the firmament, immortals, creatures of proven grandeur. Saints and martyrs had a hard time of it but they came through with flying colors, ascended to heaven and a plenteous reward, and then were written up in books where girls like myself wept tears over their sufferings, relished their triumphs. Perhaps we even relished their trials, so much a part of us they were, so without danger, so reassuring. They were romances incapable of unhappy endings, without suffering permanent or actual enough to have real meaning as suffering; St. Lawrence on his grill, Catherine breaking her wheel, even Lucy with her breasts sliced off—always magically reattached at the end of the tale.

Suffering like that of Jesus on his Cross was so automatically transcended that one endured it without harm. The Crucifixion had a special immediacy during Holy Week, then one shed real tears at the Stations of the Cross, involved oneself deeply in the imaginative sharing of his humiliation and betrayal, the crown of thorns, the flagellation, the soldiers gambling for his cloak, their hurry to lance his side and have it over and go off duty. The characters of the story, especially the women, Veronica, the Marys—Mary the mother of Jesus and Mary Magdalene, Mary the sister of Martha—one endured their pain and dismay, their loyalty, only to see them passed over in the Resurrection, but also to see all suffering transcended in miracle, even death itself. There were Easter and Pentecost to distract one from the terrible moments of Good Friday, the moment of three o'clock when one concentrated so entirely on the legendary, supernatural pain and despair, shared it, suffered it as well—all part of one's upbringing and culture and circle of known things, all shared throughout history as throughout Christendom, and always at that same moment, calendars planned around it, the pain for an instant unbearable and then transcended, part of the healing myth of the world.

In a childhood like this, no account of a saint's suffering should bring real distress, but Ripley's did. Reading Ripley one did not see a martyrdom, one saw an execution. The difference was one of faith; Ripley saw the event not only with the eyes of protestant rationalism, but through secularism. He saw a woman dragged naked through the streets and then put to death. It was even seen from the outside, bizarre, grotesque, demeaning. No longer mythical, but real. I experienced her shame, the screams of the masses. The sacred was torn away; this was a mere civil event, a real town, real streets, real roughnecks, probably real hypocrites and respectable citizens present as well. And the saint was merely a woman naked: saints were often naked during their martyrdoms as well; why did the woman seem naked in a shameful way?

Ripley had dispensed with fable and illusion. She wasn't a saint, nor holy, simply a being mercilessly persecuted—like a woman stoned, caught by a mob, a woman hunted by an entire society. To read this terrified me, brought the blood to my face, put me in a fever of fear. It was my encounter with the sexual excitement attached to and associated with the shaming of women, that cultural masochism intended for all of us.

But something else accompanied it: anger. The absurd colored illustrations, the naive historical data and drawings infuriated me. I may have been liberated by something as ephemeral as the failings of Ripley's style. Perhaps also by Ripley's secular view, surely by his skepticism. After a moment, the shaming inherent in this exemplary tale failed to intimidate. Something in me protested at the general cruelty of the situation: here was a woman made naked before a crowd who treated her with mockery and condemnation for being naked, despised her as unchaste after tearing her clothes from her, punished her for a wrong they had committed against her; this being deprived of dignity now chained and dragged behind horses. How arbitrary and unfair to interpret her nakedness as sexual and then to call it shameful.

This is a Believe It Or Not, one of those absurd pseudo-facts registered in ugly color drawings every week, tidbits on the construction of the Pyramids, the shoe size of a giant, Babe the Blue Ox. Directed at children, a weekly curiosity, an improbable event or one vaguely amusing. But in this offering you were introduced to an unfamiliar objectification and contempt for suffering. And something had gone wrong with my habitual defenses against heroic pain; the familiar fairy tales of my people and religion did not, in this one case, hold up: one was not canonized at the end of the ordeal, one was only dead.

For the first time, legend was history. Ripley had made me believe in the actual sufferings of this woman, and I was now outraged because they were mine as well. No one would save either one of us; we would have to fight off the world. I went astray in breaking out of the terrible pull of sexual curiosity and shame so carefully prepared that they at first combined as expected to make me ashamed, then feverish and afraid. But somehow it didn't stop there, went past these mysteries, dared to challenge these nearly overwhelming emotions with rage. And so began ambivalence and conflict where only submission was called for.

Instead, I got mad at the paper, at Ripley, at whatever uncaring fool had inserted this. The accusation of sexuality in the fact of sex, for the crowd has blamed her for her nakedness, for her woman's body—what other body could she have? She had not uncovered it of her own will, would have preferred to obey the general behest and remain hidden. They had uncovered her and blamed her for what they had uncovered, made it her crime, the nakedness that was her sentence. Why was her body wrong, inherently wrong? It is only a matter of time until I am like her—vulnerable, defenseless, accused. Maybe not her way, maybe not publicly, but silently, implicitly, and inside me I will know. Accepting the sentence then rejecting it. How arbitrary, how crazy, how infuriating. It lasted all Sunday, one returned to it over and over again: the sense of wrong and betrayal, the war between the sense of injustice and the sense of sexual guilt and shame, reaching out toward a generalized sense of justice one had picked up from other sources where sex and gender did not obtrude to slant the odds. I had slipped the halter, that mediated unease of guilt and shame intended for me as female.

THE image has great power over us: it is often feared, avoided, hidden. At Oxford, I saw a photograph that affected me with the cruelty of its image, saw it by accident and without preparation, for I had a terror of such pictures in those days; with forewarning I would have avoided this one as I generally did. Cruelty disturbed me; I was careful to protect myself. Browsing in *Life,* a picture jumped at me when I turned the page: a photograph of a Russian colonel hung from a meat hook during the Hungarian uprising. It was the great political event of my undergraduate days, all my sympathies were with the rebels, the best of my classmates had gone to the Austrian border and helped the revolutionaries as they escaped to freedom. But suddenly the sight of this unfortunate Russian colonel—so said the caption, he could be anyone from any side or persuasion, was only barely recognizable as human—sickened and excited me. Having seen the images of Dachau, having experienced these bodies as nothing but bodies, one was aware of another dimension here, an excitement at cruelty, at seeing what I had not intended and felt unprepared to see. Guilty for having seen it, feeling the taboo quality of such an image, as well as the unwelcome news it imparted of atrocity on the part of the rebels, my heroes, my "side." I made myself look again: it seemed the only antidote. Lest I be haunted by the image, lest it fester in my mind, lest it have power over me, lest it excite a fascination with cruelty I wanted no part of. So I forced myself to see the image a second time. And began thereby to face down an enemy within.

So often I have heard people, particularly women, claim that they did not want to see cruelty, misery, misfortune. And deliberately turn away, refuse. Not only the pictures of such events, photographs or other visual representations, but even the narrative description. I know the power of an image, and had confronted this one and felt I had won: that is, my terror gave rise to anger finally rather than despair. Rather than to that mixture of titillation, shame, and fear which ends in futility and acceptance; which is our heritage. And which is planned, predictable, the result of a hundred cultural indicators.

Ten years later I saw a photograph of a dead girl named Sylvia Likens, who had been tortured in a middlewestern basement with the words "I am a prostitute" engraved upon her abdomen, a primeval domestic execution carried out under the ideology of female sexual shame. At first the event could only torment me until shock could be absorbed, become outrage, and finally take action in writing. *The Basement* was not written until a decade after *Sexual Politics,* but it preceded it in inspiration, even made it possible.

ONE imagines one is out of this, that this is a thing of the past, the identification of the cruel with the sexual. Recently I had to face it all again. On another visit to Paris, I met and spent the day happily with a young student friend who was enjoying a year in France while studying Georges Bataille. She was wonderfully keen on him and thought I ought to look at his essay on eroticism and the visual in connection with this book. Because of the Chinese torture of the hundred pieces she said, earnest, enthralled by her subject. By this time I had spent some three years reading about torture, a malign subject I had imagined I had come to terms with; nothing about it could now sicken or shock, I was way past that, my interests were political not psychological.

But there was something about her attitude, clearly a carryover of her master's, which challenged me, frightened me, threatened—here perhaps was something to be afraid of still. Clearly the notion of such suffering excited Bataille, he had theories about it, romantic theories. My student was excited: they actually cut someone into pieces while alive, it takes a long time—the ingenuity, the ritual character—all that is terribly important, she insisted. For Bataille, it represented an ultimate of some sort; he seems to consider it the source of ecstatic experience.

I felt myself growing sick, nauseated, getting annoyed, entering that vulnerable area of shock and anger from which I had first approached the subject of torture, chosen it. As I worked, I came to understand I had to transcend all that emotionality, in order to read the subject, think it, live with it, convert it to a study of state power—and here I was losing that grip. I was also getting angry at my student and at her idol as well. She's challenging me: I've got to read this book; it's hard to find, but she'll see what she can do. I have to include this.

The hell I do, I'm thinking, how do you cut someone into pieces while they're still living, and why would anyone relish the idea in the way it seems this fellow Bataille does? Surely this is simply the most barbarous method of execution one has ever heard of; what is it my friend and her precious French philosopher find so sublime in this? She insists it's the public character of capital punishment, it's the deliberateness of it, the ritual quality. Foucault is trotted out and paraded around the tablecloth stretched between us in a café. I demur: I thought Foucault only pretended to admire public executions as an ironical rebuke to those eighteenth-century reformers who invented solitary confinement and the long torture of penitentiaries. Come on, no one could seriously recommend a return to spectacles of state cruelty.

We do agree that the Chinese torture she describes, since it is an execution, is in fact state cruelty. A cruelty evident for all to see. One that terrorizes as it expresses itself, a cruelty that need not even hide, an arrogant and secure power. I argue that the king's scaffold is even more peremptory than the mob's guillotine. They have seized power, he was given it by God. We are at an impasse. I feel in her arguments and those she admires in Bataille a turning of reason upon itself. In accusing the bureaucratic present of falling below the uses of the barbaric past, one is seduced by a corrective which is not only pointless in that it provides no usable alternative, but dangerous as well. Beginning with an ironic romanticism toward the *ancien régime,* one next succumbs to an authoritarianism which is not passé at all but current, present, and immediately available.

There are brand new brutalities to embrace, I urge, imagine South America, state crime is very physical there, consider Guatemala. Torture is not of the past and therefore something safe to sentimentalize or clothe in glamour. Torture is of the present. And the future.

All the time the figure of the Chinese victim is bombarding me as I argue, the horror of being carved into pieces before a crowd; it is happening to a human being, it is being treated as spectacle. For that matter, how much a spectacle? Surely he must be tied, immobilized. Is he gagged as well or does the crowd hear him scream the entire time? Hours of this. Who could endure the sound, the sight? This figure, this puppet suffering to provide theatre, sensation.

And when the book arrived I opened it as a gift, not even registering that it was Bataille at first, too late realizing that it would have that photograph, the photograph of the victim of the Chinese torture. Still, it was a shock to see it. To experience that vertigo, a trauma that lasted for days, many hours debilitated and infuriated by the context: why has Bataille chosen to present this abomination as erotic? I would have to face the last argument of cruelty and torture, the "turn-on."

For Georges Bataille concludes his study of erotic visual art, *The Tears of Eros,* with three photographs of this form of execution in which the victim is dismembered, through a long and gradual process of incisions and amputations, into as many pieces as experienced executioners have found possible. All so that the victim remains alive to suffer and the crowd can perceive this as suffering. To prolong the agony of the condemned man, he is given large quantities of opium—not to kill the pain but to prolong life and therefore the spectacle.

The photographs are in themselves a shock; they are particularly so in the context of erotic art and sexuality in which Bataille has placed them, informing us that his point is "to illustrate a fundamental connection between religious ecstasy and eroticism—and in particular sadism."* Bataille would

---

*The extracts that follow are taken from Georges Bataille, *The Tears of Eros,* translated by Peter Connor (San Francisco: City Lights, 1989).

deal with some obscure connection between eroticism and sadism mediated through religion, perhaps the ritualistic cruelty of religious sacrifice.

Coming upon these pictures at the end of his book, one is not only appalled by them but also surprised, the surprise of shock; an indignation that such terrible suffering would be confused with sexual excitement, would find a place in a book of erotic images. Indeed, context has much to do with shock; all that is cruel is crueler still when presented as something else, when the context has been radically altered and cruelty is exhibited as something humorous or sexy. A particular shock resides in the reality of cruelty denied; it is a sense of being fooled, of having one's own perception called into question, ridiculed.

The shock of these spectacles: a man set on fire, a boy hung on a cross, finally the image of a young man held upright by poles attached to his bound hands, while his leg is amputated below the knee. In the larger photograph, it is the victim's lower left leg which is being sawed off while a crowd watches. In a smaller photograph on the opposite page, that leg is already gone and the executioners are beginning to remove the lower section of the right leg. The face of the victim is turned upward. Drugged or not, ecstatic or not, it is a mask of suffering, augmented by the fact that below it, the victim's chest has been skinned and opened, revealing most of his rib cage; blood streams down from the ragged edges of flesh cut and peeled away as if it were fabric.

The pictures are old, originally taken in 1905 by Louis Carpeaux, a European witness to the execution of one Fou-Tchou-Li, convicted of the murder of Prince Ao-Han-Ouan and condemned to slow death by *Leng-Tch'e* (cutting into pieces). They were printed first in Carpeaux's publication, *Pekin qui s'en va* (1913), and reprinted in a scientific text by Georges Dumas, *Traité de Psychologie* (1923). The age of the photographs becomes part of their horror—the overexposed, almost blistered quality in the exposure of the victim's face, the faded gaze of the onlookers, some having lost their individual features, but many completely clear and distinct. Each of them riveted with attention. They are all men. Several wear hats and are, it seems by their activity and function, official execution- ers; the rest are humbler, wear skullcaps or are bareheaded. One guesses them to be the masses for whom this spectacle is staged.

On the surface, all the photographs I have called upon are political arguments. And one's reaction, at least my own, is visceral: the shock I am trying to fathom. Perhaps, first of all, I must deal with the very fact of my reaction: is it too strong, in some way embarrassing? One's own fault, a weakness, senti- mentality, a kind of stupidity, literal mindedness? What even occurs in this flashtide of feeling, this flush—for blood may rush to the face, one experiences a fever, sensation buzzes and scintillates, the stomach responds as it does in panic, an adren- aline response. A fear-or-flight reaction? There is a terrible apprehension of vulnerability.

There is also a blinding experience of shame, of being shamed, even personally shamed, not the grand rational man- ner of finding human behavior utterly repellent and confus- ing—how could people do such a thing, it makes one ashamed of one's species, etc. Another shame—deeper, personal, one's own. A remembrance and accumulation: the shame of being laughed at, degraded, made a spectacle of, giving way slowly to the sting of insult . . . But everything resides in that subtle shift, the difference between despair and anger, that fine line which culture and conditioning have blurred and confused.

Confusion is probably the first response I feel before these photographs and the shock they induce. What does it even mean? Since it is a mixture of responses so emotionally debili- tating it takes a long time even to sort out and understand them. And they are very possible to mistake; for it is extremely easy to err in assessing these responses, to see them in a short- sighted and literal way, even to confuse their negative energy with a positive excitement, to confuse the shame they induce with titillation, to respond to the hidden or taboo or secret (because until recently such images were secret) as if it were forbidden. To confuse the cruel with the sexual, to do it innocently and in confusion as Bataille does deliberately.

It is an easy mistake for women to make, women whose culture trains them long and carefully to respond masochistically. An education in masochism is generally part of the conditioning of any group who experience being despised; their response of identifying with what degrades and humiliates them is illogical only on the surface: in fact, it has been carefully cultivated in them.

Bataille's use of Chinese torture at the conclusion of a book on eroticism is also only superficially out of place, given the assumptions of our culture. He seems to have apprehended something basic to these assumptions. Under patriarchy, sexuality is socially controlled, limited and repressed. However private or secret, it is bounded by rules and regulations, punishments and shibboleths. Nor is it difficult to associate with violence since patriarchy depends finally upon force for its operation: rape and ravishment, defloration, overpowering and domination, are fundamental patterns of patriarchal sexuality. Bataille seems to have apprehended something basic about the way that sexual excitement is aroused under authoritarian conditions. Sexuality is a function of power for males in such situations, of powerlessness for females. It is that which Bataille can count on perpetuating as he shows us photographs of torture and tells us they are erotic; in female viewers he can advocate masochism as he can cultivate sadism in himself and other males.

Culturally, there is another habitual identification of sexuality with cruelty because representations of both are difficult of access and frequently hidden, both have long been taboo and therefore somewhat magical, the power of the unseen, the unseeable; like everything invisible, a power in itself. Particularly so for women and the young, those most carefully preserved from such sights. Bataille's book is a collection of images: most are familiar female nudity of a fairly conventional order, only a few depict torture. Taken all together the unpleasantness of the one set of images, those of cruelty and suffering, joined with the sensual pleasure and gratification of the other set, those of sexuality and eroticism, creates confusion. Because both have been taboo, both forbidden, the sadistic or cruel becomes sexualized.

The crimes of cruelty are technically illegal: does this somehow put them in the same category as forbidden sexual acts, until recently illegal as well? Recently, pictures of women suffering rape or ritual murder have become entertainment and accepted as sexually stimulating. To whom? And for what reasons? It is impossible not to inquire and thereby confront history.

FOR what assaults me with the first and last of these pictures is not only their content but the attitude with which each is presented. First my friend Catherine's apparent endorsement of *realpolitik*. And next Bataille's perception of the scene of Chinese torture, this "image of pain" as inherently erotic. There is no sexual content in these pictures of a man being slowly and deliberately dissected while still alive. Yet, inserting the question mark himself, Bataille describes this execution as both "ecstatic(?)" and "intolerable" at once. "Through this violence—even today I cannot imagine a more insane, more shocking form—I was so stunned that I reached the point of ecstasy," he reports. "My purpose," he explains, "is to illustrate a fundamental connection between religious ecstasy and eroticism—and in particular sadism. From the most unspeakable to the most elevated. This book is not written from within the limited experience of most men."

Bataille then calls upon the tradition of religious sacrifice to explain "the identity of these perfect contraries, divine ecstasy and its opposite, extreme horror." Continuing in italic type for emphasis:

THE POLITICS OF CRUELTY

> *And this is my inevitable conclusion to a history of eroticism.* But
> I should add: limited to its own domain, eroticism could never
> have achieved this fundamental truth divulged in *religious eroti-*
> *cism,* the identity of horror and the religious. Religion in its
> entirety was founded upon sacrifice. But only an interminable
> detour allows us to reach that instant where the contraries seem
> visibly conjoined, where the religious horror disclosed in sacrifice
> becomes linked to the abyss of eroticism, to the last shuddering
> tears that eroticism alone can illuminate.

These are Bataille's final words; the next four pages contain
seventeenth- and eighteenth-century engravings of dismember-
ment and a beheading, meant to further persuade.

WHAT one is being persuaded toward, the erotic character
of cruelty, its inherent capacity for sexual arousal, doesn't
work in my case; it fails to arouse me sexually, but it does
make me angry. Pained and angry, a sense of intellectual and
philosophic betrayal. A sense of betrayal old and familiar, but
nowhere quite as keenly felt as here where the sight of a being
carved into pieces is followed by reasoning both specious and
self-serving.

It was this sense of hurt, almost a feeling of being attacked,
which first brought me to the subject of this work altogether—
for the very idea of torture made me feel aggressed upon,
frightened and angry, a storm of emotions which in coming to
understand in myself I can perhaps understand the subject
better. There is a pain, followed by anger; both of these reactions seem to refer to my own experience as a woman in a
culture where women are routinely overwhelmed and dominated, emotionally and psychologically, in much the same way
they are dominated physically. The helplessness of the victim
is completely familiar. One has been taught to despair before
this, to feel one's impotence and futility further increase to
paralyze one. This is a learned response; it is also taught.

But I am also a woman dedicated to the resistance and overthrow of this form of domination, so my second response—anger—is different, even opposite in direction to my initial identification and fear, a familiar despair leading to an ancient fatality. The second response, anger, never taught and learned with much difficulty, is entirely different in character and effect: rejection replaces acceptance. Instead, one takes action, *does* something, takes arms against forces so hostile, even if only by announcing dissatisfaction, complaining of injustice, referring to and insisting upon the very humane criteria which are violated by the event of torture. Rather than permitting such violation, seeing it as fate and impossible to change, still less welcoming it as mystical or erotic, some exotic foreign custom to be respected, some necessity of state one cannot withstand . . . one rebels.

One may actually know the moment when the sight of some event that filled one with anguish, left one frozen and helpless in place, sick with what one has glimpsed—the moment when that gave way to slow-seething fury. That is the moment of liberation, the moment when one ceases to be victimized and takes the first step toward freedom. Oppression has made it possible to identify with the victim as oppressors might not, but the moment of outrage is what changes that sympathy into refusal to endure psychologically—on the victim's behalf— what the victim endured physically.

One studies torture because one hates it and opposes it, but is that all? Look inside oneself again, what is the nature of that shock one experiences, the emotional turmoil one feels—how much is fascination, curiosity? How much is guilt over that curiosity, that insight into the taboo and forbidden? Are there traces of sexual excitement in this, and if so, of what kind? What is this turmoil composed of; is it general, does it differ by gender or age or experience? If ordinary citizens are fascinated, titillated, it is important to examine the elements in a culture which utilizes our responses as a government prerogative or resource. The difference always seems to be a matter of believing in the reality of what is taking place. Not as one believes a myth, but literally as one might believe something could happen to oneself. Until one can reach that point, until conscious identification takes place, there is a certain inertia which separates the victim from those around him, a separation most advantageous to the state. If we cannot imagine torture, we can never stop it.

Staring at the onlookers in the photograph, how is this scene possible? How could people tolerate such an idea, a human creature, criminal in their eyes or not, its suffering relished as spectacle and prolonged with scientific cleverness, drugs and anatomical skill. How long does it go on? Hours, one is informed. Like the Elizabethan practice of drawing and quartering, also prolonged; political lessons presenting themselves as an art form, the executioner's craft. This is after all simply a public execution; whether the victim is criminal or innocent, the indignities committed upon his helpless body are only indignities, only the emanations of a ruler's diseased imagination. What is actually demonstrated is merely cruelty and a crude ingenuity.

And the cruelty seduces, persuades? Do the rabble, enjoying their sandwiches at a hanging, experience a gratification at seeing justice done and identify further with the wisdom of the laws? Or do they merely experience a heady superiority over the unfortunate, which evaporates toward nightfall and solidifies into a burden, the solemn yoke of the state upon the individual condition? Isn't this finally about power, indeed always about power, and never really about pleasure at all? The spectator's pitifully short orgiastic delight evaporated in an enlarged understanding of his helplessness before such enormous authority?

Perhaps it depends on who you are. If you are a woman, the first stone is thrown against all sexual activity; if you are a man, it might be actually sexual to partake. Even if only to partake psychically, spiritually: one remembers the excitement of men one has known, friends and fellow artists in the sixties discussing Richard Speck's methodical strangulation of eight women nurses; the frisson in their voices, their jokes. Given the character of patriarchal sexuality—its logic, its laws, its enforcement—what is cruel may have come to color deeply what is sexual. How else is it possible to have arrived at such an equation?

But the slender Chinese figure with the terrible gashes in its chest, the awful shape held up by two poles that pinion it aloft and in place, the terrible truncated form even now having its leg deliberately and methodically cut off at the knee—is not even a woman. How then an erotic object? Is male suffering subsumed as well into this distempered sexuality? Or is it merely a victimization which approaches that presumed to be female? An utter vulnerability, such as women are to have? If torture makes a man into a woman, as men who have been tortured often say, what does it make of a woman? Does this male victim's "femininity" derive from his emaciated, almost childlike body? So much smaller does he appear, naked, than the padded and prosperous executioners, the crowd dressed in heavy coats. How is this figure, the body rigid in the position of crucifixion even if the arms are tied behind and not extended, the whole trunk held up and above the spectators, the body lifted high by wooden poles braced by two hardworking coolies—how is this figure erotic? Hacked and bleeding, screaming in unimaginable pain, how does one come to imagine such a thing as erotic? Is it because he is a photograph, a contemporary artifact from a distant place and fairly distant in time? Is he erotic by virtue of being exotic? Would a mangled Scandinavian or a German be as erotic?

Has Bataille spoken for something larger in conflating the cruel with the erotic, illustrated a general assumption that cruelty itself is perceived as sexual, said to be erotic, seen to be so? If so, by whom and why? As you approach the picture, as you run through the pages of Bataille's *Tears of Eros*—struggling repeatedly to understand what meaning the author intends, what common ground you may share, what values are advanced that you can assent to as the stable notions of a culture—pictures follow one after another of naked female forms, full, luscious, alive, nearly every illustration a female nude, sometimes accompanied by a male or an animal; other figures where they are present are generally invading, threatening, killing, coercing. This is the familiar, so familiar, pattern of Western eroticism, its violence, its exaggerated notion of the female body as a sexual object, the only sexual object, a sexual force, a projection of sexuality itself as if its very form were an activity—an activity desired but also scorned and despised, hated and longed for, sexuality attributed almost exclusively and irrationally to women. As if the female were sex itself and therefore the single guilty party, the cause and the essence of the forbidden. And then, with utter unpredictability, one comes upon this image of an Oriental male in anguish, held aloft on a pole and carved alive. And the rhythm stops, comes to an end, is contradicted.

"Since 1925 I have owned one of these pictures," Bataille tells us. *The Tears of Eros* was first published in 1961, Bataille's last work before his death; for forty-one years he has kept and contemplated this image, possessed by it, the familiar fetish of an atrocity photo. "I wonder what the Marquis de Sade would have thought of this image," muses Bataille, "Sade who dreamed of torture, which was inaccessible to him, but who never witnessed an actual torture session. In one way or another this image was incessantly before his eyes. But Sade would have wished to see it in solitude, at least in relative solitude, without which the ecstatic and voluptuous effect is inconceivable." What but Western voyeurism could find ecstasy and voluptuousness here? It is not in the crowd for whom it was staged. They do not appear ecstatic; fascinated, utterly attentive, their eyes following the executioner's saw as it amputates a leg, there is a tension visible even in their photographed bodies and faces, each rapt and filled with concentration. There may be something else, not ecstasy but fear, certainly anxiety.

There is no rejoicing, no one is shouting or screaming, no one is in bliss over this hideous spectacle, the victim displayed like a marionette, tied to its pole, still living, still breathing, still conscious, and in what supernatural pain. But only the pain is supernatural; the crowd exhibits no transcendence, no communication with higher forces. Bataille's claims fall to the ground. One is forced to refute them, not for what they tell us of Western sexuality—the pages of female nudes did that, were an inventory of power and domination, both real and fantasized, all too familiar. But in the victim of Chinese torture one is asked to go one step further in the discovery of what is being explained as eroticism as Western man understands it. The inclusion of this photograph tells us much about Bataille but even more about his culture and his time. All its basic assumptions seem to be demonstrated in what is presented as the ultimate erotic image—the image of an Oriental in the process of being tortured to death.

What one rejects in shock is revealed, an epiphany: no longer forced to accept it as sexual or sexually exciting, one can see it for what it is—the epitome of cruelty, as Bataille says—all of that, but not erotic. In and of itself it has nothing sexual about it. Sexuality must be added through other means: mystification.

The cruelty and horror remain in the image as in the fact, but now one must remove from the image the pretension that it is erotic, sexy, pleasurable, sophisticated, an elegant taste, a philosophic *aperçu*. If cruelty and horror are not passed off as something sexual as well, the insult and the outrage from this quarter die down so that the real outrage can become clear and unconfused. It is the confusion of the two which oppresses most of all, aiding, abetting, and perpetuating oppression.

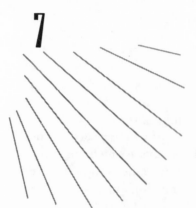

7

CLOSET LAND: STATE AND SEXUAL AUTHORITY

RADHA BHARADWAJ'S film *Closet Land* begins in total darkness, the darkness of a blindfold: only voices guide us; looking on, we are as helpless as the prisoner whose story it tells. There are only two protagonists. The film is a contest between a male interrogator, who often impersonates other voices (tough guy, nice guy), and his detainee, a woman. As we watch, we are forced to identify with the latter since we are also blindfolded, the black leader unwinding on the screen before us, only the letters of occasional credits relieving the total darkness, only the voices to guide us and set the scene.

The male voice is initially disguised, deliberately distorted to resemble electronic slowdown. This sound is later compared to a "choked gutter," a brutal sound. Its first intelligible statement is a menacing "Shut up!" in answer to the prisoner's helpless "Where am I?" For an instant the male voice becomes clear, speaking as it were to itself, "I think I have everything." Another moment further on, having given the wrong direction: "to your right"—we hear the sound of the prisoner stumbling—it excuses itself with a rhyme: "I forgot that your left is my right and vice versa, your vices are my verses." It is almost a nonsense rhyme, a rhyme by which the interrogator will eventually betray himself when impersonating other voices to deceive the prisoner in her blindfold.

The prisoner tries to sound determined, demands to see her lawyer, is irate at the treatment meted out during her arrest; finally, speaking in his own voice, the interrogator promises to "look into it." The prisoner is blindfolded all this while, and it is only when the blindfold is removed from her eyes that the audience, sharing her point of view, is permitted to see anything upon the screen. What first appears there is a burst of light, bright enough to hurt, then the face of the interrogator, orange and overexposed, only gradually solidifying into proper light and shade values as the camera mimics the eye adjusting from utter darkness to light—brilliant at first and extreme because so unfamiliar, the lens narrowing down at last to the muted shades of a large room and artificial lighting.

The room itself is broken up by a number of pillars with ornamental Ionic capitals carrying a conscious stylistic stamp of government, full of pomp and certainty like the facade of a large public building. This formalistic quality pertains throughout the film, is essential to its vision. There is no attempt at the banal workaday office of real interrogations, the dirty, deserted rooms, the provisional character of clandestine prisons: everything here is symbolic of power already absolute. If contemporary Fascist arrangements are, in actuality, messy and spontaneous, the intention here is the formal face of a state power, so entrenched that it has expressed itself on all sides and in every interior detail; not merely in its familiar monumental exteriors, but in what were once its secret places as well.

The room is high and spacious; in the center the interrogator's imposing thronelike chair, his huge desk an inverted pyramid which swivels on a central axis; surfaces are sleek, polished stone and steel. The prisoner's chair by contrast is flimsy, made of cloth and straw, insubstantial. Everything else in the room cries out with strength—the stone walls, the great stone doors with steel knobs which open electronically from a button on the desk and close with an absolute closure. The aesthetic of the security state has been realized, conveyed in arrogant lines, hard surfaces, an oppressive density of material: pompous, inflated, "futuristic."

In substance too the film is deliberately formalistic, its action a studied symbolism and allegory. There is no stated locale, the two characters are given neither name nor nationality. The interrogator is a man and "the officer in charge"; the prisoner is a woman. What she sees first—and we as well—is the man who says he is her interrogator. And the place, the room, is, he says, a state interrogation chamber.

It is established almost at once that the arrested woman is an author of children's books, someone without any interest in or knowledge of politics. The interrogator even concedes that her arrest might actually be an error; after a short interview, he agrees to release her. The great doors open onto absolute darkness: she is afraid of a trap. Becoming friendly, he persuades her to wait for a moment until the authorities have produced a letter of apology which she believes is a necessary document of safe passage.

Sitting down again, she accepts a bit of broth from his thermos to warm her up; he flatters her with the statement that he once saw her signing autographs in a bookstore. She permits herself to complain of her treatment; then, before his evident annoyance, restrains herself. She is still at his mercy, the doors have shut again. Time goes by and she complains that the man with a voice "like a choked gutter" molested her, she has the marks of his fingernails upon her, will show them only to a physician. He promises to "look into" this as well, then ignores her and reads a book. She reminds him of the letter of apology and at once he produces it from a file cabinet, a form letter. She takes it and goes toward the door. Which will not open. She panics and throws herself on the massive door, her letter in her hand. He warns her it could be "a very long time" and tosses her his suit coat to protect her against the chill in the room. "Why didn't you leave when you could?" he mocks.

"You cannot call your lawyer or anyone else from outside," he tells her now. "You must put your trust in us. I am a small part of a large mechanism. That goes for you too. Together we must seek the truth." The interrogator's pronouncements are full of double meanings, references to a higher mission, loftier planes of inquiry, the great hidden truths which those who stand to profit by them claim for the phenomena of pain and domination, the sadomasochism of the state, of the sexes, finally even of child and adult. "I will help you to the best of my ability," he promises in a solemn voice, "but the brunt of the responsibility resides with you."

This is a familiar theme in the literature of prolonged inter- rogation, particularly in Solzhenitsyn's, Artur London's, and Koestler's accounts of Soviet interrogation methods, a sifting of the soul of the prisoner, the interrogator naturally the con- fessor and judge here as in the Inquisition. The project is presented as a joint venture between the parties, the prisoner's own help enlisted in this enormous undertaking: an examina- tion of conscience, a total recall of his/her life, a complete psychological reevaluation of its every act carried out under the light of revisionist political analysis. Truth is now some- thing on which the interrogator and the state have a monopoly.

The prisoner realizes, perhaps sooner, perhaps later, that things will go better and less painfully for him the faster he apprehends the truth as "they" see it—the interrogator and those who mysteriously direct him. He must hurry to take their drift, he must discover and zero in on the version of events they have chosen to be the truth he must embrace. And quickly: torture at least will be minimized, the inevitable confession will be moved forward, perhaps a sentence will be pro- nounced, even a show trial made possible. Perhaps one will be released then into the ordinary prison population and excused further interrogation, further physical and psychological torture. Perhaps the sentence will be execution itself, a death welcome enough finally—the cheat and charade over at last, this nightmare contest where everything is weighted against him.

"Though personally I may find your lies charming," the interrogator warns his prisoner, "inadvertent blunders will be treated with firm kindness, and you must trust me to establish the ratio of firmness to kindness." His short speeches convey a great knowledge of the interrogation process, distilling the experience of thousands of pages of history and the recollections of victims. Now he formulates the casuistry of interrogation as investigation and information gathering, a necessary function of government, a job merely, impersonal, without individual responsibility. "Your best hope would be to depersonalize what is going to follow and not look upon me as your foe or yourself as a victim. Remember, we are both seekers of truth and in this quest I am your friend, philosopher and guide." This last lofty phrase ascribes a philosophical dimension to domination and cruelty, like the use of the word "firmness," and the pseudo-moral sententia later repeated over and over: "Pain ennobles both the giver and the receiver, we must break your body to save your mind." The cruelty of state power has assumed an air of transcendent wisdom, secret access to an arcane understanding of extreme mental and emotional experience. In presenting what follows as allegory, the film can examine both the nature of the victim's sufferings and the rationale of the oppressor.

The woman is now entirely a prisoner, has realized there is no way out. The interrogator removes her published works from a drawer and places them before him on the desk. From the bottom of the pile he selects something still in typescript and throws it at her. An unpublished manuscript: this is what they have unearthed against her. It is a private document; they have searched her house to find it. The interrogator protests that the search was orderly; they even cleaned the place afterward. They did, however, find blood on the toilet seat. Or so it's claimed: he must make certain. He stands and does a curious thing—he reaches into her clothing and checks to see if she is menstruating. He has her manuscript, now he must lay claim to her body as well. The manner of that claiming is absolutely sex-specific, particular not only to state but to sexual domination as well, not only a torturer's assertion of power over a prisoner, but a male interrogator's assertion of sexual ownership over a female prisoner, a form of sexual assault that is not only torture but sexual torture.

There is an epigraph at the end of the film citing Amnesty International information that more than half the governments of the world now practice torture upon their own citizens. The ambiance is consciously political, creating a parallel between male domination and domination by the state, aware of the multiplication of such inequity when the body is infringed upon. The essence of torture is its violation of the integrity of the body, an integrity which is the first guarantee of the rights of man and the citizen, bodily integrity itself so sacred, so basic a human freedom that infringement of it is constitutionally forbidden everywhere. Where the body is treated as property, not merely to incarcerate, but to hurt and humiliate, to violate and manipulate and cause deliberate pain, there is the greatest tyranny, patriarchal or governmental. Compound the two and you have the conditions which pertain in this film. In making this clear, Bharadwaj has chosen to illustrate her point with an example sexual in character but not "sexy," a man examining a woman for signs of menstrual blood. An act of sexual aggression yet not sexual activity per se, it establishes a male supremacy that other films might conventionally present through sexual activity itself.

This careful and deliberate clarification is socially and politically of special importance, since sexual activity—as portrayed in public entertainment in general and film in particular—is so often an event of violence or humiliation practiced upon woman. The subordination of women and the practice of sexual acts are two things which culture repeatedly conflates and confuses in the public mind, a confusion at the center of entertainment just now, when commercial pornography accounts for the preponderance of films produced and distributed. Even non-pornographic material is often affected by the traditionalist pornographic assumption that sex is female, a female responsibility, and subject therefore to pornography's prurient disapproval and abhorrence: sexual acts take place in order to be punished. The violence inherent in pornography itself is the inevitable punishment reserved for female participation in sex, a participation which proves that the female is dirty and horny and at fault, that she "wanted it" (isn't pure as she is supposed to be, pretended to be) and so now she's "going to get it"—sex is visited upon her as rape and mortification. Being thus aggressed upon, she is perceived as having sinned again and will be further punished by being whipped, sodomized, or even killed.

The interrogator's action, depending upon the taboo of blood and menstruation to humiliate his victim, has also deprived her of the last dignity of privacy. The nature of sexual torture depends for its cruel effect upon our traditional habits of dignity in privacy and of the integrity of the body, particularly its genitals. In checking to see if she bleeds, the interrogator violates his female prisoner; at the same time he imitates the authority of the physician in the jailor, the owner and expert, taking even the functions of the woman's own body away from her. While violating her merely with his hand and not his penis, he has appropriated all the glory of domination without even the taint of sex. And in all images of the two protagonists which follow, he will triumph in street clothes over her handcuffed, blindfolded, and half-naked body.

He is dressed in a very good suit, over which he frequently wears an overcoat with a sumptuous blue silk lining emblematic of his freedom to come and go: his clothes indicate that he is well paid and well placed. The glasses he wears suggest the look of a school principal, his manner the air of an official. In time he takes on a dead-certain masculine air of authority, and by virtue of his absolute power over his female victim, an enormous virility and power. Everything which his sexual status has given him, his civil position has magnified a thousandfold. Within this room, where he holds a woman blindfolded and handcuffed, he has the power of God himself. The woman wears only the thin nightdress in which she was arrested; later she will wake to find herself with her arms handcuffed behind her back and dressed in the black bra and panties of pornographic photography while a disembodied voice repeats over and over that women who "favor black underwear" are "closet whores."

Gradually we come to understand that the room has a skylight whose window records a night becoming dawn and then morning during the course of the film. But there is also a concurrent impression that time is eternal, that the interrogation, which the prisoner insists is still in its first night, could be taking place over months and years as the interrogator would like her to believe. This room is nearly the whole world, anything outside it will be flashback, memory or imagination; the room is the here and now, fearsome and claustrophobic despite its size. Much of it is in shadow, parts of it are mysterious; there are large cutouts in the moldings down along the baseboards which suggest surveillance from another location; visual or auditory supervision seems a certainty. Parts of the wall give way to storage areas for sound technology, and later for medical, mechanical, and electrical torture implements. The interrogator's knowledge of this room is enormous, it is not only his work place but his milieu, finally who he is; the prisoner's ignorance of it is enormous as well, a complex and subtle mechanism by which she will be hurt and frightened.

She will also be blindfolded again and again in the course of her interrogation and is therefore very easy to deceive. The interrogator is extremely skillful at adopting other voices, even the speech forms of different ages and classes. He works the large columned room like a sound studio: he has further resources in recorded material, amplifiers, tape recorders. Like any captive, the prisoner's sense of reality is being assaulted; what do "they" know of her, what do they believe, suspect, imagine? A lay person, she is utterly mystified by where she is, the procedure, the expectations of those who hold her, the degree of the ordeal that awaits her, the character of this stranger into whose absolute power she is given, perhaps for the rest of her life . . . however long that may be.

For the interrogator has the power of life and death over her, liberty or captivity, dread or hope. Already disoriented, arrested in the middle of the night and blindfolded, she will believe he is any number of other persons. The flashbacks of her arrest which come on the screen as she refers to it are curious—an officer's shirt front as she is captured and a gun put to her head, representations of the eye of memory but when blindfolded. The images are close-cropped, myopic, only the first of a number of remembered or imagined images we see on screen, fragments of her mind conveyed to our eyes, so that we "see" what she "thinks," an interesting use of the film medium to convey consciousness, even to make visible an imagined world unseen by others. Over and over certain visual motifs occur, the world of her own manuscript "Closet Land," with all their associations of a secret, utterly private reality.

But metaphors of all kinds are suspect, as the interrogator points out, might be code, even children are subject to propaganda, as he cleverly demonstrates with three still photographs. In each a child, first seen in close-up, when the camera pulls back turns out to be located in an indisputably political context: a small boy standing beside a Klansman with a rifle, the smiling face of a little girl held up in the arms of Hitler, an infant sucking a pacifier placed before three giant posters of the Ayatollah Khomeini. In an earlier exchange the interrogator had quoted at her: " 'You can do anything with children as long as you play with them'—who said that?" "Bismarck," she had replied.

The imagination becomes the battleground between them, the only uncontested space left to her . . . if he can conquer that. First he must prove her guilty, entice her to explore her own resources in the fantastic so that he may follow and chart the subversive terrain before apprehending her there. Her unpublished "Closet Land" seems fairly innocuous, the story of a child locked in a closet by a negligent and unfeeling mother. The child makes do by bringing the clothes to life and playing with them; a friendly rooster warns her when it is time to relinquish them and assume her habitual defeated posture, an animated cartoon figure of a little girl seated dejectedly on a closet floor.

"When you write for children, you pretty much have to be direct. There's no room for hidden meanings . . . my stories are harmless, cheerful pieces of fluff," the author insists. And seeing the animations pictured brightly on the screen in pure blues and greens as the friendly rooster appears or the cat with green wings flies into the empyrean—images of sky and outdoors and freedom in contrast to the shadowed values and chiaroscuro of the interrogation room's sealed indoor space— one is inclined to agree that these huge animations filling the entire screen, recognizable and conventional creatures of children's fiction, are in fact hardly worth the interrogator's time. But then their metaphoric aspect is revealed as autobiography: the prisoner was the child in the closet, her stories all originate there. The interrogator would have them portend much else: "I don't trust lonely people, life's eternal spectators, watching, waiting . . ."

He astonishes her by playing a tape recording of her own voice denouncing her mother while visiting her a year ago in a hospital room: " 'I've done all I could, I've been there for you, but you were never there for me, you never noticed. You just never noticed.' . . ." "And then you stormed out of the hospital," the interrogator accuses her, " . . . and that night your mother died." The woman is aghast: "You've been spying on me." A common occurrence, he assures her, government policy in fact: "All conversations in all hospital rooms are taped, without exceptions. We gain access to confessions, guilts, longings—you name it—that we wouldn't otherwise be privy to. Most of it is sentimental drivel and it's destroyed. But the conversations between writers, artists, political activists, these are never destroyed."

State control of private life and government paranoia have gone far here. The interrogator rises and without warning strikes his prisoner a practiced blow upon the ears, a common technique in torture: it produces a trauma much like the loss of consciousness. "Come on, it was just a tap," he scolds her. "It'll pass." "Put your head on your knees," he instructs, waiting for the pain to subside so that he will have her entire attention again. Was she in good health, was she on any medication he should know about, he had asked earlier in seeming solicitude. Medical information, like the presence of physicians at torture, is a matter of drawing the line, preventing death or illness through which the victim might elude his tormentor.

After suddenly burning her hand with a cigarette (in the beginning he had assured her he didn't smoke), he gives her something for the pain and presents her with a wine bottle in a bucket of ice: she drinks eagerly, only to discover it is urine. Each blow and insult is followed with fatherly, friendly commiseration. He continues pursuing her guilt: "Closet Land is a place where people go for secret meetings. Remember, the clothes don't even come alive until the child is alone . . . when the Friendly Rooster who is on the lookout, gives the warning cry, they scatter and run away. When mother comes back she can't find anything. You have made the child a martyr and the mother a tyrant. Your sympathies are with the child of course because you resent any authority."

The author disclaims responsibility; this is after all merely his interpretation. "People get turned on by passages in the Bible," she points out sensibly. "Closet Land is a simple children's story." But it is not a simple world, he argues. "Just think, skeletons rattling in the closet. It's a place where people hide, we say 'closet homosexual,' 'closet intellectual.' A dark, secret world. Like the basement, the space under the bed at night." All children's fiction has an element of horror, she argues—dragons, witches—"children's authors aren't political creatures because children aren't. Politics means big things. Anyone who knows children knows they live for themselves and the present moment."

Nevertheless, he warns, children are "far more receptive to suggestion than adults," and children can be taught to "find themselves and the present moment within an ideology." She shrugs. "You are guilty of subliminal indoctrination," he thunders. "Absurd," she protests. "You're not a member of the underground?" he presses on. "No," she answers, insisting she knows nothing about politics. "Do you support us then?" he asks on a note of closing in: Is she not for "order and stability"? Seen from here, the outside world has shrunk to two camps; there is no neutrality.

The interrogator proceeds to take her story literally. Where is Closet Land? he demands, sure of himself. "We already have two turncoats," he threatens, a kindergarten teacher and a physicist, fellow conspirators. "Who is the Friendly Rooster," he demands, "Is he in the government? We have a few suspicions." He has got the scent now, is willing to use any subterfuge to achieve a collar. He places before her the confession he has kept typed and ready in his drawer all along.

> I confess that my story Closet Land is an allegory for the struggles of the various underground groups which are resisting the government. The child protagonist of the story stands for the uninformed reader whose views I wish to mould. I am consciously representing governmental authority in the character of the mother. The clothes are all underground insurgents: the Friendly Rooster is a government official.

As she points out, even if she did confess to this "pack of lies," "How do I know it will stop here?" For the first time, she weeps.

A voice-over comes on and the screen shows us the interior of a closet, the closet door swinging shut leaving only darkness and the expressive voice of the professional storyteller employed to read or recite children's fables.

> The closet child knew that she'd missed her chance when she could have opened the door. Whatever could the poor closet child do? Badman gives her nothing to drink, she's so parched that she'd even drink the urine he offered her. So closet child will do what all children do when they're trapped, she shut her eyes hard, and pretended that she could glide out of hell. She knew that there was a passage of brightness right outside hell and that the elves had left a large pitcher of fresh dew just for her.

We see a radiant passageway, accordion-pleated like an airline jetway, flooded with light, the woman walking along it confidently, her hair brushed, her face serenely floating toward a large frosty pitcher of water; in a single frame it transforms itself into a tumbler of cool liquid held out to her by the hand of her interrogator. She drinks. The imagination works: it has produced a real glass of real water. Then he knocks her out.

PRIVATE and public life intersect in this film in a manner familiar to women, persons who have so little acknowledged citizenship or public existence that investigation by the state might not stop with imagined political connections but proceed toward the perceived crime of female sexuality. The woman wakes to find herself clothed only in black underwear, the recorded voice of her persecutor tediously repeating, as if it were a news item or a scientific fact, a series of figures, beginning with "96.8 percent" and ending with "105.9 percent of women who favor black underwear" are "closet whores." Her clothing humiliates her in a sex-specific way only intensified by the fact of bondage in such an outfit. A great blotch of lipstick is smeared over her mouth, her cheeks are rouged in a clownish manner, and her hair is tied in childish pigtails with large ribbons of mismatched and foolishly gay colors, one yellow, one blue. She is now disfigured with the pornographic iconography directed toward the sexual violation of children, the merging of female sexuality with "little girl" imagery, a costume of depraved stupidity. The self is being destroyed.

The woman is then aligned before a bright light against a projected image of herself in bed with a lover, photographs obtained through surveillance: there is a repeated flashback image of shirts hanging in a closet, a naked lightbulb. The interrogator's recorded voice announces that certain "friendly neighborhood sex watch reports" reveal that she is no good with men, has not slept with one for a year. Nothing in her life belongs to her any more, the state has complete power over her past, complete access to it and to her most intimate moments. The voice of authority announces that she no longer merits a name or identity and will henceforth become the label "AB 234."

The interrogator enters the room, pretending to know nothing of her change of clothes. Alas, he must blindfold her again since his replacement ("I'd advise you to be straight with him, he's not very patient") will take over, an undercover agent whose face she is not permitted to see. Fearing still greater evil, she is reduced to begging this interrogator to stay. "They're watching me too," he lies to her, throwing up a bridge of complicity between victim and victimizer.

He then pretends to leave, a pretense that encompasses the viewer as well at first, since we see only huge shoes coming down the stairs when the "newcomer" enters. A moment later this "newcomer" is revealed to be the same interrogator speaking in other voices, using a variety of devices: loudspeakers, taped dialogues, a mixture of words and sound effects where he takes on several voices—those of both interrogator and prisoner, the tortured and the torturer—each deception clear to the viewer but perfectly effective in deceiving the woman imprisoned in her blindfold.

Then he pretends to leave and enter again as himself, now in the role of sympathizer, offering to remove her blindfold, unlock her handcuffs, and assist her in escaping. A moment before, while impersonating a prisoner with an aged working-class voice, he had praised himself as interrogator: "he's a different sort," just beg him, fall at his knees, and he will let you go—the voice had tipped her off. She tries to follow this advice. And the interrogator appears to be as good as advertised. He removes her blindfold. But as he goes through his pockets for the key to her handcuffs, he removes, deliberately and for her to see it and understand, the clove of garlic he had chewed a short while before, impersonating "choked gutter"—garlic he had mixed in his mouth with tomato and then, with studied insult, emptied into her mouth when she was blindfolded and helpless, unable to understand what was being forced down her throat.

She is sighted now and the sight of the garlic clove reveals his deception and the fact that he has toyed with her, staged her fears, intimidated her through falsehoods and charades. Still in handcuffs, she kicks him in the genitals. "You have no right to make a joke of this," she charges him. He quotes policy: "Our aims are to purge society of negative influences, that end justifies the use of certain unorthodox means." "Your aim is to humiliate and debase a human being; there is no justification for cruelty." They state and restate their positions, at checkmate. Finally he begins to remove her handcuffs.

The moment she is free, she fights for her life. Only gradually and with difficulty is she overpowered and subdued by force again, handcuffed, and then pinioned by the steel hoops at the sides of his great stone desktop, the interrogator repeating his charge that the underwear in which she has been dressed makes her a "closet whore," bringing to a close this section of the interrogation, a section of sexual indictment.

/   /   /

WHILE deceiving her with impersonations, the interrogator had staged an atrocity, a "barbecue" where a red-hot skewer is pushed up the anus of an imagined male prisoner who might really be present in some other interrogation room and whose scream reaches us through a speaker. On that occasion, we watched as the interrogator wheeled out the grill from its place in the wall and enacted the scraping noise of the skewer. We had also heard the shriek of the victim, in which, completely persuaded, the woman joined in sympathy.

Things have moved to a different plane now, however, with her attack upon the interrogator. There will be no mercy now, no quarter, no more staging; this will be real. This time we see the grill really plugged in, the red-hot iron filling the screen; the skewer smokes, the woman is spreadeagled upon the stone table awaiting the brand. We hear but are spared the sight. From now on the prisoner is completely at the mercy of her tormentors, bound upon the table and subjected to the fiercest torture and indoctrination.

The interrogator's desk with its steel "restraints" also functions as an operating table where drugs are administered by a crew of paramedics whom we never see. We do hear them; a number of male voices having a long, warm conversation about a new baby:

"He wakes up only once at night. He sleeps . . . like a baby."

There is a laugh and another voice: "And then they grow up and they're nothing but a heartache."

"I'd try for another, but the wife says she wants to wait awhile."

"My daughter who swore she'd never have another—she's three months' pregnant."

"We're giving him stewed fruit now."

More laughter. "Go easy on that, you don't want him having diarrhea. I still remember when my daughter first discovered bananas."

"The supervisor wanted me to work another shift next week, but I said no way . . . I miss him when I don't see him. He looks like a little monkey. . . ."

This piece of dialogue is extremely effective in conveying the normality of state interrogation. The hands that remove the humiliating smear of lipstick from the woman—the pierrot circle of rouge from her cheek—are hands belonging to a functionary who has a new baby at home. Or to his fellow employee who also loves his children, or to a third whose daughter is pregnant again. They may or may not know that the woman they work on now has just been tortured, they may or may not have witnessed the interrogator's insertion of a heated metal skewer into her anus, followed by a hypodermic. The long needle in their hands will silence her again, their rubber-gloved hands reaching for a sedative in a cabinet of medical supplies, another gloved hand placing the tape recorder by her head, the tape recorder whose cassette message will repeat over and over that her body must be broken to save her mind, and that "Pain ennobles both the giver and the receiver," words the functionary hears clearly as he finishes his work.

There is no real contradiction here between these events and their implicit commentary on the inevitability of female suffering in childbirth, its pain and subjugation, overtones that relish a satisfaction with destiny. The fond parents we have overheard in conversation are witting or unwitting parties to a crime which they stolidly regard as employment. We may be consumed with curiosity to know whether they are fully or only partially aware of the cruelties in which they participate, yet such issues may be of no concern to them at all. The figure before them has ceased to be human, is an enemy or a patient; whatever suffering or humiliation she endures is no affair of theirs. The fact that they discuss the fate of women while working over the body of a helpless woman prisoner may be an irony which entirely escapes them.

/ / /

THE woman is now to be punished for outright resistance. She is increasingly held in restraints, physical or chemical, frequently pinned to the table, handcuffed when permitted to rise or stand or sit in the interrogation chair. She refuses to fall asleep to the sound of the tape-recorded message: "Discipline will remain government policy as long as you resist." In retribution she is forced to stay awake in the "arabesque," suspended in the position of a ballet dancer, one hand tied above her head to a rope attached to the ceiling, one foot extended and tied behind her, the other foot bearing all her weight. From within this prolonged suffering she chants an antiphony to the tape-recorded messages, defying her captors. "Pain ennobles both the giver and receiver," it announces. "Pain will only strengthen my will," she replies. "Resistance is futile," the machine recites. "Resistance is my only weapon," she answers it.

This has become a contest of wills so unequal as to be no contest at all. The prisoner has nothing but determination and a capacity for suffering, a limited capacity, after all. The state has every device and all the time in the world. Generally it is only a matter of time before an individual's limits of endurance are reached; various as they may be, they are still finite. This prisoner seems to be entirely innocent of politics, and like a great many persons arrested and tortured in our time, she has no preparation or training for her ordeal and meets it equipped only with personal honor and principle. The politically committed have their cause to support them, an ideology and comrades. The citizen without political commitment, when caught in the meshes of the state, is, in the absence of constitutional safeguards and guarantees, utterly helpless on the physical plane. There are other planes, however.

IN the worst moments (it is not the blows, it is the suspense, the interrogator warns, that will exhaust her) she is cheered in her ordeal by the sight of her beloved cartoon characters, her imaginary personae. One of them is real enough to swoop down, pick her up, and carry her off so that the wave of electroshock to her genitals is frustrated entirely, transcended. At such moments she hears as well as sees her allies, hearing a particular sound, the sound of whistling. It could be real or imagined: the viewer is never sure, although the interrogator appears to hear it as well. And so she continues to resist, pinioned and solitary but answering the tape-recorded message quietly with a litany of her own. All around her there is the swelling and magnificent sound of a musical whistling which she has in some sense or other created and brought into being. She begs the sound to continue.

"They tell me you're being stubborn," the interrogator, exhausted himself, complains. "It's a waiting game then." He takes off his coat; torturers have forever to prove their point. Over and over, he reasons with her: her signature on the confession is meaningless as the confession is meaningless—it is only a word, a lie in a world of lies—surely it hardly matters, why bother to hold out? But she holds out, maintaining her sense of time and place even when connected to electrodes which the interrogator activates simply by pressing a button. She refuses to give the correct answers, matching the word "government" to the word "abuse," and backing down only when he administers shock: "Resistance," he says; "Futile," she dutifully replies. She will respond to pain but still refuses to sign a confession.

"Doesn't it bother you to see someone stretched out before you," she upbraids him, "aren't you worried that this is your job and you do it without question; other men work in offices and factories, but you come here . . . What made you this way?" They recite their lines to each other—"Just sign, come on, give me a break." "No." "Why do you refuse this small thing?" he asks. "Just a signature; think of it as an autograph." She smiles but she will not sign, her integrity is radiant.

Exasperated, he opens his tool chest and extracts a pliers.

Earlier, while play-acting, he had described the process of extracting a nail: "The toughest part is getting a good grip. But once you have the nail steady and firm, then you just tug. You keep tugging until you hear a crack and the nail is on its way out. The flesh underneath is pink as a baby's ass. Like yours, AB 234, before the innocence was gone, before it knew the world, or a man's touch." She had screamed then in sympathy with the torment of a prisoner the interrogator had conjured up for her with his talent for ventriloquy and mimicry. A whistle followed her scream, a whistle that seems to come from beyond the room, perhaps from an ally.

A real pliers is now in the interrogator's hand; we see him attack her foot, we hear her screams, she is frantic for rescue, for the mind to escape the body, image after image of her cat character appears, his eye, his claw—but he cannot save her, she is near despair in her pain . . . "whistle," she begs the air around her, but there is no sound, the whistling has failed her.

Her screams are terrible, that sick begging sound of someone in great pain demeaning themselves by petitioning for mercy, the sound of the beaten child whose reappearance in the present is the real purpose of torture. But then, suddenly, the cat with green wings swoops onto the screen, we see an animated drawing of the little girl caught in a vortex, spinning and then ascending with the flying animal. "I got away," she reports—the man who has just maimed her is appalled, he falls back in disbelief. "Where is Closet Land?" he asks solemnly. "It's in my mind," she smiles, triumphant: "You can break my body but you cannot break my mind"—she has just proven it to him.

As long as she can go to Closet Land: this ability to escape is something she has had since childhood, since all the times she was locked in the closet. Finally she reveals to him that she was also sexually abused there as a child: "A man. Mama's friend. They used to have breakfast on Sunday. I'd take the coats and scarves and hang them up in the closet. . . . When I was in the closet hanging up his coat, that's when it first happened. He used to smile like it was a secret between us. I was five." Her mother never suspected: "poor foolish Mama, strutting around." The mother has failed the child, failed to strengthen or protect from male predation. The man of course has threatened the child, she dare not tell, he will chop off her head. But imagination offers an out, even here: "I'd shut my eyes tight . . . and my friends came to me, the flying cow, the cat with green wings . . . I was even able to forget he was there, with his hand under my dress."

"I wonder if you know, really know the strength of your mind," the interrogator marvels. "Most people break down in a matter of hours. You escaped from us on the back of a flying cow and a cat with green wings"; it is an ironic and amused admiration, the facile admiration of professional torturers before outstanding courage, a taste their calling permits them to cultivate.

A young Iranian woman, arrested and tortured under the Ayatollah Khomeini's regime, told me not only of her own torture by falaka where the vulnerable instep of the foot is beaten with a whip or wooden rod, administered by a security officer in the presence of a mullah or Islamic priest, but also described the fate of another woman in Evin Prison during the same weeks, a woman famous for her bravery under torture. This bravery fascinated her tormentors. She earned a certain reputation for it, a nearly reverential regard among the soldiers in the prison; this amazing endurance of falaka, inflicted upon her over and over again, her legs every day more and more swollen as the blows to the soles of her feet finally destroyed her ability to walk at all. And still they marvelled at her endurance, her courage, and beat her more. By the time they killed her, they almost regarded her as a saint.

Such admiration is dangerous, compliments to a victim are always hardwon . . . and the interrogator, by insisting now that she come with him to Closet Land, is only heaping more suffering upon the prisoner. To remind us of this, we catch sight of the blood on his hand from extracting her toenail. Since she can no longer walk, he drags her toward the great stone doors and into the darkness beyond them. There one sees again the naked lightbulb and the clothes on their hangers, a door opens and the legs of a man's trousers approach. The political enters another dimension of the personal in female experience as he reveals himself to be her first tormentor, her mother's admirer, and responsible for her being locked up during his Sunday morning hours of courtship. While she was imprisoned in the closet, he took the opportunity of visiting her to molest her.

He's the one; he even knows the rhyme about chopping off her head, a voice from childhood whispering endearments in one breath, accusing her of being a "whore" in the next: a tiresome masculine obsession with "purity." "Pink as a baby's ass," he had described the injured toe after the nail is removed. "Like yours, AB 234, before a man touched it." A possessive brutality comes over him, a hostility toward the flesh and sexuality itself characteristic of the prurient or pornographic vision. "Scream!" he orders her three times. But she does not scream. So he berates her with original sin: "Such a knowing look in such young eyes," fondling again the very fragility of her childhood. "Tiny ribs like a sparrow's bones I could have broken with one rough caress." "You took away my innocence too," he accuses her, self-pitying, projecting onto her the evil he has indulged in himself.

THERE is a great narcissism about the figure of the interrogator: the victim exists to indulge it, to assist him in exploring the dark depths of his soul, an avocation, the subtle "philosophic" dimension of his profession. The knowledge of evil is one of the fringe benefits of the experience of state power, soldiery, masculine pursuits in general: women and children function as soundingboards here, foils, mirrors, means of comparison. " 'Because thou hast the power and own'st the grace, to look through and behind this mask of me,' " he recites, a verse he has recited before, in his self-absorption implying that only through abusing a victim can he catch sight of his goal, " 'my soul's true face.' "

"Why?" the woman asks. Understandably—it is a sensible question—why would anyone set such a train of events in motion, a train begun long ago in her childhood? The interrogator chooses to insist instead on his public function: "You're here as a dissident. Part of the tribe who think too much. If you'd continued writing about . . . flying cows and winged cats, you'd have been safe. But then we found Closet Land." "Then I'm back where I started, aren't I?" the woman concludes, seeing the unfairness of it, the predestined guilt, "I invented Closet Land when you beat a child. And I'm being punished now, after all these years, because I invented Closet Land." The whole chain of events assaults her now: "The intrusion at night, the arrest, the senseless charges, the brutality of it."

This merging of state interrogator with child molester is a daring device and could only succeed in a context as metaphoric as this, where pattern is everything. The woman as victim has been replaced by the child as victim, the duality of man and woman, state and citizen, running now on a female continuum, stages of oppression from the sexual exploitation and abuse of female children leading to female arrest for sexual activity rather than overtly political charges: as a woman, she is below the level of citizen. Under torture one is first reduced to a woman, then to a child, and as the torturer creates a woman out of any human material being tortured, he also creates a child, the citizen as child, frightened before the great, all-powerful, adult sadism of the state. There is a logic to this finally, and the film's substitutions and surprises are necessities. Once the state has conquered opposition to its authority, the entire citizenry becomes docile as women, frightened as children; further resistance is impossible.

But it happened so slowly, freedom was relinquished almost without noticing. Recalling it now, the woman begins to understand:

> I never knew. Or else I didn't want to know. Or at least I didn't want to see. I shut my eyes like I did in the closet. The woman down the street. About a couple months ago she disappeared, vanished. I remember going to lunch with my publisher who knew this woman I never really knew; I remember saying hello to her on the street. They came for her mother next, an eighty-year-old woman. Men were searching this missing woman's house while this old woman sat there like trash waiting to be picked up. We all passed her on the way to work, I know I did. And the old woman looked at me, in the eye, and I looked back. And I didn't see her . . . I just didn't notice. It's the same thing, shutting a child in a closet, and shutting the people away. You can frighten a child into silence; you can frighten the people too, with time. They'll shut their eyes and not scream. I never screamed in the closet, did I?

Civil life goes on, no one comments, she continues, "while their neighbors disappear around them. And then they will become like children, scared of bad men who will chop off their heads. That's what so terrifying. Because children are so powerless, they make such easy victims. . . ."

"If I told you," the interrogator begins, "that this is your last chance, that everything is at stake, everything, everything, would you sign?" The woman goes toward the desk. We do not know if she will capitulate finally or continue to refuse; surely she must see that whatever her insights may be now, they have come too late. "How do you shut a mind away?" she had challenged him, sure of herself. Now, at the end, he will show her. Dragging her back inside the room, he goes to a drawer; shaking with fury and excitement, he presents her with a photograph of the man he calls the physicist. "They cut out his tongue, but he found a way, he whistled. Then *they* found a way. That's why he couldn't whistle to you today. One little injection—he was a physicist—look at him now, not a care in the world, not a thought in his head. And look at his eyes. His empty, empty eyes."

It is all there in a photograph, the broken creature pictured is destroyed. He could have signed and lived on. Now he is a vegetable, condemned to live on, better off dead. His humiliation will continue even beyond his comprehension of it. Guilty or innocent, conspirator or layman, he has been consumed by the force of the machine. There is no resisting; this is absolute power; the will is nothing before it. Here is what could happen to her . . . "It's all lies anyway . . . so sign it!" the interrogator shouts. He has won his battle of wills, he's exhausted. She approaches the table where the confession lies, picks it up, reading as she holds it; then slowly and methodically she tears it in half, and then into smaller and smaller pieces. They flutter to the ground around her.

She has held out. He puts the handcuffs back upon her wrists, she does not bother to resist; somewhere in the battle of wills she has won, conquering her own fears and thereby conquering him. There is a transference of power which he seems to recognize as he leads her toward the great stone doors. This time they open and the camera is poised at the threshold, looking back upon the room. The scraps of paper on the floor announce the end of an event. The woman turns and goes through the doors by herself, not onto darkness but onto a causeway, dark at first, then brighter and brighter. Throughout the film the causeway has been the symbol of the conquering imagination. She will enter it alone, the light brighter and brighter until her photographic image fades and there is only a great white light upon the screen. She has gone into freedom, possibly. Should there be no other freedom at hand—there is still the freedom of death.

Words appear on the screen to comment on this final ambiguity:

"I can see that in the midst of death, life persists. In the midst of untruth, truth persists. In the midst of darkness, light persists."

—*Mohandas Karamchand Gandhi*

8

THE EXTREME EXPERIENCE OF SOLITUDE: AUROBINDO, NGŨGĨ, NIEN CHENG

ONE is struck by the waste of confinement, the waste of hours and days, months and years of human life suddenly seized and imprisoned, taken over and appropriated by the state. All one has, this single existence, this time on earth. Stolen from so many; for it is the scale of this waste, the size of this confiscation, the multitude of lives uprooted, transported, torn from millions of hands in the course of this century. The thing done casually, routinely, mechanistically. As if some great machine or natural power, some "act of God," as the law terms it, had intervened: for in a sense it had; an irresistible force had intruded upon the course of a life. The machinery of arrest had reached out from the web of those watching and classifying, implementing the orders of new legalist procedure put in place by malign unblinking intention. Somehow accepted nevertheless, permitted without effective question or resistance until there was finally no resisting.

And one's life is taken away, one loses all control of it, it belongs to the authorities; one is lucky to stay alive sometimes,

sometimes lucky to die quickly and with the least suffering. A train arrives and you are penned into it, a truck takes you somewhere in the dark, you are stuffed in the trunk of a car. Carried, hidden, tormented, held away against one's will. Those who see release are sent forth into emptiness, the future is pale and blank and threatened by memories. Citizens reduced to nomads, refugees, beggars. Persons once going somewhere, their minds intent upon a direction, a trade, the usual path of work and children, relatives. Unpredictably, catastrophe intervenes and all their intentions are thereafter thwarted, their abilities and skills destroyed, wasted. Time passes them by while they are caged like animals, driven in drudgery, marched, converted into slave labor, packed into cells or isolated alone. Their lives drain away, they watch them escape, hemmed in by obdurate structures, locked doors, the guard on duty, the barbed wire, the gun tower, the electrical cable, the overall control at checkpoint and depot, police radios on the roads, the supervision of employment and residence, house arrest. One becomes a thing placed to wait, perhaps to survive, perhaps only to suffer.

But you have lost the use of your life, the individual mind enduring this knowledge, seeing its body confined. All these holding cells, penitentiaries, concentration camps, detention centers—full of conscious awareness of the passing moment. The precious time of human life wasted on an inconceivable scale.

AT imprisonment, life stops. Then it goes on again, without meaning. Creating meaning, imbuing meaningless time with meaning, is the terrible challenge of confinement, particularly solitary confinement. When Aurobindo Ghose was arrested on suspicion of terrorism in 1908, he was taken to Alipore Jail south of Calcutta and put in a stone cell five feet long and five feet wide, a cave fronted by bars. The steel bars are set in a frame which is hinged and, when unlocked, opens onto a tiny

cement court surrounded by high cement walls at the end of
which is a brick wall with a small wooden door. "On top of
that door, at eye level, there was a small hole or opening. After
the door had been bolted the sentry peeped from time to time,
in order to find what the convict was doing," Aurobindo tells
us in *Tales of Prison Life.** Inside this claustrophobic space,
under conditions of appalling heat and thirst, Aurobindo was
finding God.

> Friday, May 1 . . . I did not know that day would mean an end
> of a chapter in my life, and that there stretched before me a year's
> imprisonment during which period all my human relations would
> cease, that for a whole year I would have to live, beyond the pale
> of society, like an animal in a cage. And when I would re-enter the
> world of activity, it would not be the old familiar Aurobindo
> Ghose. . . . I have spoken of a year's imprisonment. It would have
> been more appropriate to speak of a year's living in an ashram or
> a hermitage. . . . The only result of the wrath of the British
> Government was that I found God.

Perhaps it was not, after all, such a strange thing to do in
India at the time of national insurgence. God was the Mother
for religious Hindus, India the Motherland. Though he was
part of the agitation for Indian independence, had dedicated
his life to political activity since his return to India after an
education in England, Aurobindo had no connection with the
conspiracy for which he was arrested. He is innocent of the
bombing he is charged with, but he has been arrested before,
acquired some experience with "legal" quibbles; aware that he
has been taken into custody without a warrant, he has refused
to make a statement and looks forward to a trial without any
pretense of fairness or justice.

Now he is isolated in what is actually a cage, given a bowl
and a plate, and forced to feed on rice "spiced with husks,

*The extracts that follow are taken from *Tales of Prison Life,* translated by Sisur
Kumar Ghose (Poudicherry, India: All India Press, 1974).

pebbles, insects, hair, dirt and other such stuff." It is a fairly desperate situation; desperate measures are required to meet it.

AUROBINDO GHOSE had meditated for years, had sought "direct vision," but the force of a "thousand worldly desires," an "attachment toward numerous activities and the deep darkness of ignorance," had always caused him to fail. Prison was his opportunity, his turning point, his place of transformation. Leaving it, he quit politics, founded a religious movement, and began life again as a mystic.

The way there lay through unbearable mental anguish: he tried to meditate longer, "but the mind pulled in a thousand directions." He proceeded anyway, reached an hour and a half: the mind rebelled, the body was exhausted. He is starving inside this place, baked in the sun, flooded when it rains, pelted with dust when there is wind, concentrating past his powers. "Afterwards, devoid of human conversation" and feeling "an insufferable listlessness due to the absence of any subject of thought, the mind gradually lost its capacity to think." It is terrifying; but he has no choice, must continue the struggle.

"There was for a time a condition when it seemed a thousand indistinct ideas were hovering around the doors of the mind but with the gates closed; one or two that were able to get through were frightened by the silence of these mental states and quietly running away." In this "dull state," he suffered "an intense mental agony." Initially he had been comforted by the sight of a tree, a rare and wonderful thing to see in prison, even a cow and a cowherd: if they left the door to the courtyard open, and if he crouched down near the bars of his cage, he could catch sight of these things. Before coming to prison he had been, he realizes, "confined to a rather narrow circle"—the intense political work he shared with other young men of all castes and all corners of the Indian subcontinent, sleeping on floors, eating the normal food of the poor, sharing a sense of "nationwide brotherhood" with peasant, iron-

monger, businessman, and potter, a faith in socialism and
unity "putting its stamp" on his "life's dedication." But in all
this world of activity, "the closed emotions would rarely include birds and animals." He had once come across a line in
a poem describing a boy's love for his buffalo, found it forced,
felt a note of exaggeration in it, artificiality—were he to read
it now, he would feel differently: "At Alipore I could feel how
deep can be the love of man for all created things, how thrilled
a man can be on seeing a cow, a bird. . . ."

In his present anguish he reaches again for this solace: "I
looked at the beauties of nature outside, but with that solitary
tree, a sliced sky and the cheerless prospects in the prison, how
long can the mind, in such state, find consolation?" It doesn't
work: the "sliced sky" only confirms his condition.

Try nothingness, then: "I looked towards the blank wall."
A dangerous choice: "Gazing at the lifeless white surface the
mind seemed to grow even more hopeless, realizing the agony
of the imprisoned condition the brain was restless in the cage."
At the end of his resources, he tries to meditate again. It is
impossible, "the intense baffled attempt made the mind only
more tired, useless, made it burn and boil." Looking around
his cell he notices some black ants, then some smaller red ants
whom the black ones set upon, biting and killing them. "I felt
an intense charity and sympathy for those unjustly treated red
ants and tried to save them from the black killers." This gives
him a respite that lasts several days.

Things get worse after that: "Day after day the mind rebelled and felt increasingly desolate," time itself is an "unbearable torture"; it becomes a physical condition, he can't
breathe, feels as though he's being throttled by an enemy in a
dream and hasn't the strength to move. Busy as he used to be
in his old life, he had still spent long periods in "solitary
musings"—"Had the mind become so weak that the solitude
of a few days could make me so restless?" He is afraid now,
at the end of his resources: it is one thing to be alone at home
and able to call on friends or books, even the "noise on the

roadside." "But here, bound to the wheels of an iron law, subservient to the whim of others" and "deprived of every human contact," he recalls the saying that one who can stand solitude is either a brute or a god.

The example of the Italian regicide Breci haunts him now: instead of execution, Breci was sentenced to seven years of solitary confinement. "Within a year he had gone mad. But he had endured for some time! Was my mental strength so poor?" God, Aurobindo decides, has deliberately shown him the state of mind in which prisoners in solitary move toward insanity.

Prison has already taught him much, a young man of privilege and education, the superior of his tormentors in every way. They have sent him to the bottom of the pit, where he has discovered an overwhelming charity, a new and enduring love of life and every life form. His eyes have been opened on "the nobility of the vulgar, the attractiveness of the repellant, the perfection of the maimed and the beauty of the hideous." Out of his suffering he has acquired "an excess of kindness and sympathy for the victims of human cruelty and torture." Solitary confinement has turned him "wholly against the inhuman cruelty of western prison administration," knowledge he must use to turn his "countrymen and the world from these barbarous ways."

This is his first lesson. The second is more immediate: he has learned his mind's weakness so that he could "get rid of it forever." The third lesson is that he can do nothing by his own effort; yoga is not the product of "personal effort": a spirit of "faith or reverence" and "complete self surrender" is the only route to wisdom and faith. He is not there yet. Aurobindo's agony goes on within his cell: "One afternoon as I was thinking streams of thought began to flow endlessly and then suddenly these grew so uncontrolled and incoherent that I could feel that the mind's regulating power was about to cease." When the turmoil lessens, he discovers that although the power of "mental control" had ceased, intelligence itself was not lost. In fact, it "did not deviate for a moment." Actually it was as if intelligence was "watching quietly this marvelous phenomenon."

This was an understanding that came later. "At the time, shaking with the terror of being overcome by insanity," Aurobindo throws himself on God and prays in desperation that he will not lose his intellect. "That very moment there spread over my being such a gentle and cooling breeze, the heated brain became relaxed, easy and supremely blissful such as in all my life I had never known before." At the moment of transcendence he sleeps secure as a child "on the lap of the World-Mother." He has attained a state of grace which will remain with him, comfort him in his innocence, and carry him right through his trial. "From that day all my troubles of prison life were over." Aurobindo has been rescued by the miraculous. It is a magnificent gift, whether his own or God's, but not given to many.

IT is not given to the Kenyan dissenter Ngũgĩ wa Thiong'o, detained at Jomo Kenyatta's pleasure for a year at Kamiti Maximum Security Prison between 1977 and 1978; he must rely on other resources. "I have borne with misfortune until I have discovered its secret meaning," the Arabian poet Anitar wrote in slavery. Ngũgĩ is a writer too, writing is all he has here and he must do it in secret; tonight he is pushing himself to finish a novel before dawn, while enduring "interior segregation" in solitary confinement in a cell block with eighteen other political prisoners. "Here I have no name. I am just a number in a file: K6,77." "It is past midnight . . . I am at the desk, under the full electric glare of a hundred-watt naked bulb, scribbling words on toilet paper," he says in *Detained: A Writer's Prison Diary.**

He is pushing himself hard tonight, but the manuscript

---

*The extracts that follow are taken from Ngũgĩ wa Thiong'o, *Detained: A Writer's Prison Diary* (London: William Heinemann, 1981).

which is his lifeline will be discovered by a guard in the coming months and taken from him. Jean Genet wrote *Our Lady of the Flowers* on toilet paper in a French prison; when it was found and destroyed, he wrote it over again. Toilet paper is a literary tradition in prisons, where it usually comes in small separate sheets of recycled paper, stiff and harsh to the touch, but easy to write on: I have seen five hundred words inscribed on a piece of it only three inches square and smuggled out of Armaugh Jail by Irish women prisoners. When Ngũgĩ began using it, he thought of Wole Soyinka and Dennis Brutus at Robben Island. Writing in these circumstances he can draw on a collective experience, predecessors; nearly everyone in his block is writing something. In time he discovers that there is actually a committee on his behalf in London. Meanwhile he is captured in a maze, with no idea how long it will last: there are political prisoners here who have been detained nine years already; men have been broken here, he will live to see some die.

This is a maximum-security prison; though it is near three large cities and "next door" to Kenyatta University College, the men buried within this modern construction could "as easily have been on the moon or Mars," scientifically isolated, "quarantined from everything and everybody except for a highly drilled select squad of prison guards and their commanding officers."

The idea of maximum security had always filled Ngũgĩ with horror: now he lives inside it, contemplating its political significance. He had been chairman of the Department of English at Nairobi University, a novelist who had recently produced a play, working impromptu with non-actors in the countryside; its democratic character has offended the authorities. Ngũgĩ is never charged with a crime and never faces trial. The paper that deprives one of freedom is a dry, single-page form:

The powers conferred by regulation 6 (1) of the Public Security (Detained and Restricted Persons) Regulations 1966, the Minister

THE POLITICS OF CRUELTY

for Home Affairs, being satisfied that it is necessary for the preservation of public security to exercise control of [here Ngũgĩ's name
is filled in] (hereinafter referred to as the detained person), HEREBY
ORDERS that the detained person shall be detained.

This dull statement ends with a date and a signature that closes
off Ngũgĩ's life.

THEY came at night, assured him he was not under arrest,
promised he had only to answer a few questions, gave their
word he would be back by morning; his wife remembered to
get the car keys, he forgot to give her the checkbook. The
intrusion is a ritual, institutionalized, a program of intimidation. Ngũgĩ could have been summoned to the station by telephone; they could have sent one unarmed policeman to fetch
him. Instead, they arrive in force and with machine guns "to
abduct a writer" whose only acts of resistance were "safely
between the hard and soft covers" of "imaginative reflec-
tions." In an "awe-inspiring" silence they search his library for
incriminating works, content with a few ordinary texts publicly sold in bookstores. Given the circumstances of a police
state, they could easily supply whatever banned material they
chose: Ngũgĩ quotes Victor Jacinto Flecha's poem "It's No
Use."*

> They'll come to find you
> In lorries piled high with leaflets,
> With letters no one ever wrote to you
> They'll fill your passport with stamps
> From countries where you have never been
> They'll drag you away
> Like some dead dog
> And that night you'll find out all about torture . . .

*Flecha's poem "It's No Use" (translated by Nick Caistor) appeared in *Index on
Censorship,* VIII:1 (London, January/February 1979).

No one will hear of Ngũgĩ's whereabouts for two weeks; arrests are supposed to be published in the papers, but the news of his was never released. Even though he had gone willingly into custody, he is put in chains and as he is driven into Kamiti Prison, bystanders are beaten away with batons. Why all the mystery, Ngũgĩ wonders, no one is going to free him by force.

Detention without trial is not only an assault on one politically committed person but also "a calculated act of psychological terror," which is aimed at everyone, a program for the "psychological siege of the whole nation." It's important therefore that it be conducted as a ritual, a ceremony, a calculated exercise directed at an entire people as well as at the individual detainee, part of the strategy of breaking him, making him feel cut off from others, from the group, from the sense of solidarity with purpose and principle that gives him strength. "He must be made, not just to know, but to actually feel with the links cut, he is now adrift in an ocean of endless fear and humiliation," thrown into that ocean to "stay afloat any way he knows how, or else to plunge into the depths and drown."

Ngũgĩ is in the same prison where the British confined the Mau-Mau. Kenyatta, once a revolutionary, now a dictator, was once a detainee himself. The circle changes but does not break: colonial methods have become neocolonial. British Preservation of Order and Emergency Powers acts have been updated as Kenya's Public Security acts; one is no longer innocent until proven guilty, there are now crimes of thought and intention. Kenyatta has killed and jailed his former comrades. Token but still lucrative directorships and corporate shares have been distributed among the Kenyan upper echelon to ensure the unrestricted freedom of foreign economic interests and a cheap labor supply. The familiar comprador paradigm of neocolonialism has been put in place. To the original British economic interests, American influence has been added; Israeli commandos have been permitted inside Kenya to make strikes on Uganda.

The culture of the new Kenyan elite has taken on an imitative caste; economically and politically dependent upon outside sources, it began to foster "an incurable wish for permanent identification" with what was distant, wonderful, beckoning. A kind of corruption had set in that hankers for "the imagined grandeur" of colonial style, up-to-date cosmopolitan luxury, fast new money. Security of all kinds has become an issue, a thriving business, a product necessary not only to foreigners but to the Kenyan upper class. Fears grow. Dissent is suppressed. People are watched and investigated by the General Service Unit.

Perhaps someone has gained access to Kenyatta, read a few passages of Ngũgĩ's poems out of context and told him that this fellow was teaching subversion at the university. His play has been banned, future performances were cancelled, this is all he is really sure of. A "people's play," organized in his old village, the village he grew up in and returned to find demoralized by poverty. The cooperative project he has made of the play changed and revitalized village life: first came literacy and the restoration of the local language, then hard work, the building of a cultural and community center, audiences of thousands. Suddenly the district commissioner cited "public security" against the project. Now it is forbidden, even the theatre it built is destroyed; what was licenced and performed in the open is now banned. Perhaps the pool of cheap labor this population represented was becoming too aware.

Ngũgĩ sits in solitary considering history, analyzing the forces against him, using his perception of injustice to fight off the impression of wrongdoing which his situation would impose upon him. Over and over he examines his nation's history, locked in his cell with two dialectically opposed versions of it and having to conclude that "any awakening of the people" to their liberation from either internal repression or external exploitation "is always seen in terms of 'sin' and denounced with the religious rhetoric of a wronged, self righteous god." The security state has appropriated all morality under the rubric of law and order; around it is a sea of anarchy and sedition: agitators become "devils whose removal from society is now portrayed as a divine mission."

Detention is an exemplary fate for the dissatisfied; it will silence other objection. The security state cannot arrest the whole village, it must select for detention and surround that example with portentous formality. Detention is efficient and expeditious; in fact, it is probably the only way to maintain the pretense of legalism. For above all else, detention is how to "deal with" the innocent. There is neither crime nor evidence, there cannot be a trial; a trial would be embarrassing. So one is simply jailed without accusation. And since there is no trial, there can be no appeal. The state has expressed itself in its power. Now it is up to the imprisoned to hold on any way they can. Ngũgĩ does it with his mind, meditating on politics, the "culture of silence and fear" that has abducted him.

Survival is in intellect, still more in writing, making something: "Free thoughts on toilet paper," he laughs to himself, remembering how strange it had once seemed to him that Kwame Nkrumah's autobiography, *Ghana,* was composed on this stuff in a prison cell; "romantic," he had thought, even "a little unreal," despite the photographic evidence reproduced in the book. Now he understands how "paper, any paper is the most precious article for a political prisoner," and especially one imprisoned for his writing. With paper he can "pick the jagged bits" embedded in his mind; partly to "wrench some ease" but also—always history and the hope it holds out—"partly that some world sometime may know."

Among the political prisoners there is one who has been kept in solitary confinement so long, isolated so effectively (the guards even refusing to speak to him, merely gesturing) that he began to doubt himself, grew terrified that his execution was imminent, finally could speak only in a whisper. One is appalled to learn that the prisoner's offense was merely an attempt to register a new political party, a right guaranteed by the constitution. As I write this, news bulletins report that Kenyatta's successor Daniel Moi has arrested Wangari Maathai, Kenya's internationally renowned environmentalist, for virtually the same thing.

Ngũgĩ is forbidden to speak with his fellow prisoners, but they get word to him anyway: their example and support are priceless. Wasonga Sijeyo, the strongest of them all, veteran of nine years of political detention, reminds him that it is a good thing for Kenya's intellectuals to be imprisoned; it will rouse them from their illusions: "Some of them might outlive jail to tell the world." His fellow sufferers surround him with history, immerse him in their collective dream of Kenya's past and future. "Just watch your mind . . . don't let them break you and you'll be all right even if they keep you for life . . . but you must try . . . you have to, for us, for the ones you left behind."

They have given him his mission. Immured in a room where the light is on twenty-four hours a day, in a world deliberately deprived of color, surrounded only by white and gray, "the colors of death," like an animal in a psychological experiment, "cut off from any part of the skyline of trees and buildings which might give us a glimpse of the world of active life," suspended in this loathsome monotony, his writer's soul protesting, "I need life to write about life," even here he must make his stand, try a novel. And brave enough to take on Gĩkũyũ, one of the disregarded African tongues, rather than English—stung by a guard's taunt that he doesn't even write in his own language. Composing at night, fighting loneliness, silence, every form of discouragement, the "dominant method" of thinking like a force filling his cell to convince him it is futile, "There was only one way of looking at things, there was only one history and culture which moved in circles so that the beginning and the end were the same": oppression is old, power wins. History is for him or against him, but maximum security is now—"What was the point of making the effort?

We were all the children of Sisyphus fated for ever to roll the heavy stone of tyranny up the steep hill of struggle, only to see it roll back to the bottom."

"Prison defeated him," warders are fond of saying with a shrug, or more often, "He was defeated by prison," discrediting those they have broken in their double-walled compound, yet speaking as if they were some "neutral referee in a gladiatorial contest between the prisoner and the prison, a contest that the defeated had freely and willingly entered with the sure-to-win braggadocio of Muhammad Ali." Unfair as it is, prison is a test, and there are two types of political prisoners, Ngũgĩ decides: the ones who say yes and surrender, and the ones who say no. To say yes is to be overcome by the vision of doom prepared by their captors; these are graciously offered mediation if they will denounce their previous stands and actions. They have decided not to resist evil. They have seen the evidence of the moment and concluded the other side is bigger than they are.

But there are so many extenuating circumstances. New to it all, Ngũgĩ goes over the ground of his predecessors. Harry Thuku, the labor organizer of the twenties, was broken by nine years of lonely detention; when released, he formed an organization whose members pledged loyalty "to his Majesty the King of Great Britain." Ngũgĩ comes to feel that Kenyatta was not only broken by prison but also undermined by his own background, an insecure petit bourgeois ambivalence toward revolution. Released and put in power, Kenyatta hunted down the remaining Mau-Mau guerrillas—"these evil men, vagrants"; responsible ultimately for the death of Kariuki, the last Mau-Mau symbol, tortured, then murdered in 1975. Now Ngũgĩ is Kenyatta's prisoner, a detainee under a regime "headed by an ex-detainee who had finally given in" to the corrupt forces he had once opposed. The problem of history is the latitude a yes-man will permit a no-man. "Would he release a detainee who dared say 'No' when he himself had said 'Yes?' " Ngũgĩ may be here as long as Kenyatta is alive.

Those who have said no are consciously repudiating a culture of fear and submissive silence. They acted out of principle, but they also had hope. "They were sure that a million hands united in struggle would finally break the rock of oppression." They might fail as individuals but the effort would continue and they would forever be part of it. For those with this faith, "detention would not break their spirit, it could at most only break their bodies." It is a war of good and evil, a contest of forces, a long shot against terrorization and compliance.

INTELLECTUAL acceptance of this is one thing, "emotional reconciliation to the stark reality was another": Ngũgĩ must find a way to keep his faith, which is his sanity; he must continue to say no to detention itself, to "any and every infringement" of his human and democratic rights—here in this place, a maximum-security prison where at night even the guards are locked in and the keys taken away. He makes his stand by refusing the chains prisoners are required to wear when they are permitted visits. By resisting, he loses the visit, the sight of his wife, news of a daughter born in his absence. Prisoners are chained even on the operating table. Still refusing to wear chains—he has never been convicted, never even accused of a crime—Ngũgĩ is given no dental care when his gums develop abscesses.

Psychological torture is very sophisticated in this type of prison; every avenue of denial has been carefully followed up. Disease is used against the prisoner, medical treatment is withheld or given often not to effect a cure, but merely to be recorded. Families are used against prisoners; because of the intensity of family emotions, prisoners are most vulnerable here, easy to manipulate: prisoners are told that their wives are deceiving them, relatives are enlisted to persuade them to give in.

Against all these forces the detainee has only his refusal.

Ngũgĩ has writing as well, a covert hide-and-seek composition at which a guard may discover him at any moment through the rectangular slit at the top of the door. Tonight he is working as hard as he can to bring a certain character to life. This is a book about a man writing another book, the novel he struggled to compose in prison: it is at the same time an essay on politics and history as comprehended in detention and reflected upon later in freedom. Soon the manuscript will be confiscated and for the three weeks it is missing Ngũgĩ will be nearly destroyed by grief. One remembers how many books have been written in prison, beginning with classics like *Morte D'Arthur, Don Quixote, Pilgrim's Progress,* Wilde's *De Profundis.* But later in this century that small stream has become a river. In so many places around the world this writing goes on now, the words of prisoners rising from South America like prayers, the accounts of witnesses coming off the presses of Amnesty—as if writing alone were a remedy, the only remedy at hand, the beginning of remedy.

Kenyatta will die one night while Ngũgĩ is his prisoner. The warders are forbidden to tell the inmates; the news is kept from them for weeks, but a guard will give Ngũgĩ a clue tonight by calling him "Professor," congratulating him that right now his "star shines bright in the sky." When, months later, late at night he hears the words at last: "Ngũgĩ, you are now free," and sees the cell door finally open—"The first thing I do is to rush to the compound to hug darkness (which I have not seen for a year) and to look at the stars."

WRITING will not provide Nien Cheng with any solutions inside prison. In fact, it is dangerous to write—and yet one is forced to. Day after day she is provided with a roll of paper and set to the task of writing an autobiography which is in effect a confession. Since she insists doggedly that she is innocent, when signing her name she will add the words "who has committed no crime" to the word "criminal" printed already at the bottom of the last page.*

At the top of the first page there will be a quotation from Chairman Mao, a Supreme Directive, in her case the words: "They are allowed only to be docile and obedient; they are not allowed to speak out of turn." Imprisoned for six and a half years of solitary confinement in Shanghai's Number One Detention House with nothing else to read but the collected works of Chairman Mao, Nien Cheng has her own quotation to add: "Where there is counterrevolution, we shall certainly suppress it; when we make a mistake, we shall certainly correct it." Her imprisonment is just such a mistake, she is convinced, and she will not accept the automatic assumption of guilt under which she is being confined without trial or evidence during the Cultural Revolution.

The state holds the body prisoner, but it wants one's past as well: you cannot make a draft or discard an error. Psychological invasion has been perfected here: "If you omit anything we will think you are not sincere." All around her people are convicting themselves in their own handwriting; if one autobiography fails to go far enough, they will have to write another one tomorrow, or next week, or a few years from now when things settle down and the interrogators are on the job again. At one point the interrogators themselves are reduced to cleaning the halls.

During the course of her detention several different factions take over the Detention House, as the Red Guard and then the army and then the proletariat take it upon themselves to decide her fate while luminaries at the top of China's power structure battle for power; Liu Shaoqi falls, then Chen Boda, and finally Lin Biao as Mao establishes his place in history and the Gang of Four contest with Zhou Enlai. Though it takes her a decade

---

*The extracts that follow are taken from Nien Cheng, *Life and Death in Shanghai* (New York: Grove Press, 1986).

to unravel all these maneuvers, her life and millions of others hang in the balance.

Locked in a cell with a single industrious spider for company, Nien Cheng is the victim of power politics: a widowed mother with a good job, she was an assistant to the manager of British Shell, for nine years dealing correctly with the Shanghai municipal government under Communist rule in an era when China needed this contact. Shell has departed and handed over its assets to the regime; she is out of a job. But the very policy of contact with the West is now under retroactive attack, so it will be necessary to discredit those who had authorized it. Ultimately, Zhou Enlai authorized it, Mao and the Gang of Four oppose it; Zhou is still powerful and beloved, so nothing can be done directly, but if contact with imperial capitalism can be proven to be espionage as well, then . . .

At an early "struggle meeting," Shell's accountant Tao wears a dunce hat and admits to a variety of unlikely crimes: after two and a half years of imprisonment, sleep deprivation, hard labor, abuse, and family pressure—his son is a Party member—Tao capitulates and declares that he was a spy. The case against Nien Cheng would usually be good enough now, but she reacts like one without fear, does something unprecedented by laughing loudly and derisively at Tao's performance, spoiling the whole occasion and failing again to confess. The year before there had been the possibility of using her daughter Meiping to denounce her, but Meiping was recalcitrant under questioning, things got out of hand, the Maoist technique of "exhaustive bombardment" went awry and turned into one of those "accidents" of "mass enthusiasm." The militia abducted her to the ninth floor of a building on Nanjing Street in downtown Shanghai, where Meiping's interrogators "overdid it": her death by torture was passed off as suicide.

Before she leaves China, Nien Cheng will actually start the process by which one of her daughter's murderers will be brought to trial and condemned to death. But since he is a Party member, his execution will be stayed for two years and he will go free. Here she failed. Everywhere else she succeeded; through miraculous patience and integrity she prevailed in detention and lived to be released, insisted upon and obtained official "rehabilitation." And after further years of waiting, she was actually accorded the apology she had demanded as a condition for leaving the Number One House of Detention—without it she had refused freedom and had to be forcibly ejected.

THIS is a very strange story of the individual pitted against enormous forces yet courageous enough to endure, even prevail. The regime has robbed her of her house, imposed over six years of suffering upon her, and taken her daughter's life. Through all that she has endured, Nien Cheng burns like clear light, resolute, reasonable, an understated feminine heroine. Her own existence is shattered, beginning with that moment when the Red Guards invade her house and begin to destroy her blue and white china, her white porcelain, their "impatient feet" grinding bits beneath them. She is further annihilated at "struggle meetings" held in public schools before duped audiences of fanaticized citizens, in the early years fascinated and credulous through propaganda, later on bored but remaining obedient to the orchestration of chants and "big character" posters, still ready to trample her to death as she is brought around for show time after time. More than six years of interrogation, solitary confinement, and near starvation in an unheated cell should have broken her too.

All the classic techniques of isolation are employed—the conviction that she is alone, utterly friendless, a member of the wrong class, guilty by her very history, her family background. She is consumed with fear over her daughter's fate, hidden from her until the terrible moment in the sixth year of her imprisonment when Meiping's clothing is unceremoniously delivered to her cell. Her health fails her, she suffers two serious cases of pneumonia, a disease of the gums that will cause her to lose all her teeth, frequent and massive hemorrhaging which is diagnosed as cancer—it is assumed that she is terminally ill, perhaps the reason that she is finally released at all. In fact, she has conquered through sheer willpower and her belief in her own complete innocence, which no amount of abuse and injustice can destroy.

Where everyone confesses, she has refused to confess. Her colleagues have all complied and incriminated her; finally her brother betrays her with a false confession: "It is useless to resist," he explains. "If they say something happened, it happened." Years into her interrogation a young worker, part of that day's panel, asks her in astonishment: "What can you be thinking about? What is it you pin your hope on?" It is a reasonable question in a system that does not envision error, is always right. Here accusation is tantamount to conviction, needs only the ritual of confession to come to a conclusion, here no evidence is necessary. She demands evidence. Interrogators pound the table before them and demand she confess: she dares to pound the table back at them, calling for a piece of paper where she writes a vow that if guilty she will accept the death penalty.

A middle-aged woman of culture and understanding, tact and compassion, a "lady"; she will, over the years, at moments of near despair and when it is necessary to keep up her "fighting spirit," deliberately dispute with her guards until they beat and kick her. No one has ever seen anything like her: "we have never had a prisoner . . . so truculent and argumentative," the prison doctor remarks on her release. "Are you glad?" he insists. "Six and a half years is a long time to lock up an innocent person," she answers simply.

Nothing can destroy her insistence on honor, on justice, her set determination that this system must act correctly. Even though it cannot, is no longer set up to do so. Everyone explains this to her: interrogators spend time explicating "dialectical materialism," how the courts are simply the tools of repression for whatever class is in power, the proletariat being now in power must use them against its enemies: there is no justice, only victorious classes. She refuses to accept, and clings to ideas like evidence and proof. Several years into her imprisonment, guards who once assured her she was guilty simply because she had been arrested, grown bewildered by the upheavals of the Cultural Revolution as it affects everything, even prison administration, now admit themselves that they "don't know anymore what's a crime and what isn't."

TOTAL moral confusion has taken over: that had been Nien Cheng's point all along, the very reason why she had decided not to confess to lies, never to deviate from the truth. It is reality, sanity. Lies are confusion, they complicate, prolong.

When the finger of suspicion first points to her and she is made to watch Tao's confession at the first "struggle meeting," she experiences "disgust and shame that such an act of barbarism against a fellow human being could have taken place in my beloved native land, with a history of five thousand years of civilization. As a Chinese, I felt degraded." She perceives the spiral of untruth ahead: "These men gave me the impression that they wanted a confession from me, even if I made it up." This is exactly the case, her old friend Mr. Hu assures her on his last visit to her house; there are in fact quotas: "In each organization three to five percent of the total must be declared the 'enemy,' because that was the percentage mentioned by Chairman Mao in one of his speeches." If interrogators fail to get confessions, "they may be accused of not supporting the movement."

By supporting it, by eager participation in the line, one stays out of trouble, even gets ahead. Mysterious and changeable, the line must be followed carefully. It is written everywhere, it is inscribed on ribbons, it hangs in banners, is on posters— there is a glut of propaganda, often inscrutably metaphoric ("dig deep tunnels," "pluck out weeds"), in time so omnipresent and confusing that finally all slogans are suspect: "official lies" indulged in this long ultimately serve no purpose "except to create the impression that truth was unimportant."

Instead, you listen for rumors, you test the wind, you read between the lines of the newspapers, you "interpret," as Nien Cheng must when the government newspaper is delivered every day to her prison cell and loudspeakers lecture on political correctitude or announce the names of those to be executed that night.

Hu had decided there is no defense against lies but the truth, carefully phrasing this conclusion so that it is not a personal directive: "no individual should make a false confession, no matter how great the pressure is." To lie is dangerous because the Party is never satisfied; it will demand more and more admissions of guilt; in the end there will be such a tangle of untruths that one can no longer extract oneself. He has seen it happen to many people. To stand by the truth is an old Chinese ethic; it will be hers too.

To lie is what most will do to save themselves, it is what the authorities want: by lying, one acknowledges their authority, replaces one's own reality with theirs, submits to the reality of their power. Everything is directed toward this end. The accused kneels through "struggle meetings" with his head bowed, hands shackled behind his back: humbled, mortified, crushed. During the fiercest period of her interrogation Nien Cheng is handcuffed in this position for eleven days, unable to sleep or eat, an ordeal she barely survives. It is expected that she will starve to death and be labelled a counterrevolutionary. "That's the customary procedure for prisoners who die before their cases are clarified," a guard explains to her.

Of course the hope of clarification is why she has clung to life, the boon she has begged for a thousand times, her goal as heaven is for the devout. The guard hints that there might still be a way to eat and stay alive. Nien Cheng considers it all night and breaks the riddle: Tomorrow when the food is put through the little door, she will not just shake her head and demonstrate that her hands are tightly handcuffed behind her back. Instead, she will turn around and ever so carefully take hold of the container, and, carrying it behind her back, place it precariously upon the other unused bed in her cell which functions as her table. Then, still not spilling the precious rice gruel, her hands captive behind her back will invert the container and empty out its contents on her clean towel. Then she will turn around, bend down, and "eat like an animal." She will survive even this.

The unheated cell, which everyone was certain would break her long ago, has ice on its window now. Her hands are a mass of blood and pus: though she cannot see them—tied behind her back—their stains cover her quilt. It seems likely she may never have their use again. She is overcome by fever: in moments of lucidity she tries to discipline her mind with simple arithmetic; a few seconds later, "my ability to concentrate would evaporate and I would get confused again." She can no longer understand the guards who come to the door, has reached the point where she no longer has the strength to feed herself. Yet after using the toilet she still raises her trousers and closes the zipper: since this involves extra pain and injury to her wrists she might have forgone the movement out of necessity, yet to have left them unzipped would have "demoralized" her. It would have undermined the force that sustains her, her "fighting spirit": her survival only possible because they failed to break it.

She faints at the end of the eleventh day and the cuffs are removed at last. Finally able to see her hands again, she discovers they are "swollen to an enormous size." "The swelling extended to my elbows. Around my wrists where the handcuffs had cut into my flesh, blood and pus continued to ooze out of the wounds. My nails were purple in color and felt as if they were going to fall off. I touched the back of each hand, only to find the skin and flesh numb. I tried to curl up my fingers but could not because they were the size of carrots." She prays that she will not lose the use of her hands; she must heal them herself because "the doctor does not give treatment when the prisoner has been punished."

This is a common torture. The cuffs are not only tightened to the utmost but the prisoner is often further weighed down with chains, shackled to a window bar from which he cannot move to eat or drink or relieve himself: the authorities deny that this is torture and call it "persuasion" or "punishment." It has probably been put to use again against the student demonstrators of Tiananmen Square in China's most recent wave of repression. The moment Nien Cheng is released, she is required to show herself in the exercise yard so that three mysterious figures in army topcoats watching from a window above may see her condition and be satisfied with her suffering.

THERE is always someone watching through a window. When she faces the interrogator, there is a little window just behind her head which opens onto a face she cannot see. The interrogator, looking past her, gets his signal and begins. Because someone else is looking on, someone invisible, the interrogator is not the final interrogator but an intermediary. She will never see the pair of eyes that control her, though she often hears the little door behind her head slammed shut in disgust. When the concealed window closes, there is no point in continuing and the interrogator stops; nothing important can happen without this surveillance. Nien Cheng's "real antagonist" will always be invisible, though she wishes over and over that she could deal "face to face with the man who had treated me so unjustly and have his features carved on my memory, never to be forgotten."

It is likely there are many of them, supervisors, "higher-ups" like the high-ranking military officers around Lin Biao who eavesdrop on big "struggle meetings," the telltale wire of their recording devices attached to the microphones which the

Party speakers shout into: the moment these invisible presences depart, it is over. The crowd picks up its belongings and files out. Her head forced down in the obligatory servile position, Nien Cheng hears them "chatting" as they leave the building. " 'Getting rather chilly, isn't it?' 'Where are you going for supper?' . . . They sounded no different from an audience departing after a show in a cinema or theatre."

Truth obsesses this woman: she has pitted herself against a regime that controls a quarter of the earth's population and remains undaunted before it. Fortunate and exceptional as well—ten thousand died in Shanghai alone during the Cultural Revolution, her own daughter one of the victims, but this only strengthens her resolve. In her first view of the long corridor of Number One Detention House, she registers its full weight of despair: "In subsequent years, in my dreams and nightmares, I saw again and again, in the dim light, the long line of doors with sinister-looking bolts and padlocks outside and felt again and again the helplessness and frustration of being locked inside." But her first act once inside the cell is to clean the place. Thoroughly, as a woman house-cleans, managing to get water and use it wisely so that every inch of its surfaces, the bed frame, the wall, the cement toilet, is immaculate. The wall beside the bed is beyond cleaning: she papers it over with toilet paper again and again, sacrificing food to make a paste out of rice, counting the grains. The guards tear it off, she replaces it. After she has "tackled" the dirt, a ration of hot drinking water is issued. "I sat on the clean bed and drank it with enjoyment. Plain boiled water had never tasted so good."

A MIND with such a clear perception of reality is a thing of great beauty. Nien Cheng is resolute even from the beginning, the moment when "the man in the tinted glasses" who has dogged her for weeks finally places her under arrest and forces her into the usual black jeep which will take her to prison: her mood is neither fear nor defeat but a determination that if they do not kill her, she will not give up, well aware how many people, "even seasoned party leaders, made ritual confessions of guilt under pressure, hoping to avoid confrontation with the Party or lessen their immediate suffering by submission. Many others became mentally confused under pressure and made false confessions because they had lost control. . . . It seemed to me that making a false confession when I was innocent was a foolish thing to do. The more logical and intelligent course was to face persecution no matter what I might have to endure."

One is astounded by her endurance beyond even what she endures: the labyrinth of deception and psychological manipulation, the exhortation on every side to surrender and confess, the threats and blows, the terrible weight of time and illness and physical deterioration. Believing in truth, she believes in reason, asking to see the penal code and lawbooks, just as she had composed herself to be the "picture of Chinese fatalism" as she greeted her first Red Guard with a copy of the Chinese Communist Constitution in hand. He waves it aside, it has been abolished, replaced by Mao's little book. She won't accept such unreason: she challenges the prison interrogator not to behave like an "hysterical" Red Guard adolescent, but to conduct himself like "a trained man with a sense of responsibility, able to distinguish a guilty person from an innocent." And when he lies that he has evidence against her or boasts that evidence is irrelevant, she answers him that she would rather die than confess to lies.

"To want to live is a basic instinct," he insists, threatening that if she does not lie, that is, confess, he will shoot her. "Firstly, do not fear hardship," she quotes Mao to him. "Secondly, do not fear death." "That was for the Liberation Army Soldiers," not for the likes of her, he responds contemptuously. She replies that "The teachings of our Great Leader have universal significance and are applicable in all circumstances," quoting Lin Biao, still in favor at the moment. In fact, she will hold this system to its promises; having accepted Communist rule as historically inevitable, she refuses to let it perish in chaotic unreason. For all her intellectual perception she refuses to give way to cynicism, expediency, the brutal authoritarianism that surrounds her, demanding instead that authority behave responsibly.

Her insistence on evidence saves her, since there is no evidence against her. "Lay out the facts," Mao says, "let them lay them out." Much as she deplores the evil he has done in wasting so many lives, she is fair enough to admire his essay on the tactics of guerrilla warfare. Consummate and admirable representative of the bourgeois way of life, she has an appreciation of the good that the regime has accomplished, its superiority to the Kuomintang corruption which preceded it. And as it now constitutes legal authority, she will hold it to account. She will not permit its representatives to ignore and ridicule the idea of justice: it is justice she will have from them. A mere woman demanding this. Maybe it is all she can do. Short of dishonor—her own consumed in their's; short of that disorder into which the regime and its vast subject population have plunged—lies and denunciations, confessions and executions, a barbarism that burns books and destroys art, recklessly laying waste to its past as it turns the present into a nightmare of economic shortage and ruined hope.

In a sense, Nien Chen becomes China, embodies it before her opponents. Even when she leaves for Hong Kong and the West, carrying one suitcase and the permitted sum of twenty dollars, she brings her country with her so that she can finally record the experience of the Cultural Revolution. When the Red Guards arrived that first night to loot her house, her own *Kristallnacht,* she had been reading William Shirer's *The Rise and Fall of the Third Reich.* Catching sight of her copy of the Chinese Constitution, she brings it along as she goes downstairs to open the door. Useless at that moment, it is priceless at other times, consistently and inherently valuable, like the classic Tang poetry she systematically reconstructs from memory to comfort herself in prison while holding Mao's quotations on her lap. When a few pieces of her porcelain collection are restored to her again, precious objects whose enthusiastic destruction she was able to prevent only through an appeal to the militants' greed after appeals to history or workmanship failed, she donates them to the Shanghai Museum.

Then Nien Cheng takes reluctant leave of the city itself, escaping the constant surveillance that is her lot even after rehabilitation, launching herself at sixty years of age into a new existence, knowing she will never return, knowing she will die on foreign soil. Reading her work, one comes to know this woman's spirit, not only to appreciate its fortitude but to experience its rich and fragrant sensibility. Nien Cheng epitomizes the stoicism and philosophic distance, the balance and wisdom, the finished grace she has absorbed from her culture and which her book will represent for the rest of time.

PART THREE

RECENT
POLITICS OF
CRUELTY IN
ACTION

9

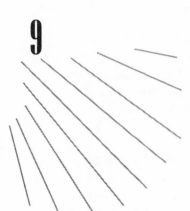

THE LITTLE SCHOOL:
ARGENTINA AND BRAZIL

"THAT day, at noon, she was wearing her husband's slippers; it was hot and she had not felt like turning the closet upside down to find her own. There were enough chores to be done in the house. When they knocked at the door, she walked down the ninety-foot corridor, *flip-flop, flip-flop.* For a second she thought that perhaps she should not open the door; they were knocking with unusual violence . . . but it was noon time. She had always waited for them to come at night."* She had nearly answered the door out of habit, but the knocking grows so loud—it has to be them. Realizing this, she makes a run for it out the backyard.

The narrator in Alicia Partnoy's *The Little School* is Partnoy herself, and not only had she always expected "them" to come at night, she had slept a great many nights with her shoes on, waiting for them. That she is wearing a comfortable house

---

*The extracts that follow are taken from Alicia Partnoy, *The Little School,* translated by Alicia Partnoy with Lois They and Saundra Braunstein (Pittsburgh: Cleis, 1986).

dress at the moment of arrest is an unexpected convenience, and even if the accident of wearing "his slippers" is comical, there is also something reassuring in it.

But they are no good for running: "She lost the first slipper in the corridor," before reaching the place where Ruth, her little girl, was standing. "She lost the second slipper while leaping over the brick wall." By then the shouts and kicks at the door were brutal. The child burst into tears in the doorway. While squatting in the bushes, Partnoy hears a shot. "She looked up and saw soldiers on every roof. She ran to the street through weeds as tall as she. . . . When the soldiers grabbed her, forcing her into the truck, she glanced down at her feet in the dry street dust. . . ." She would be arrested barefoot.

Alicia Partnoy's account of her experiences in a clandestine Argentinean prison under the military government were published piecemeal and anonymously in human rights journals until they appeared together in the work entitled *The Little School*. Though narrated in the third person, the arrest is her own abduction on January 12, 1977, when she was taken to the headquarters of the 5th Army Corps and then to a strange little compound hidden behind it, a few shabby trailers parked around an old house about a mile from the You and I Motel (Tu y Yo) on Carrindanga Road, a belt highway outside the town of Bahia Blanca. It is remote, dusty: one hears the traffic, a few trains, even the lowing of cattle. Handcuffed, Partnoy was brought with a blindfold over her eyes, but by tilting her head she was able to read the letters A.A.A., the initials of the Alianza Anticomunista Argentina, a paramilitary group "with whom the military has since denied any relation."

THE term "Little School" (*La Escuelita*) is military humor, a name the victims of this clandestine prison heard all the time, the name they used in their own minds, whispered to each other when they dared to break its rule of silence; a mocking irony remembered as the experience itself by those who survived. "I knew just one Little School," Partnoy warns the reader, "but throughout our continent there are many 'schools' whose professors use the lessons of torture and humiliation to teach us to lose the memories of ourselves. Beware: in little schools the boundaries between story and history are so subtle that even I can hardly find them." In Argentina, more than thirty thousand persons disappeared during the "dirty war" between 1976 and 1979, four hundred of them children kidnapped with their parents or born in captivity. The vast majority of the disappeared remain unaccounted for.

Partnoy's Little School is in fact a little hell: there are two small rooms where an average of fifteen prisoners are forced to lie prone on campbeds. They must remain in this position twenty-four hours a day in a continuous condition of helplessness and inactivity. They are always blindfolded and their hands are bound. Between the two rooms there is a small tiled hallway where guards are on duty to ensure that they will neither speak nor move. Crude circumstances but absolute: the captive is totally immobilized and utterly forbidden to communicate. Blinded, deprived even of sight, he or she is reduced to an object. Move or speak and you are beaten with a rubber truncheon. Partnoy endured this parody of an authoritarian classroom regimen for six months from her arrest in January till the following June, unable to move, to speak, or to see.

To be imprisoned under these conditions is torture itself. But there are further tortures: past the guards' room and their kitchen and bath down the hall, a door opens onto the patio where the "torture room" is located, just before the latrine and the water tank. The torture room is equipped with an iron bed frame, standard equipment in such places; humble object made for other purposes but used here for the torment of electric shock. The metal conducts, and it is strong; prisoners can be bound to it. The guards sleep in trailers; in time a few more trailers will be added for more "disappeared."

It is the ordinary squalor of this bizarre homemade jail that makes it so real. The roof leaks: "When it rained, the water streamed into the rooms and soaked us. When the temperature fell below zero, we were covered with only dirty blankets; when the heat was unbearable we were obligated to blanket even our heads. We were forced to remain silent and prone, often immobile or face down for many hours, our eyes blind-folded and our wrists tightly bound."

It is as if, by covering the captives with blankets, they are made to disappear within their hidden prison. For six months Partnoy's family had no idea where she had vanished; the military denied that it had her in custody just as it had denied thousands of others. The ability to "disappear" a human being is such an awesome power that the verb itself, grammatically intransitive, becomes transitive and now takes an object. A new passive is also created: one does not disappear, one is disappeared. The word is further detached from its nearly abstract connotations of perception or impression and trans-formed into a specific act: "to disappear" someone is to erase a presence, perhaps even an existence, through capture.

But in a very special manner; this is no ordinary kidnap, this is an act by authority. Government now causes its citizens to exist or cease to exist. These magical feats of appearance and disappearance, the condition of being seen or being invisible, present or not present, border on conjuring. The state's very efficacy in abducting its targets not only has the effect of making them cease to be but perhaps also to have never been. Since the fact of their detention is not recognized or recorded officially anywhere, the "disappeared" can be killed with the same ease as they can be detained until broken through torture. When broken they may be tried, used as witnesses, or mur-dered.

To practice torture, the state creates the usual preconditions for torture: on coming to power in 1976, the junta annulled the constitution. During the three years that followed, the most oppressive years of military rule, thirty thousand Argentineans simply vanished from among their fellow citizens. Government statements consistently denied this; the last official pronouncement, the Final Document of the Military Junta on the War Against Subversion and Terrorism of April 1983, denies it categorically: "There is also talk of 'disappeared' persons who are still held under arrest by the Argentine government in unknown places in our country. All of this is nothing but a falsehood stated with political purposes, since there are neither secret detention places in the Republic nor persons in clandestine detention in any penal institution."

A few months later, the dictatorship collapsed; by December 1983, a democratically elected president had come to power. Partnoy returned to Argentina the next summer to find a country where "hundreds of unidentified corpses were being exhumed, most of them with signs of torture." She testified before the commission appointed to investigate disappearances and helped to identify the location of the Little School. But for all the crimes of this government and despite overwhelming evidence against it, only two military leaders, General Jorge Videla and Admiral Emilio Massera, were given life sentences for their part in the disappearance and torture of this enormous number of victims.

Partnoy is stunned with disappointment by the results of the junta's trial: "Only three others were convicted and four military officers were acquitted of all charges. The rest of the criminals enjoy complete freedom." She is fully aware that this trial could have set a precedent in Latin America, only the second considerable trial for torture since Nuremberg.* Nuremberg however was a case of the victor judging the vanquished; here was a case of a nation judging itself: "It is true that a very important trial has taken place against the generals who presided over the country, the men responsible for the

---

*When the Greek Junta fell in 1975, its torturers were tried, in the beginning with great success; the United Nations Declaration Against Torture was drafted in the same year. However, the Greek courts soon lost their impetus to convict, and methods of implementing the UN Declaration have not been developed. The 1975 UN Declaration Against Torture has been strengthened and augmented by the 1984 UN Conventions Against Torture, but that too has not been implemented.

massive assassinations. But it is also true that not until justice is brought in cases like that of the Little School will there be a safeguard against the recurrence of these crimes in the future."

Indeed, the results of the Argentinean trial are deplorable, virtually an exoneration of the military and all its brutality, a brutality in which thousands of uniformed members of the armed forces took part, together with thousands more paramilitary and covert actors who were never censured or brought to trial. Out of all these only five convictions, three of them minor: crimes as it were without consequence. The outcome was very reassuring not only for the Argentinean military but for all other military regimes in the region. A great opportunity has been lost. What began as a trial of the military ended as a surrender to military intimidation. In capitulating to the army by failing to try or punish the torturers among its ranks, Argentina may have made their return not only possible but easy. Justice seems further away than ever and the squadrons of Little Schools throughout the continent operate as usual.

How differently justice dealt with Partnoy and the occupants of the Little School, subjected to months of terrorization and torture, bound and prone, blindfolded and forced to remain silent, beaten constantly by the guards around them. Beaten even if their plate tipped and a bit of soup spilled as they ate isolated in the frightening dark, surrounded by soldiers waiting to strike them for any infraction of this mad regimen.

Although no one responsible for their suffering has been or will be accused, Alicia Partnoy has pursued the fate of those imprisoned with her because each is representative of thousands of prisoners throughout South and Central America and because these facts are so disregarded. Her close friend Graciela Alicia Romero de Metz was five months pregnant at her arrest. Graciela was beaten and tortured with electric shocks to the stomach during her transfer from another prison.

She gave birth at the Little School and her child was given to one of the interrogators. Graciela was taken away on April 23, 1978, and never heard from again: she is on Amnesty International's list of disappeared persons. On the night of April 12, 1977, Maria Elena Romero and Gustavo Marcelo "Benja" Yoti were taken from the Little School and shot: the newspaper reported the following day that they had died in a "confrontation" with military forces. They were both seventeen years old.

There was also Carlos Maria Ilaqua: "Guards dislocated Carlos' shoulder during torture by hanging him by the arms in a well of water"; he was taken away the next day and has disappeared entirely. The biochemist Ana Maria de Maisonave and her husband Rodolfo Maisonave were both tortured, then condemned by a military court to twenty-five years in prison. Néstor Junquera and his wife Maria Eugenia Gonzalez de Junquera were also tortured at the Little School: "Maria Eugenia, who was recovering from an abortion, was in danger of dying from torture"; both were taken from the Little School in December 1976. Nothing more is known of them.

Juan Carlos Castilla and Juan Pablo Fornazari were captured in their pickup truck in the fall of 1976, tortured at length upon arrest, and then brought to the Little School, where they "endured many hours with blindfolds over their eyes, standing naked outside in bad weather and surrounded by trained watch dogs that would not allow them to move." They were then "savagely tortured," and when "extremely weakened with torture by electric shock, Juan Carlos Castilla had to remain standing on his feet, while his testicles were tied to the window grating of the building." By December, they were reported to have died in a "confrontation" with the military, the phrase generally used to cover a murder in captivity. Their pickup truck was taken over by the military for use at the Little School.

There were also a dozen high school students, some of

whom were tortured by electric shock. Their treatment illus-
trates the character of fascism: they were abducted because
they disobeyed a teacher.

> The students were finishing classes and there was a happy atmo-
> sphere in the school. The professor, a Navy officer, ordered the
> students to stop making noise. When they did not comply, he
> expelled the students from the school. The students' parents com-
> plained to military authorities and requested that their children be
> readmitted. The authorities warned them to stop complaining or
> "they would regret it." Some days later, heavily armed masked
> groups invaded the houses of the students and kidnapped them.

There are other prisoners whose fates, even whose names,
Alicia Partnoy does not know: a twenty-six-year-old gardener
tortured by the guards with a blowtorch and kept outside the
building in a trailer, and a young man with a deep chest
wound, the result of torture: "I heard him begging to have his
wound dressed for several days, but, according to the guards,
by the time they finally dressed the wound it had become
severely infected."

For those who have disappeared into the Little School and
the darkness inside its blindfolds, the world has disappeared as
well. Perhaps because of this, Partnoy is poignantly aware of
color. At the very moment of her arrest, she had looked up:
"The sky was so blue that it hurt." On her first morning in the
Little School, she wakes to find that "someone had retied her
blindfold during the night" and now "the peep hole was
smaller but still big enough to see the floor; blood on the tiles
next to a spot of sky blue." She is being led from one wing of
the Little School to another: "While they opened the iron grate
into the corridor, she thought for a minute of the sky blue spot.
She could have sworn that it was a very familiar color, like the

sky blue color of her husband's pants; it *was* him, lying on the hall floor, wounded."

Blindfolding is many things at once. For the one blind-folded, it is disorientation and vulnerability brought to a pitch of disability and dependence. One is physically helpless and psychologically intimidated. A blindfold achieves all this with a simple piece of fabric once the hands are bound. Although those who are blindfolded can see nothing, they are absurdly visible: objects, marks of scorn and abuse. Each figure in the circle who abuses them remains invisible, protected against discovery and any possible prosecution, even if what he does is now only technically illegal, even if his office does indeed provide the absolute impunity he has always been assured. He still feels safer if those he torments are blindfolded, just in case he were to face revenge one day or legal accusation. Improbably remote circumstances at this moment, the blindfold giving the blinded a sense of doom and impotence, the privilege of sight giving the captor the feeling of omnipotence before his handicapped and sightless victim. In some places practitioners rely entirely on blindfolds, keeping them in place continuously and not removing them for years at a time.

In the Little School, the blindfold is not a temporary conve-nience resorted to when a prisoner is brought from one secret place to another—it is a permanent state. Partnoy was blind-folded during her entire six-month stay there from January until June. Prone, still, silent, and in the dark. Prisoners even eat blindfolded, sitting on the bed, their plates on their laps: "When we had soup or watery stew, the blows were constant because the guards insisted that we keep our plates straight. When we were thirsty, we asked for water, receiving only threats or blows in response. For talking we were punished with blows from a billy jack, punches or removal of our mat-tresses. The atmosphere of violence was constant. The guards put guns to our heads or mouths and pretended to pull the trigger." All this violence in the dark while one is of sightless, the sound of a friend being beaten, the vulnerability of being next, but unable to see it coming.

THERE are "sides" here as in warfare. Partnoy and her friends in the opposition are powerless captives, but the state chooses to perceive them as dangerous enemies, subversives. Everywhere the state is at war with subversion, real or imagined. "Closet Land is a place where people go for secret meetings," the interrogator had claimed (see Chapter 7), interpreting his prisoner's fable for children in political terms, the story of a lonely child locked in a closet who converts the clothing hanging there into imaginary companions. "The clothes don't even come alive" until the mother leaves and "the child is alone," he insists; "when the Friendly Rooster who is on the lookout, gives the warning cry, they scatter and run away. When mother comes back she can't find anything. Your sympathies are with the child of course because you resent any authority." The interrogator is intent upon getting the author's signature to a confession that her story is "an allegory for the struggles of the various underground groups which are resisting the government. The child protagonist of the story stands for the uninformed reader whose views I wish to mould. I am consciously representing governmental authority in the character of the mother. The clothes are all underground insurgents: the Friendly Rooster is a government official."

Would these statements mollify the fury of state power? How would it react to the admission that "The clothes are all underground insurgents"? As a convenient absurdity or the final proof of conspiracy? Would it be satisfied if assured that the Friendly Rooster is really a government official, therefore a spy and a traitor to the system of "order" it represents. One is dealing with a mind-set here, *mentalité*. And with the infinite. Infinite distrust, suspicion, duplicity, enmity. If the prisoner is politically naive and without commitment, there is a certain bleak humor here, madness of a comic sort, were it not

so powerful and dangerous. If the prisoner is politically sophisticated, committed to one degree or another of opposition and
resistance, the situation is altered drastically.

The state may still be utterly off the mark in its accusations.
It may be on a fishing expedition. Or it may be at the moment
when the code is broken or revealed. Because while there are
utter "innocents" in the world, there are also those who are
"guilty" of opposing the state, who may indeed have committed the acts of which they are accused, criminal acts in the view
of their persecutors, acts of protest in their own view, but still
specific acts, some covered by the traditional criminal code,
others merely political activities which the regime has banned
without reference to constitutional or comparative law, activities such as printing and distributing leaflets, calling and attending meetings, making statements or speeches—activities
arbitrarily defined as criminal.

There may be no act in question at all, merely attitude, a
crime of the heart, thought crime. A detainee may have no
strong opinions or convictions whatsoever upon arrest, yet
find imprisonment a revelation, an unlooked-for but exhaustive political education. Not even the innocent are permitted to
remain ignorant; those with some insight are likely to improve
upon it through custody. Theory becomes practice, the abstract hardens into the concrete, principles are brought to
apply.

There are the innocent and there are the "guilty"—the
politically uncommitted and the political opponents of the
regime—persons whom the regime would automatically judge
to be guilty because in opposition to it. Irrespective of other
activity, legal or illegal, criminal or warlike or defensive: attitude alone is often automatic proof of guilt.

And since "guilt" is so frequently theological rather than a
matter of legal proof, one cannot trust the state to represent
justice any more accurately than the detainee represents
wrongdoing. Let us call them by different terms, terms which
reflect their present positions of jailor and jailed, powerful and

powerless. Taking a longer view, let us call them "incumbents" and "insurgents," a competition between an insecure present threatened with an uncertain future. In constant and internecine warfare, they can be either diametrically opposed or potentially alike, the two camps coming in time to merge or exchange identities, as power changes hands.

Change itself however, real change, will not come about unless these elements change as well. Until then, insurgent may even become incumbent through the rule of force, the vagaries of warfare, the accidents of coups, the successes of propaganda and advertising. It is only through the creation of a new ethic that the insurgent cause actually distinguishes itself and affects the bystander public, persuading it to dare even against odds, surely against power. The degree of difference is crucial, a matter of the will to change rather than merely the will to power.

Alicia Partnoy's companions in the Little School represent this change in values very well. They are young, university-trained, caught up as she is by the Perónist call to social justice, economic independence, and political sovereignty, an end to the neocolonial influences which had helped to bring about the coup and military rule. Alicia is a graduate student in literature; so is her friend "Vasca" (Zulma Izurieta), who works in a literacy program in the shantytowns. Vasca and her eighteen-year-old companion Braco will be taken from the Little School and shot, having first been anesthetized with an injection and wrapped in blankets; this too will be called a "confrontation."

Many of those in the Little School have been touched by liberation theology, like Néstor: "If you don't believe in God, how do you find strength to risk being killed by the military?" Partnoy herself is a Jewish agnostic; except for religion, she has everything in common with Néstor and his wife Mary: "We followed each other's steps from our teens to the very same doors of this concentration camp: marriage, children, political activism." Alicia read from the Gospels at their wedding. The night her uncle was abducted she took refuge at their house and ended up reading their Bible to stay awake on watch; a towel draped over a lamp so no one could see inside the house, a blunt kitchen knife in her hand. The two women chatted about their children, their marriages, "the political work of women," imagining that by staying awake they would have time to get away. "When, later, three Army trucks arrived at my home, and I ended up here, I realized how naive we were thinking we could possible escape. At Néstor and Mary's house there were three children, three knives and a Bible. By any stretch of imagination we were a lost cause."

There is anti-Semitism at the Little School, endemic in the military; when the guards discover Partnoy is Jewish, they bait her that they will make soap of her. But it is not for being Jewish that she is here, any more than Néstor is here because he is a Christian; the priests have blessed the junta's weapons again and again, rabbis have praised the coup for averting "chaos." They are here because they are the opposition. Alicia's offense was to have produced and distributed information on the economic situation, workers' strikes, and the repression. She knows of disappearances; everyone knows, but of course no one really knows: there are no lists, no admissions. Jacobo Timerman, whose *Prisoner Without a Name, Cell Without a Number* describes his own torture and confinement, was detained in a clandestine cell for over two years merely for printing the names of the disappeared in his Buenos Aires newspaper, *La Opinión*. Then the mothers of the disappeared began to demonstrate in silent procession in the Plaza de Mayo, carrying placards with the names of their missing children, although they too were subject to repression and disappearance; protest had entered a new stage, one finally more difficult to suppress. Their courage had its effect and added immensely to the pressure which human rights groups were having upon world opinion. Opposition is a slow, difficult, and dangerous effort. Injustice works swiftly and from power; those who oppose it are vulnerable, barely organized.

But they operate from principle, understanding, outrage, a

shared ethic. Seeing the bright blue of her husband's pants from under her blindfold, Partnoy realizes that he is now a prisoner too: "Her heart shrank a little more until it was hard as a stone." " 'We must be tough,' she thought, 'otherwise they will rip us to shreds.' " The guard pushes her on along the hall, she steps down onto the cement floor of the "machine room," catching sight of the iron frame bed used for torture: fear "carved an enormous hole" in her stomach.

There is so much to fear—torture, blows, the final bullet. Blindfolded, Partnoy lies on her bed imagining her death, sending her mind out to count the bullets that will end in her body. She spends a day trying to remember her child's face, unable to get it right; perhaps just as well. Were she to see a picture, she would cry—"And if I cry, I crumble." Another day she tries for hours to reach her parents through telepathy and reassure them that she is still alive, visualizing them through an effort of will: her mother in the back room painting, her father making tea, her younger brother reading a book. The tea boils, the boy turns a page. There in freedom, normality, peace, so far away.

Here in this tedium of inactivity, blindness, arbitrary blows, soldiers shove their guns into the prisoners' mouths to express the perverse sexuality of their power. But even here there are moments which are precious, moments of subtle communication among a band of friends constantly forbidden to communicate, yet able for a second or two to whisper, to share some perception. After mealtimes there is sometimes such an occasion, and what one says is important, words are carefully chosen. "Vasca," Partnoy whispers. "They gave me slippers with only one flower." "At last," Vasca whispers back: Partnoy came here barefoot. But this is not the point: "Just one flower, two slippers and just one flower," Partnoy emphasizes, wanting her friend to visualize and understand "that one-flowered slipper amid the dirt and fear, the screams and the torture, that flower so plastic, so unbelievable, so ridiculous," like a stage prop, "almost obscene, absurd, a joke." Blind-folded, Vasca sees it too and they laugh.

The guards make fun of them, amuse themselves by invading their privacy, watching them in the latrine, demanding kisses by putting a knife to the throat of women prisoners, endlessly molesting them with their hands or suggesting sexual intimacies between prisoners so that they might look on and masturbate. In the corridor, Partnoy is made to bump into another prisoner, then ordered by a guard to slap the man's face. She cannot see the face, but caresses it as one of her own. She is slapped twelve times in punishment. In the midst of this indignity she realizes it was Hugo's face, Hugo who has been tortured more than she: "I wasn't going to hurt a pal." During another game the prisoners are made to hold hands and run around the room, unable to see where they are going. Alicia can hold Vasca's hand, a "handshake of complicity." In her other hand is Hugo's—"Our palms conveyed a message: 'Courage. For today and for the rest of the days we'll have to endure here.'"

They are young, and given a chance they will laugh and make faces, tease, even pretend to flirt for the fun of it. Mostly they will give comfort in their growing horror as one by one the members of this band of friends are brought in. Alicia hears Eli's voice and knows they have her too. Then Maria Elena. Benja, the youngest, is brought is one night and chained to the end of Partnoy's bed; she feeds him the cheese they got today, reaching it to him with her toes. They are making him stand there shackled all night; she remembers his quick young hands passing out leaflets, his earnest attempts at political analysis. They used to do graffiti together: "Down with the military killers. We shall overcome!"

"We are all here, all of us. What did these motherfuckers do to catch us all?" Of course they did it slowly, detail by detail, "each pebble of information helped create the avalanche that would crush the rest of our friends": little by little they have come upon the alias, the hair color, the inflection of the voice. When the avalanche reaches her, Alicia Partnoy will be calling herself "Rosa," not knowing which name they come for, "but it was for me they came." Benja will be shot, and Maria Elena; Néstor and Mary are taken away and never heard from again. And Hugo.

Patichoti is in the bunk below her. By pretending to admire her ankles, he tries to make Alicia laugh. "What's wrong, Skinny?" It is her birthday, the guard had promised her a soda, in this unbearable heat and tedium even hatred doesn't prevent her "from wanting to feel the tickle of bubbles" travelling down her throat. There will be no soda; instead, the radio will be turned up and the torture will begin down the hall, the screams audible only in the breaks between popular songs. "I read Patichoti's lips: 'Take heart,' he says." She knows he is remembering his own torture.

When Partnoy's husband is tortured, he tries to block it out by concentrating on a familiar children's song he used to sing their little girl, a nonsense rhyme about frogs and rabbits, repeating the words over and over in the midst of his pain, his mind disordered, rambling: "don't make me believe I'm an animal," "that's not my scream, that's an animal's scream." At one point he gives in: "I told the torturers if they took me to the meeting place I would point to him," but when the moment comes he cannot betray another. "When I saw him I didn't do what I'd promised. Afterward the electric prod again and the blows." The words of the rhyme go on in his mind. "We all hear him when it rains . . . Nobody knows where he hides," more pain, the realization that he may never see his child again, never live through this, his kidneys are mangled now, there is blood in his urine . . . "I smell like a caged animal."

There is a hellish surrealism to the Little School, a dizzy cruelty that conveys the feeling of life under fascism: as Partnoy is forced to urinate in an aluminum can she hears, along with the "almost musical sound" of her urine, the sound of a guard whipping someone in the next room. There are announcements on the radio advising citizens that if they see any family groups travelling at odd hours of the day or night, they should report them at once to the military authorities: "The number to call is . . ." There is the sound of the guards' television set, the kitchen noises of their wooden salad bowl and wine bottles, the screams from the iron frame bed. There is the gauze to tie and retie the prisoners' hands after each meal, there are all those blindfolds. It is the prisoner's responsibility to be sure the blindfold is tight: if it gets loose, you must call out "señor"—here the word has the force of "lord" rather than just "mister"—and request that it be tightened.

The only thing one can trust here is the bread that comes every day with the sound of the bread bag sweeping across the floor; it is consolation, even riches. It is the only "reliable" thing, besides "the belief that we have always been right, that betting our blood in the fight against these killers was the only intelligent option." Bread has a special meaning: you can trade and exchange and share it. It is how they tell each other of their affection and solidarity, offering to share their only possession. When the bread is gone and someone asks for more, there are always voices that call out: "I have some bread left, can I pass it?" If permission is denied it is passed covertly, worth the risk because it is communion: feeling their isolation growing and the world they seek "vanishing in the shadows," bread becomes a "reminder that true values are still alive."

The prisoners of the Little School are suffering and dying for these values, conserving a humanity being destroyed all around them by the dead forces of coercion and obedience. They still believe in mercy and kindness, generosity and honor. They can recognize a plastic flower and know real bread. They have the courage and integrity systematically being uprooted by the regime they oppose.

How do such systems come into being? The case of Brazil is a comparable model for study, since the politics of cruelty are now part of life in the region and many countries can furnish an example: Uruguay, Paraguay, Bolivia, Peru, Venezuela, Panama, El Salvador, Guatemala. It begins with an ideology, the doctrine of the national security state. *Brasil, Nunca Mais,* the historic secret Report of the Archdiocese of São Paulo, published in English as *Torture in Brazil,** is based on a five-year study of the official court records of military trials from 1964 to 1969. The Report gives a careful account of how such an idea develops and proliferates, how it originates in economic conditions, takes over politics, and permeates the legal system, resulting in the web of police apparatus that enforces abduction, interrogation, and torture.

Although portions of the Brazilian military were first seduced by Nazism and impressed by its early victories, Brazil finally joined the Allied forces in World War II and its expeditionary force fought on the Italian front under U.S. command. That connection was strengthened as generations of Brazilian officers thereafter came to the United States for military courses. They returned profoundly influenced by a new theory of national defense. They had learned in America that fortifying their national system against external attack was "far less important than shoring up institutions against an 'internal enemy' that might be trying to undermine them."

In 1949 the Superior War College was founded in Brazil, modelled upon the National War College of the United States, further adapting this interpretation of American Cold War strategy. U.S. national defense policy focused upon an exterior enemy, the Soviet Union, communism. Brazil could imagine no such external danger. But since any threat to U.S. economic interests in Brazil was perceived to be communism as well, a substitution was made: the enemy in Brazil's case was interior rather than exterior. At the Superior War College this was developed into an elaborate political program, and military personnel were trained for political and administrative office

*Translated by Jaime Wright and Joan Dassin (New York: Vintage Books, 1986).

in government on the assumption of the military coming to power.

This idea was developed into a political program by the Brazilian military in the years it prepared for the coup of 1964, when the reformer President João Goulart was deposed by the army with the assistance of the United States through covert operations, destabilizing propaganda, and repeated assurances of support from the U.S. Embassy and its military attaché.

The new military government proclaimed itself a "victorious revolution," which "confers its own legitimacy upon itself." Then it set about changing the laws, enacting a series of "Institutional Acts," five in all, which cumulatively granted it dictatorial powers. They were necessary: given the unpopularity of its economic program, only force could implement it. Every door was opened to foreign investment incentive, easy credit, land purchase; huge projects were undertaken, massive indebtedness was built up as the living conditions of Brazilian citizens deteriorated. This neocolonial situation where one nation holds sway over a formally independent country, extracting economic and political benefits, gradually requires greater and greater military enforcement.

And therefore the need for "security" grows ever more urgent. Upon taking over, the new government drove ten thousand civil servants out of office, then instituted a General Committee for Investigations; five thousand investigations, affecting a total of forty thousand persons. Within months it had created a National Intelligence Service, extended the jurisdiction of military courts to the civilian population, abolished most political parties, developed the ability to suspend the legislative branch at will, rewritten the constitution, and given total license to the executive.

Through a barrage of acts, decrees, prohibitions, it had nearly silenced dissent, but sporadic resistance gave it occasion to restore the death penalty and to develop more and more "organs of security" until it had a great machine of repression, what came to be known as "the System." By the time that

General Emilio Medici followed Marshal Castello Branco into office in 1969, the System was well developed: thousands were being sent to prison, abducted in the street or seized in raids upon their homes, interrogated, tortured, and murdered.

The "internal enemy" is hunted everywhere and with a thousand arms, one after another variety of police force is established and locked into an interconnecting grid: the army, navy, and air force police powers, the political state police, the federal police, the civil police, the military state police, and the civil guard. It is not an open war but a secret one, carried out through interrogation, surreptitious investigation, telephone taps, the storing and processing of information; clerical at one end, brutal at the other. The System proliferates and expands into acronyms, gathers autonomous and officially unacknowledged paramilitary units under the umbrella of OBAN (Operation Bandeirantes), which gains support in the business sector and funding by numbers of multinationals, among them Ford and General Motors, its headquarters a police precinct where every type of police organ is represented and coordinated.

The very fact that OBAN was extra-legal gave it great flexibility and impunity with regard to methods of interrogation; this in turn empowered it for important victories in the "fight against subversion." This conglomerate is so successful it provides a model for the next step in the System, DOI-CODI, the Center for Internal Defense Operations, which coordinates every police and paramilitary organ region by region, culminating in DEOPS, the State Departments for Political and Social Order—the most important forces of political repression and responsible for the most investigations, abductions, interrogations, tortures, and murders.

Once the enemy is the citizenry itself, there is no end to fears for security; dissent is treasonous, opposition criminal activity. The System is a pyramid extending upward from its base of interrogation rooms to its apex with the Council of National Security; its chief holds cabinet rank and meets each day with the president, its budget expands exponentially. Directed against its own people, it must be paid for and supported by them as well, a luxurious burden of paranoia, a great useless expense undertaken to ensure their oppression.

In designing the National Intelligence Service after study in the United States, General Golbery do Conto e Silva had foreseen this. In his *Geopolitica do Brasil,* which became a manual for military government, he concluded that there was no alternative: "There is a new dilemma, that of well-being versus security. This was pointed out by Göring in the past, in an imprecise but highly suggestive and well-known slogan: 'More guns, less butter' . . . there is no way to escape the need to sacrifice well-being for security, once the latter is truly threatened." Göring of course had been speaking of a country at war with an external enemy; Golbery is speaking of one at war with its own population. They must not only endure poverty so that the military can remain safely in power over them, they must sacrifice every right as well.

Ultimately only the military is safe in the national security state. Everyone else is at risk; any life may come under suspicion and unbearable persecution. Living in a protected world of their own, the military are a separate caste enjoying great privilege and unlimited power, a world of state crime and lawlessness completely protected by the specious legality of its own laws. The doctrine of national security is an absolute one; it has decreed from the beginning that "internal opposition could not be tolerated" if its own security were to be maintained: toward that monopoly on authority it has dedicated its entire armory of force, every gun and roadblock, every listening post and agent. But its greatest weapon is torture: arriving at total control, it acknowledges this as its surest avenue.

TORTURE is institutionalized under regimes like these, a deliberate political and social policy, a calculated strategy of widespread intimidation which goes far beyond the old abuses of police interrogation. The secret character of torture is only ambiguously maintained: protests against it in the congress or the press are rare and swiftly punished, but when suspects are arrested it is routine to beat them in the sight and hearing of their neighbors. The population at large must know something of disappearance, enough to be afraid: the opposition must know more, enough to despair. There are circles of awareness, but within the System itself, there is hardly any pretense: the Report of the Archdiocese, compiled from the official records of the military courts themselves, gives a frank and open picture. Once in the custody of OBAN or DOI-CODI, very few escaped torture; but most victims did not refer to it when they finally reached the courtroom, silenced by their own fear or a well-grounded sense of futility as well as the advice of council. Nevertheless, of the seven thousand defendants tried in this period, nearly two thousand had the temerity to speak out in such a court, testifying that they had been tortured and protesting against it. Although their courage had no effect and allegations of torture were ignored and dismissed, the information they provided, information the military regime did not even think to suppress, is invaluable and gives us an understanding of the process.

Torture had a budget and staff, training procedure, study and teaching methods, was regarded as a science. There are classes, classrooms, visual aids, technical terms, and apparatus: slide photographs of torture are followed with practical demonstrations on prisoners. The classes are described in the testimony of the prisoners who were used as live subjects in classes where acknowledged experts like Lieutenant Hayton would instruct large groups of eighty or one hundred army personnel, the lecture and photographs followed with practical "hands-on" exercises. Dulce Pandolfi, a twenty-four-year-old university student, was used as a guinea pig for torture classes in the barracks on Barão de Mesquita Street in Rio: "stripped naked and subjected to beatings and electric shocks and other torments such as the 'parrot's perch.' After being taken to her cell, the defendant was assisted by a doctor, and after a while, was again tortured with exquisite cruelty in a demonstration of how torture should be carried out." One student prisoner was even used as a subject before an audience of military cadets at a preparatory school. Another prisoner was told as he was being used for demonstration that his torturers were exporting their sophisticated knowledge of the technology of pain and "owed nothing to any foreign organization" in their expertise.

Perhaps they overstated their case: the practice of using live subjects, according to the Report of the Archdiocese, was introduced by the American police instructor Dan Mitrione in the early years of the regime: "Mitrione took beggars off the streets and tortured them in classrooms, so that the local police would learn the various ways of creating, in the prisoner, the supreme contradiction between the body and the mind by striking blows to vulnerable points of the body." When Mitrione was transferred to Uruguay to teach policemen there, the use of live subjects could be refined upon.

The methods of torture reported in the military court records are now common throughout the continent. They have names like the "parrot's perch" and the "ice box" and the "dragon chair." In the first, the prisoner's wrists and ankles are tied to an iron bar anchored between two tables, suspended just above the ground. The body is then beaten or shocked with electricity. The dragon chair is a device into which one is strapped for the same purpose. It has a metal seat to increase conduction and an iron bar that pushes the legs backward with each shock, causing deep gashes. Electric shock is produced by army field telephones and various rotary devices called "the little pepper" or "the doubler of tension." Ice boxes are any number of cold and restrictive spaces where the victim is confined for long periods to endure deafening noises, strong light, or lack of ventilation. Insects and animals are also used: snakes, dogs, cockroaches. Every sexual orifice and organ is invaded through these methods: electric shock is typically directed at the most vulnerable parts of the body—the fingers and mouth, as well as the penis, vagina, breasts, and anus. The experience of drowning is created in many ways as water is forced into the mouth through tubes or towels; strangulation is approached by hanging or with a garotte. Victims are made to stand precariously on aluminum cans, or hung on beams as if crucified.

Torture is routinely practiced for a considerable period even before interrogation begins, for its own sake and without the excuse of obtaining information, to induce terror and despair and to bring about the victim's moral destruction. To complement this, friends and relatives are captured so that emotional ties may be called upon. From the records of the court it is clear that "children were sacrificed before their parents' eyes, pregnant women had miscarriages and wives were subjected to suffering to make them incriminate their husbands." Women prisoners were raped, penetrated with objects, and ritually humiliated by groups of males before whom their vulnerability was ingeniously exploited.

Beatings are consistently the main method, the most constant and aggressive, hostile and personal form of intimidation and destruction. Beatings are carried out by groups, with clubs, paddles, rubber thongs, and other labor-saving instruments—systematic assaults protracted over hours and days, often with the intention that the screams of the victim will be heard by other prisoners. Ten hours after the journalist Wladimir Herzog had voluntarily entered a police station to clear his name of suspicion, he was dead, beaten to death in the hearing of many witnesses: it was reported as suicide, and the cause of death on Herzog's certificate was listed as "asphyxiation by constriction of the neck." Fraudulent medical reports were standard practice, the real causes of death disguised as suicides, automobile accidents, shootouts, and confrontations.

Medicine played a large part in the operation: there were staffs of doctors and nurses whose role was not merely to prevent the prisoner from escaping through accidental death, but instructing the torturers in the most vulnerable parts of the body, and prolonging and enhancing pain by administering drugs to revive the victim so that the torture could go forward. Over and over there are accounts of injections and stimulants so that pain can be renewed; practitioners are named, even specific doses and pharmaceuticals. One instance describes an injection of Cepasol in 25 milligrams, as well as muscular tranquilizers so that the victim's body "could again become sensitive to the pain of the beatings to which he had been submitted" when, following a heart and respiratory stoppage, "he became insensitive to all pain." Medical personnel were full participants in torture, part of the team, not mere consultants; torture had become a branch of scientific knowledge, a specialty.

Of the seven thousand tried by military courts in Brazil, an average of fourteen might be tried for one offense, sometimes as many as two hundred. An additional 3,600 listed persons were interrogated but not charged; these were used as witnesses. Two thirds of them had been subject to torture in detention. Taken to one of the locations of the System, whether an official center or a clandestine offshoot, one was helpless. According to the Report of the Archdiocese, "Persons were interrogated with hoods over their heads, while the interrogators used code names or nicknames and did not identify themselves to the prisoners. Virtually no prisoner who passed through their hands escaped torture."

Torture is effective in obtaining confession, any confession, however false or spurious. And confession was virtually the only evidence the court recognized, frequently having no other. Interrogation could ultimately produce confession from someone; even if it was later disavowed as coerced, the confession remained as the persuasive element. Every type of false confession was made; to end their torture, people signed statements that were dictated to them or depositions they were not even permitted to read. They also agreed to sign blank pages, broken as this victim of the clandestine prison in Petropolis: "I was overcome, sick, reduced to a worm and obeyed like a puppet." She was made to accuse her innocent sister, appear on television declaring herself a paid agent of the government, submit to photographs where the marks of her torture were presented as the results of a traffic accident, even to sign a work contract and be filmed counting the money she was paid.

After the right to file a writ of habeas corpus was denied by Institutional Act Five in 1968, there was no hope at all. "Without the right of habeas corpus, without the power to communicate his detainment, and without a fixed time limit for the conclusion of the inquest, the political prisoner, once inside the security organs, was absolutely defenseless, from the day he was abducted to the moment he appeared in military court. The prisoner—subjected as well to long torture sessions—had little choice but to confess everything his interrogators wished." That so many endured in silence is remarkable; that others could not is to be expected.

"This is not the Army, Navy or the Air Force, this is where hell is," a voice shouted from outside the hood that pharmacist Jose Cavalcante was forced to wear when he arrived at a clandestine prison he could never locate again. The impression that store clerk Ednaldo Silva had on arriving was that he was hearing his own screams: as he returned to reality, he realized he was hearing others scream, "other persons like myself" inside an "authentic hell." When lawyer Affonso Monteiro, a former councilman and congressman, was brought to the clandestine prison in the military school in Belo Horizonte, he was informed that "no one could rescue him and that his hour had come."

Such secret prisons offered the System the greatest impunity and were the worst fate of all. Here death waited and mystery brought greater terror. Persons detained never saw their prisons from outside; only a few details could characterize them as what they might once have been: abandoned farms, empty country houses, warehouses. One arrived on the floor of a car, blindfolded, counting turns, trying to locate and memorize landmarks, guessing at distances and directions. Sometimes if you lived and were lucky, you could even return and find them and give testimony to a succeeding government: Jacobo Timerman searched tirelessly and rediscovered his private prison in a discreet white house in the suburbs of Buenos Aires. But he could never bring his captors to trial in Argentina; neither could Alicia Partnoy.

In Brazil, the effort was never made: the Amnesty of 1979 closed all cases of the regime's crimes against its citizens, and the long list of the 440 torturers printed at the end of the Archdiocese Report—names obtained through the military court's own records of its procedures against their victims—is a list of men now beyond the reach of the law, which includes many still "in service" to the republic.

Force remains immune to justice, even the "moral justice" the Report argues for, having despaired of any other and anxious not to be accused of "revenge." If the rule of law and democracy has returned to Argentina and Brazil, it may be only temporarily; meanwhile it has been extinguished elsewhere. The screams of victims sound somewhere else, but they echo still in testimony. Four different people—an engineer, a radio technician, a salesman, and a teaching assistant—all prisoners, listened inside São Paulo's DOI headquarters to the sound of geology student Alexandre Vannucchi Leme's death. The first witness heard the screams of someone who had already been in solitary confinement for fifteen days before his own arrival: "In the beginning his screams had a certain intensity which gradually diminished until they became weak." The second witness was in the adjoining cell and heard Alexandre Leme's tortures and beatings. The third saw his corpse: "During two or three days I heard his screams and, at last, late in the afternoon of 19th March . . . I saw his corpse being taken out of the solitary cell, spreading blood over the entire inner court." The last witness, the young schoolteacher Neide Richopo, having been told that if she did not sign her deposition, "the same thing that happened to Alexandre might happen to her," has pondered this death: "Screams were heard throughout the day . . . on the second day he was dragged, already dead, from the cell where he was."

Leme's death was presented as a suicide; in fact, as Richopo observed, there were originally several versions of this suicide, although the "official" version presented at the end is totally implausible: "It was that he had been run over by a vehicle . . . he could never have been run over because he was already dead when he left the DOI."

Somehow the official version is always a lie, and even the most informative reports fail to produce results. Because if a trial ever takes place, the court fails to convict: the witnesses come forward, the bodies are exhumed and analyzed for evidence of torture by experts, yet somehow the military always escapes unscathed. Somehow the national security state maintains its immunity; it is such a general phenomenon now, such a widespread ideology, so essential to the military element and its unchallenged power in the society of the region and its neocolonial mission, that, like a colony of bacteria temporarily in remission, it simply relocates and continues to operate with impunity.

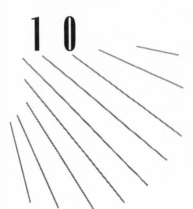

10

The Death of a Guatemalan Village. El Salvador

The whole nightmare began with an absurd mistake. A mistake about uniforms: they were used to the uniforms with the speckles of camouflage printed on the fabric—that was the army, you had to obey them, they run the country. But the men who approached them wore light green instead: they must be guerrillas. The villagers of Tzalala in Huehuetenango, a tiny Mayan Indian settlement in the hills of Guatemala, have been organized by the army into a civil patrol. This way they can be watched, in fact made to police themselves, forced to cooperate, their culture eroded as they are gradually militarized, hardened, turned against themselves and each other, separated from any contact with the resistance. Because they cannot be trusted with arms, they have nothing but sticks to carry, polished clubs, sometimes pieces of wood shaped like guns, even painted black to resemble rifles. They also have slingshots and stones.

Unfortunately, there is one rifle among them, an old one, but when the man who carries it dutifully fires, imagining he

is obeying orders and attacking the "enemy" against whom he
has been trained for a few weeks now to defend the village, he
brings down carnage on them all. The army answer with their
Galil submachine guns and six villagers are killed; the rest will
be rounded up and punished for their mistake. The schoolmaster looks on, watching out over the village plaza, his children
lying on the floor of their classroom, listening to the gunfire
approaching, seeing the soldiers arrive and the disconsolate
civil patrol members herded into the public square with its
basketball court. The schoolmaster is Victor Montejo, and his
Testimony: Death of a Guatemalan Village is an account of the
terrible afternoon of Friday, September 9, 1982.*

It is all a stupid mistake, the blunder of farmers playing
soldier. The Indians of Tzalala are innocents, untouched by
the great struggle around them; they have no real connection
to the resistance. "The guerrillas had passed through the village now and then and those who had seen them said they wear
rubber boots and cause no harm to anyone," the mother of one
of his students tells him: a soldier in leather boots has just
broken down the door of her hut where she is crouched over
the body of her son, the first casualty of army fire. People are
their clothes, their uniforms, the players are what they wear;
the day's events are senseless to her. The man in boots will
pillage her hut, loot it before her eyes, steal her silver earrings
and even the ribbons she has woven. Then he will force her out
into the square, where she will be rounded up by the sergeant
and corralled into the church with the rest of the women.

Montejo has been schoolmaster here for ten years, he lives
in a neighboring town and goes home on the weekends to his
wife and children. For a moment he considers flight; his own
brother has been murdered by the army in an arbitrary, almost
accidental shooting in a park. An educated men, he is far more

---

*The extracts that follow are taken from Victor Montejo's *Testimony: Death of a
Guatemalan Village,* translated by Victor Perera (Willimantic, Conn.: Curbstone,
1987).

politically sophisticated then the Indian villagers around him, who have no frame of reference. The neighboring settlement of Coya was bombed into extinction two summers ago, nearby villages were destroyed by massacre earlier this year, the countryside is under attack and invasion in the last most desperate "Offensive Against Subversion" waged by President Rios Montt. The guerrillas had finally built up a base of support in Indian communities: unable to defeat them in the field, the military has taken another course—it will destroy the base of support, the Indian population itself. It will occupy the villages, execute all sympathizers, massacre entire settlements, destroy their thatched housing and their small corn fields, sell their communal lands, imprison starving refugees in camps of forced labor called "model villages," and organize the surviving Indian communities into civil patrols.

This is what happened in Tzalala. At first the villagers refused: they needed a road, they didn't need a patrol. The military commissioner permitted them to be organized as work parties and then simply converted these details into civil patrols. Each villager was issued an identity card and given a shift. They are still very new at this when catastrophe overcomes them. But they have already been forced to kill. Ten days ago, on August 30, under orders to find suspects among their neighbors, they "prowled the vicinity like a pack of wolves after a scent, searching out subversives." Most cooperated out of fear, but by now a few were enthusiastic about "wiping out the ones from the mountains." The propaganda of their training is paying off. "Communism is bad; they will take away our lands. We have to protect our lands," one sad young man proclaims, though he owns no land; the Indians in the area share their lands communally in the traditional manner.

The captives plead with their neighbors for their lives—they have children. " 'We promised not to release anyone who fell into our hands,' replies one of the chiefs of the civil patrol. 'Not even if it's our own father or brother.' " Hearing this,

Montejo is observing a culture and a way of life die out: "This was the first time the civil defenders had begun speaking in these terms. How sad it is when a man loses his own identity and is easily indoctrinated." The "defender" is repeating to his own neighbor "what the military had drummed into his head: Destroy, kill, even if it includes your own family."

Between coercion and belief, between their fear of reprisals and their persuasion by power, the self-importance of their duties, the new authority of their office, the swagger and masculine privilege, the macho elation the patrol has encouraged, community has been eroded. "This military doctrine had gradually undermined the foundations of an indigenous culture, causing the Indian to act against his own will and best interests and destroying what is most sacred in his ancient Mayan legacy."

And so it happens that the captives are brought to the square, beaten and tortured by the army, and then turned over to their neighbors of the civil patrol for execution: they will be forced to prove themselves.

"All right now, senores defenders," the army officer challenges them, "I want you to execute these two subversives yourselves. You captured them and now you must finish them off." They recoil, they look at each other and draw back. The officer calls them "sissies," "spineless scum." "We are not used to killing. We are Christians," one dares to say. "Like the great whore's mother. You will get used to killing or I will finish you off myself." The officer points his gun at them.

A veteran civil defender, the most callous among them, stepped forward first and aimed a telling blow on the head of the first kneeling captive, Jesus. He was joined by the villagers who had planned the capture and then by the others who formed the circle. They began to pummel the condemned villager with their polished clubs. He tried to scream but all that came out was a horrendous gurgling of the blood in his chest.

They tire and are urged on: "Once more, all of you go to it and get it done right."

The defenders returned to their macabre homicidal task, their assorted clubs and sticks dripping warm blood. The sounds produced by the blows that fell on the luckless man's head and body were like those made by a cracked coconut. When the skull was beaten to a pulp and the face disfigured beyond recognition, the participants in the sinister drama stepped back once again to contemplate the horror.

"This fucker doesn't want to die," the officer comments drily, and a soldier finishes him off with a knife; the next one they must do by themselves. "Do you know this man?" "He is an outsider," they answer. "What are you waiting for?" "The defenders wasted no time in throwing themselves on the newcomer and beating him without respite." It goes faster now, they are better at it. They have crossed a line. And the officer can claim that the army does not kill; "It is the Indian defenders who are doing the butchering."

A few days later they are called upon to give a demonstration for another community, carrying out an execution in a cemetery "to show the people there how they deal with enemies of the government." Even that first time, the event was "indelibly imprinted on the memory of the community, which feared that the spilling of blood would attract further calamities"—but they were still completely unprepared for what happened today. They had been willing to cooperate with their oppressors; they had not intended to attack an army patrol in unfamiliar uniforms, they were genuinely trying to obey orders by firing on what they imagined were guerrillas. The women and children are confined in the chapel, the men stand aghast in the square. "In the faces of each of the civil defenders I could see fear. They seemed dazed and unable to grasp their situation. Or perhaps they understood and regretted their mistakes.

They had gone out determined to wipe out an unknown enemy and had met the very men who had professed to be their friends and protectors. Even the dimmer ones had occasion to reflect on their actions."

Nor were they prepared for the blacklist that followed, where each had to present his identity card which was checked against this new sergeant's list, a list prepared by one of their own number, someone who remains anonymous, for now anyone can denounce a neighbor to settle any score or grudge. Five men are singled out and tied to the oak posts of the basketball court, the village's only amusement center. When these five have been executed by the soldiers, the survivors will be forced to hack down the posts so that a helicopter can land. They do it carefully, hoping to be able to restore the precious handmade court with its hoops and backboards.

The schoolmaster still looks on. He had tried to explain the mistake of the attack, the confusion of uniforms, but now he is under suspicion: a young man has denounced him under torture, said his voice was the voice that threatened him the other night in the dark. The soldiers refer to torture as "telling jokes": it goes on till a confession is made, even if it is all lies. The young man, Manuel, lies in a pool of blood; he has given a name, it is written on a matchbook. He has accused the schoolmaster; they used to play soccer together, he has a reputation as a loudmouth and perhaps someone else had threatened him. Montejo pleads with him, "What will you gain by killing me?" "I want them to kill you too. We can die together," Manuel answers, arbitrary, spiteful; the soldiers go on beating him. Then they all go outside, Montejo sees the sky again, hears the women screaming, sees that all those prepared for the firing squad have been beaten as well; but no one could provide information. One more defender is denounced and then saved by a report that he is well off and therefore innocent.

Montejo realizes that there is now a rope around his neck. In fact they had intended to remove him by helicopter gunship, but in their endless inefficiency the ship lands twice and fails to take him both times, the sergeant calling out in fury after the pilot. When the executions have been completed, Montejo will be marched over the hills to town. "I turned my back to the plaza and could not recognize the faces of my acquaintances. My vision was blurred by the tears that had sprung from my eyes; I looked at everyone as though in a dream. Wherever I looked, the men crouched and avoided my eyes, turning to one side."

THE route to this demoralized moment is long but has a certain logic, the logic of conquest. The first uses of militia in colonial Guatemala were consistently directed at the suppression and control of the indigenous Indian peoples, who still compose the majority of the population in a rigid race/caste/class hierarchy that progresses "upward" to ladino or mixed blood, Spanish, and European. Throughout its decades of army rule, rural Guatemala has been controlled by a system of "military commissioners" who provide the state with conscripts and surveillance and private landowners with a docile labor force.

Guatemala has undergone only one period of reform in this century, the decade between 1944 and 1954, the presidential terms of Juan Jose Arévalo and Jacobo Arbenz Guzman—a period of popularly elected democratic government where labor organization was permitted, even encouraged, and a beginning was made at land reform. The moment of Arbenz's fall is the moment history stopped in Guatemala or took another course, the army withdrawing support for an elected government that had relied upon it, joining in a CIA-supported coup replacing democrat with dictator, and beginning forty years of military repression. Land reform would never again be considered in an agrarian economy of staggering disparities, the larger holdings accounting for as much as 90 percent of the land in export agribusiness; as the great plantations swell, the peasantry's communal land and subsistence plots contract and they are forced to travel to the coast to perform as migrant labor several months a year at wages that barely sustain life. The big plantations reek of chemicals, toxins, insecticides; crops are sprayed by air while Indian laborers are exposed in the field; workers' living conditions and their shack housing are described by the International Labor Office as "totally unacceptable with regard to hygiene, health, education and morality."*

Arbenz's agrarian policy offended United Fruit with plans for appropriation of unused portions of its vast holdings. The American firm demanded twenty-five times the sum Arbenz was offering in compensation and registered its claim directly with the State Department: a head-on collision with the U.S. government. Direct threats to U.S. corporate interests were totally unacceptable. Arbenz's modest reforms were now considered "Communist," the Arbenz government toppled, and the new military government was very careful to appeal to United States investment as well as its Cold War ideology.

THE doctrine was American; so was the advisory planning, training, and instruction, the military aid and materiel. In Guatemala, the doctrine took the form of counter-insurgency. a variant on the ideology of the national security state. Perhaps also an intensification, especially if one remembers that counter-insurgency is also described as counterterror. So while the huge repressive machinery of the national security state tends to lie in wait for transgressions against its authority, poised and ready to pounce, counter-insurgency assumes that the mischief is already going on, that an insurgent force is present, that it has dared to organize and band together, that it is out there, ready to be attacked, even to attack authority

---

*Cited in George Black, Milton Jamail and Norma Stoltz Chinchilla, *Garrison Guatemala* (New York: Monthly Review Press, 1984).

itself, the military state. This is to assume not only that the enemy is internal, the population itself, but that there is a real enemy with a face, the guerrilla, the armed resistance. In the first period of counter-insurgency in the sixties, when U.S. Special Forces were used in training and advisory and perhaps even in some combat capacity, some eight thousand persons were killed by the Guatemalan government, although the guerrillas themselves did not number over five hundred. In the eighties there may have been ten thousand insurgents, but something like eighty thousand persons were killed. The other victims are considered support, accomplices in some sense: they were there, they were in the neighborhood, it is difficult to tell the guilty from the innocent, and these people, like the Viet Cong—for counter-insurgency was built on American strategy in Vietnam, the "model hamlet" method of invading and controlling alien populations and the "Phoenix" pattern of assassination—these people must be crushed, if necessary exterminated. One begins with deception, spreading lies and disinformation, "fooling them, finding them, attacking them, annihilating them," as Rios Montt's four tactics outline it in his "Standing Orders for the Development of Anti-Subversive Operations" in the so-called Victoria 82 Plan of Campaign.

It is interesting that in the case of the doctrines of both the national security state and counter-insurgency, Latin American military could accept a U.S. version of their military situation and their relationship to their own population, without objecting that American strategists did not apply these doctrines at home. Only the U.S. Special Forces operated on the same dynamic toward civilians as did Latin American regimes, since this was a unit dealing with foreign nationals or a teaching branch for export. There are consequences in the fact that the U.S. military did not posit an enemy within its population or a hostile dynamic toward its citizens: what was appropriate for export was not acceptable at home. There is an unconscious racism and imperialism inherent in such a double standard. It is related to privilege, or what has become privilege in the face of deprivation, that narcissistic glow U.S. nationals experience in their certainty that their civil rights are still intact, respected. Others elsewhere have lost or never had the traditional "liberties" they continue to enjoy—together with their recent economic hegemony. Observing their own good fortune in comparison to the fate of other citizens under other governments may be so satisfying that scruples about equity or causation do not arise.

The American counter-insurgency doctrine was formative, all-pervasive: lives were lived and lost behind its perceptions. Its effect was a nightmare brutality of clandestine executions and mutilated corpses, yet acceptable to Latin American militarism for reasons of its own. One might guess at a colonized sense of inferiority before the glamour and wealth of empire, the young officer dazzled by study abroad. But far more important is the balance of power at home, preserving that. Through such necessity they have arrived at a particular form of bad faith which accepts any terms in order to maintain power. That these are one's own people is not material: the ideology of anti-communism has made them estranged, foreign, contaminated, possessed by a diabolic force that makes them more remote than foreigners, less sympathetic, less human. The rules of combat do not apply here; the rules of war are military, not paramilitary. There is nothing too cruel or outrageous in this combat, there is no restraint, no mercy, no quarter. Counter-insurgency becomes counterterror.

In the city, one is always dealing with "unknown assailants," "masked men," and nameless or anonymous "death squads," "vigilante groups." In the countryside, where the army openly confronts the peasantry, there are other forms of manipulation and distancing: Indian foot soldiers deal with Indian peasants, but by careful design they are never from the same provinces or language groups. The soldier's training has been a systematic denial of his natural sympathies, part of it a deliberate brutalization whereby he has been beaten routinely, endured it, and been taught to beat others. He has been thoroughly conditioned to believe there are "Communists" everywhere and to regard them as anathema. He has been lied to and suborned and estranged from his origins and background. Although he was conscripted by poverty or even impressed and kidnapped on market day, the army has in time become his home, his whole sphere of experience now: its male culture is familiar and agreeable. It is an entire institution, secure and reassuring, full of authority and prestige, a path of opportunity far above what fate would have presented otherwise; promotion is frequent, sometimes every four months, there are extra awards for guerrilla deaths, executions.

One is fighting a crusade, warring with a pure evil. Counterinsurgency was always understood to be a "dirty war": beyond morality, magical and abstract. Everyone is pretending: there is no Communist threat, the opposition is indigenous, a broad-based spectrum of worker, peasant, and middle-class dissatisfaction arising out of traditional commitments to democracy and religious values where the Communist Party is an insignificant minority. But the specter of communism has been used successfully to justify military rule and then dictatorship. Doctrine, dogma, myth, convenience. The army grows richer and more powerful, no longer the servant of the propertied classes but their partner. The political parties are eviscerated; elections are fraudulent. Measures are more and more extreme, the military proliferates through every institution, controls more and more of the social apparatus, declares frequent states of siege which suspend the constitution and all other civil guarantees.

There is no place for resistance to go; it is stifled by the end of the sixties after ten years of secret and open repression and intimidation: the guerrillas have disappeared, the students are quiet, the trade unions do not protest. And then it begins all over again, greater dissent, larger strikes, cooperatives, Base Christian communities, huge peasant unions, a unified armed struggle. Then further mobilization of the army, more death lists and disappearances, a chaos of brutality, the ultimate massacres of the countryside.

There is a fever in the struggle, a psychotic violence which appalls, grows monstrous, colors everything. For forty years bodies have been turning up beside the road, in ravines, in sandpits and dumps, in "clandestine cemeteries" found by accident in the countryside or at the city limits: the bodies uniformly show signs of torture, even mutilation. Hands, ears, noses, genitals are cut off. The victims are students, teachers, lawyers, journalists, labor leaders, even centrist political figures, members of the Christian Democratic Party. Many victims are persons with significant credibility whose death and disappearance now make the hope of political or legal redress still more distant and unobtainable. The intention is to wither all hope of dissent or opposition, to induce a collective despair.

One feels it in the bewildered fatigue of human rights workers, endlessly vulnerable to assassination of character, death threats, death, and disappearance itself. The current president, a civilian, has again failed to stop the torture and murder euphemistically referred to as "human rights abuses"; instead, he has granted another amnesty to the army, extending it complete immunity. Disappearances continue, forced labor, civil patrols; human rights groups like Mutual Support go through months of paperwork and red tape to open one clandestine cemetery, its original informality suddenly formal, government victims now government property. Everywhere there is surveillance, strangers are watched, there are "ears" and the ears are paid. In the countryside one might need permission from the military commissioner in order to have an overnight guest. The army envisions a more perfect regimentation of citizens through the civil patrol system, entire military supervision of rural life.

People who have worked in the cooperatives are under suspicion now; so are medical workers, especially those who go back to the health "promoter" groups that sprang up at the time of the earthquake in 1976. In David Schwantes's *Guatemala, A Cry from the Heart,** a human rights worker explains to a visitor what life is like for one of these paramedics:

> When the violence began, he was suspected of being a subversive, as were most leaders of efforts to improve the lives of the peasants. He went into hiding. A few years ago, he decided it was safe enough for him to live openly. In the last year, however, he had to quit his work with the clinic and the health promotion programs and had gone back into hiding. He had become "much burned," which meant he was identified as a subversive, a risk to political stability, a man whose name was on "the list" . . . it is now "just a matter of when they'll get around to him." A man like this is simply waiting to be murdered.

"He won't survive the next round," the speaker concludes in exhausted futility.

The ideological seems every day more specious in such a contest, the doctrine not even paranoia now, merely a cover for a brutal hold on power. Conquest is through sheer nastiness: the model is not a warrior or officer ethic but the mafia, criminality. But it is a highly technical and completely sophisticated criminal force, enjoying every advantage of governmental prestige and cohesion: its very mechanical heart the great communications center in the National Palace where all intelligence information from every source is coordinated and the orders go out for death squad killings. This great complex, the Regional Center for Telecommunications *(La Regionale),* a gift of U.S. "development assistance," not only puts Guatemala in twenty-four-hour contact with the police and security of six other neighboring states and the Southern Command of the U.S. Army in the Panama Canal Zone but also functions as the command center for the supposed random killings, the thousands of tortured bodies which the regime passed off as inexplicable crimes by unknown assassins or persons beyond

*(Minneapolis: Health Initiative Press, 1990).

THE POLITICS OF CRUELTY

the law, zealots whom it claims it cannot control or identify.

On February 18, 1981, Amnesty International published a report which concluded that "no pro-government groups existed independent of government control and that government agencies were directly responsible for the killings and kidnapping which the authorities ascribed to extremist death squads." Amnesty's conclusions were based on a variety of testimony, including that of Elias y Barahona, former press representative of the Ministry of the Interior, whose duty it had been to present such deaths as savage infighting between the extreme left and extreme right, utterly disassociated from government. Deaths ascribed to much-publicized squads like White Hand, ESA, and NOA, groups which advertised themselves by leaflet and claimed "credit" by crude notes pinned upon disfigured bodies, were and still are the work of the government itself: the Ministry of the Interior was said to keep a supply of blank stationery from the chief death squads.

Executions by the various police forces are routinely performed by groups of demoted policemen forced to atone for past irregularities by assassination duty with short pay and some chance of reinstatement. Executions by the military itself are also conducted by government personnel, the assassins generally two *confidentiales* or secret military intelligence agents in one part of the country, who are provided with tickets and photographs of their victims either routinely approved from the lists in the central regional files by the heads of the detective corps and the military police or, in the case of the prominent, decided upon at meetings of the Departments of Interior and Defense. Duty is temporary and hard to trace; the agents return at once to their own locales and are disassociated with the crime.

Surveillance is highly developed through *La Regionale;* electronic information from any government data base can be correlated to intelligence. Whatever may be learned from the state-run telephone company, the ministries of Labor, Finance, Immigration, and Passport Records. Everything is on hand, ready for "when the time comes to pick them up," as the historian Michael McClintock demonstrates in *The American Connection*, Volume 2, *State Terror and Popular Resistance in Guatemala.** Tens of thousands have met this fate. There is very little detention; nearly everyone who disappears in Guatemala is murdered. Combined with torture and mutilation, it is a very hard death.

By the time counterterror reached Tzalala in 1982, it carried the freight of nearly thirty years of fear; another decade has been added since, the incomprehensible machine still descending, godlike and terrible from the sky upon unsophisticated people who have no weapons against this force, are paupers before its glittering expense and its brilliantly equipped soldiers, whom they face empty-handed without resources or technology. The American helicopter gunship. One is defenseless before its noise, its mounted machine guns, its slicing overhead propeller.

In Chiapas, on the Mexican border, I listened to accounts by Guatemalan refugees of how the ships had descended upon their villages—Indians for whom the surprise was still fresh, the trick of promising electricity and schools on the first visit, the ploy of rounding up the headmen in the plaza still effective, their shock when the soldiers machine-gunned the elders of the community still resounding in the air of the wattle shelter where we sat, the same thatched structure they had at home. When the soldiers came in the ships the second time, they sternly ordered the people to stay inside and then set these structures on fire: sitting inside this fragile structure made of sticks you feel how it would burn, the speed and heat and entrapment of it. The familiar spy and cinema glamour of urban disappearance, our imaginary realm of foreign intrigue and tropical adventure, dissolves in the brutality of burning

*(London: Zed Books, 1985).

simple people alive. The fire is inescapable, yet some broke out and ran; these few around me survived the machine-gun fire. The fruits of ideology: listening, one is astounded at how this scrap of military myth, counter-insurgency, has taken on the power to create such suffering, such inhumanity.

In the memory of El Salvador, the seminal moment of modern history is the massacre of 1932, when General Martinez suppressed a great peasant revolt in the west. Within forty-eight hours thirty thousand people were executed wholesale from a population of a million. That was the turning point. Buried under a pile of bodies, Miguel Marmol, one of the great labor leaders of the era, survived a firing squad and lived to tell of it. In *Miguel Marmol,* the poet Roque Dalton has seen to it that Marmol's entire personality has survived as well, perfectly conveyed in his subject's own voice, the entire biography of the man one long monologue rich in lust and obscenity, insight and honor. Dalton didn't even use a tape recorder, but transcribed by hand during weeks of patient listening. For Marmol, everything began in 1932: "Since that accursed year, all of us have become other people, and I believe that El Salvador has become another country. El Salvador is today above all a creature of that barbarity . . . the basic way of thinking that still governs us is that of the perpetrators of the massacre."* Decades of military repression followed under the ominous control of the national police and National Guard, a police state complete with photo identity cards, checkpoints, travel restrictions, and internal passports, greater and greater control building toward the advent of the death squads in 1975.

But the instant when Archbishop Romero is murdered with one bullet on a church altar while saying mass on March 24,

---

*Roque Dalton, *Miguel Marmol,* translated by Kathleen Ross and Richard Schaaf (Willimantic, Conn.: Curbstone, 1982).

1980, is also crucial. By then it was civil war, a mass popular movement against which the army was at war; and by then Romero himself would be so incensed he would not only admonish the soldiery to disobey orders to torture fellow peasants but go on to justify open rebellion, perhaps even the armed struggle: "when a dictatorship violates human rights and attacks the common good of the nation, when it becomes insupportable and all channels of dialogue, understanding and rationality are closed, when this occurs, the Church speaks of the legitimate right to insurrectional violence." At his funeral, a hundred thousand mourned Romero in the cathedral square and the military opened fire on the crowd with machine guns. Things had gone this far.

And by then U.S. efficiency in intelligence and communications had speeded up counter-insurgency repression with paramilitary forces in a proliferation of state terror which had produced the bodies of the disappeared, victims of the death squads described so often in books and newspapers, yet perhaps for many of us first and most hauntingly in Joan Didion's *Salvador:** "A mother and her two sons hacked to death in their beds by eight *desconocidos,* unknown men. The same morning's paper: the unidentified body of a young man, strangled, found on the shoulder of a road. Same morning, different story: the unidentified bodies of three young men, found on another road, their faces partially destroyed by bayonets, one face carved to represent a cross."

"These bodies," photographed by the archdiocese Human Rights Commission and kept on file for relatives to try to identify, were "often broken into unnatural positions," Didion goes on, "and the faces to which the bodies are attached (when they are attached) are equally unnatural, sometimes unrecognizable as human faces, obliterated by acid or beaten to a mash of misplaced ears and teeth or slashed ear to ear and invaded by insects," sometimes better identified by remnants of cloth-

---

*(New York: Washington Square Press, 1983).

ing—"white shirt, purple pants, black shoes"—since "the photograph accompanying that last caption shows a body with no eyes, because the vultures got to it before the photographer did."

These are not forensic photographs because there will never be a trial. Counter-terror is in place now, has taken over, its consequences are everywhere, but its product is the corpse itself, the exemplary object. Bodies appear on the roads every day. Didion saw one herself on the way to Gotera; there had been one in the same spot the morning before, five others before that. There is El Playon and Puerta del Diablo, body-dumping grounds on the outskirts of San Salvador. There is a daily horror to life now, a psychotic terror; an enormous security apparatus reaches into every corner of the country, coordinating death lists. One person in fifty is an informant.

COUNTER-INSURGENCY has produced this, the American doctrine, the American training and advisers, the American aid and war materiel in congressional appropriation after appropriation. Archbishop Romero had begged that the repression come to an end and that U.S. military aid come to a halt: another appropriation was voted the day after his murder. One must go back to the beginning of counter-insurgency theory and implementation, the article of faith that all forms of opposition and protest are subversion: trade unions, student demonstrations, opposition parties. Every form of dissent has been criminalized, converted to communism, to treason: for economic reasons, if no other, since the disparity in wealth is so enormous, the oligarchy of the "fourteen families" so powerful, the role of the security forces to guard the elite so manifest. "Development" and "civic action" were supposed to balance the role of "coercion" in counter-insurgency; but this would involve basic economic change, undesirable and therefore unfeasible, so they remain public relations gestures, words and phrases.

What is created instead is a vast network of security forces and political police, the product of twenty years of U.S. training. Organized beside it is a secret paramilitary force, faceless bands of men mobilized under patronage, low-level government workers who must "volunteer" to keep their jobs, army reservists and veterans retrained as part-time assassins in the city and the countryside, who in the jargon of the U.S. Defense Department, CIA, Public Safety Program, and U.S. Army pronouncements cited in Volume 1 of McClintock's *American Connection* form the "basic civilian counter-terrorist organization." "Young elites," they are called flatteringly, "who have a stake in the community, because they have a family, own a house or a piece of land, are ambitious to get ahead in business, profession or politics." The selection of such men is the "first priority after the military have cleared an area," training them for guard duty, nighttime roadblocks, surveillance, and to act as informants and guides for the military, not excepting assassination squad duty. U.S. advisers created this web of counterterror in ORDEN and a number of other Salvadoran paramilitary organizations, civil defense patrols, and death squads.

In forming such units every interest and prejudice can be played upon, every mercenary or ideological connection, religious belief, ethnic identification, class consciousness, incorporating employees of the landlord class, lesser relatives of property, recipients of patronage, and especially families identified with the National Guard. It is a volatile mix: once organized and empowered, once citizens are permitted and encouraged, trained and directed to break the law, to carry arms and to commit murders and assassinations, it is hard to stop this process, modify or moderate it. Directed and controlled by the army and security forces, the identity of paramilitary individuals is secret to the rest of the population, just as their deeds are obfuscated and confused in the press, blamed on "extreme elements of the right or left." Constant confusion is necessary, references to mysteries, unknown assailants, masked men, vigilantes, fringe groups, persons "out of control," with "no official ties," phantoms, independent and "unaffiliated" bodies. A language of the indefinite comes into being, the unaccountable: there will be no accountability, only power, fear.

Yet for all this, as one U.S. Army study puts it, "paramilitary forces are primarily political." An astute observation; even when the message is merely intimidation, "Their function is to provide visible and effective demonstrations of the power of the state." Even when the source of the violence is muddied, the message is still effective: one gets the point. Responsibility and blame are avoided at the same time.

On another, formal and public level, lies, censorship, and "disinformation" are still important elements. The real nature of events must be concealed from public opinion in the United States, or at least disguised by vague and distancing terms like "human rights abuses"; persons on the spot fully aware of government collusion must be paralyzed with fear. Everywhere there is a blasé indifference to the fact that counter-insurgency terror is in direct contravention to the laws of the land in the American democracies and all the international agreements to which both governments are party. Governmental crime has been traditionally recognized as excess and aberration, but this brutality is accepted as something different, a sophisticated and innovative policy.

Torture and detention have a new legality: detention is completely legalized under Revolutionary Government Junta Decree 507, torture is nearly legal in that confessions under judicial interrogation are admissable. There is a frequent state of siege, with curfew restrictions where anyone may be shot on sight and other summary executions whether overt or covert become routine. Counter-insurgency brings new standards and perspectives: when people are thrown out of helicopters or their houses are burned, it is now part of a subtle new program. It becomes a crime to report human rights abuses inside or outside the country. El Salvador's only medical school was occupied by the military, then closed; death squads invaded hospitals to murder surgeons in operating rooms and shoot patients in their beds; nurses and health care workers "disappeared." Dr. Charles Clements in his *Witness to War** describes how he was first introduced to Salvadoran interrogation techniques by treating a woman whose breast had been cut off with a machete.

Violence has a way of escalating; state violence once given rein develops into a dizzy and terrible way of life but one that tends to backfire: the more repression the state applies, the greater popular resistance. Ultimately, counter-insurgency is counterproductive and may bring on the very revolutionary activity it purportedly intended to prevent but finally produces as sheer force creates greater and greater resentment. As government plunges into crime, it loses its way and finally its authority.

The irresponsibility inherent in counter-insurgency has placed the prestige and power, the moral authority of the United States, its military and material assistance of all kinds behind the thinking of U.S. Army handbooks which can describe an imaginary Latin American country called "Centralia" where counter-insurgency techniques are considered with this single limitation: "You may not use mass counter-terror, as opposed to selective terror, against the civilian population, i.e. genocide is not an alternative." McClintock cites this source, and one is forced to consider with him just how high a percentage of the population may be exterminated under the term "selective."

UNDER the massacre conditions of army counter-insurgency, that percentage could go very high indeed. Over and over in counter-insurgency thinking the armed resistance is conceived of as being like fish in the sea; failing to catch the fish, the army will drain the sea instead by destroying its base

*(New York: Bantam Books, 1984).

of support in the local population, if necessary by exterminating that population itself. The term "civilian" has no meaning now, the entire citizenry in some regions may be bombed and machine-gunned; strategists like Colonel Ochoa deny even that civilians exist in certain zones—even children there are military targets. By the eighties, emboldened by the Reagan administration, the army itself had become a death squad. The people flee on foot, following trails in the mountains without food or shelter, dragging the children and the aged along with them, only to be ambushed and strafed at a river crossing, hundreds at a time. McClintock quotes an American graduate student, Phillipe Bourgois, who was a witness on one of these flights and provided testimony to the U.S. Congress: "for the next fourteen days, I fled with the local population as we were subjected to aerial bombardment, artillery fire, helicopter strafing and attack by Salvadoran foot soldiers. In retrospect it appears as if the Salvadoran government troops had wanted to annihilate all living creatures (human and animal) within the confines of the 30 square mile area."

At Copan, in May 1980, at least six hundred unburied corpses were reported, prey for dogs and buzzards for several days. At the Lempa River, thousands of villagers fleeing were bombed and strafed in March 1981. There were two massacres along the Sumpul River a few months later, and later that same year a series of "clearance" operations in Cabanas and Morazan; the Salvadoran Human Rights Commission (Socorro Juridico) documented that one of them "resulted in the murder of forty-four minors, the capture and murder of ten family groups and the murder of thirty-three women. A total of 147 noncombatants were either killed by the security forces or taken away by them. People in the area saw corpses floating down the river after the operation."

Massacre after massacre is attributed to the Atlacatl Battalion, trained in El Salvador by U.S. Special Forces from Fort Gulick in the Canal Zone, or to the Ramon Belloso, trained at Fort Bragg, North Carolina. The El Mozote massacre, reported in the U.S. press and by the Americas Watch Committee, took the lives of a thousand civilians from a number of villages in Morazan; the main strike force was again the Atlacatl Battalion, comprising three thousand army and security forces as well as paramilitary irregulars.

In El Mozote itself there was only a single survivor, a thirty-eight-year-old woman named Rufina Amaya. The troops arrived early in the morning and rounded up the villagers, locking the men up in the church and women in a house nearby. At noon the men were blindfolded and executed in the town center, Amaya's husband among them, who was nearly blind. Then the women: in the afternoon the young women were taken to the hills and raped, then killed and their bodies burned. Next the old women were taken and shot. "The soldiers had no fury," Amaya explained, "They just observed the Lieutenant's orders. They were cold." Hiding among the trees, Amaya heard the soldiers discuss how to kill the children; they seem to have decided to choke them, because later she heard their screams and calls for help but heard no shots. Three of her own children were among those dead; all were under ten years old.

CONDITIONS like this have produced mass resistance, a popular front in the cities, and the occupation of parts of the country by armed guerrilla communities, conditions of war, finally even negotiations for peace. One of the leading elements in the struggle is the emerging force of women, particularly the Co-Madres, a Salvadoran group growing out of the demonstrations first inaugurated by the Argentinean Mothers of the Disappeared; subjected to escalating repression, arrest, and torture, but increasingly politicized and internationally effective. The biography of one of the founders of this group is a summary of the life of the poor in El Salvador brought to consciousness and hope through the ideas of liberation theology, the Base Christian community, and cooperative movement. They define a life of grinding poverty and unremitting governmental persecution before which they cannot capitulate. A desperate necessity requires that such adherents remain undaunted by the massive powers arrayed against them by wealth and military power in El Salvador itself and the virtually limitless might of the United States upon which they can draw. There is both irony and optimism in the fact that this biography has been translated into English and is distributed by the Co-Madres office in Washington, D.C., where the group now have offices and are calling upon American feminist and human rights opinion.

My name is America Sosa.* I am originally from San Miguel, El Salvador. I am forty-nine years old. I have studied up to the sixth grade. I am a widow and have seven children, ages nineteen to thirty. I now live in Washington D.C. in Sanctuary with the Dumbarton United Methodist Church in Georgetown.

From 1973 to 1979 I was an active member of the leadership team of the Base Christian Community of San Antonio Abad; of the Executive Board of a saving and loan cooperative; and of a community parochial clinic. . . . Some of my duties and responsibilities as one of the leaders of the community included: maintaining unity and harmony in the group, teaching catechism, giving pre-baptismal and pre-matrimonial counseling, counseling couples with marital problems, coordinating Bible study groups and giving courses in cooperativism.

In January of 1979, a group made up of members of both the Army and the security forces assaulted the community retreat house "El Despertar" and assassinated, on the spot, Father Octavio Ortiz Luna and four youths (aged fourteen to sixteen) who were celebrating a spiritual retreat. After that, the village of San Antonio Abad was occupied by the military, and some of the leaders and members of the Christian Community, including my

---

*America Sosa, "Autobiography." Testimony of the Representative of the Committee of Mothers and Relatives of Political Prisoners, Disappeared and Assassinated of El Salvador, Monsignor "Oscar Arnulfo Romero." Distributed by the Co-Madres, Washington, D.C.

oldest children and I, were sought by the authorities. I felt obliged to abandon my house and my community activities in San Antonio Abad.

In December of 1980, one of my sons, Juan, was captured at a roadblock by agents of the National Police. He was taken, along with others that had been arrested, to the general headquarters of the aforementioned security forces. For three days he was disappeared because the National Police denied his arrest. My son was fourteen years old at the time of his detention. He was studying in the eighth grade and was a volunteer for the Green Cross. He remained incommunicado for three months in the National Police Headquarters, where he was frequently tortured, beaten and insulted. There they forced him to sign an extrajudicial statement which they would not permit him to read and which claimed he was guilty of the murder of a colonel and the burning of several buses.

Afterwards, without any previous trial, without investigation, without right to an attorney, he was sentenced to prison. He went to Santa Tecla as a political prisoner, whence he was released seven months later. Immediately after his release, my son sought refuge in the Mexican Embassy because he was afraid he would be assassinated, as had occurred in many other cases. The Mexican authorities granted him political asylum and he is currently living in Mexico. I have not seen him in seven years.

It was at that time, when I was searching for my son in the hospitals, in the jails, in the streets, in those times of pain and desperation, that I came to join the Committee of Mothers. They provided me with information and legal and financial assistance. But, the most precious thing I found there was the moral support of human solidarity that all of the mothers offered me. They understood well my anguish since the same experience had already happened to them.

In November of 1981, three months after my son was released from prison, my husband Joaquin was arrested by the Treasury Police as he was returning from work. My husband was forty-nine years old and he was a construction worker. He never worked in political issues or organizations, since he was afraid to get involved. His only objective in life was to assure the well-being of his family. Again, I had to relive the anguish of the disappearance of one of my loved ones. In all the places where we sought my husband, they told us they had never seen him, that they didn't know him. One week after his arrest and disappearance, my husband sent us a message through a former prisoner who had just been released, saying that he had been detained in Sotanos (secret prison) of the Hacienda Police.

After many petitions and pleadings to the director of the security forces, my husband was released. The day he left prison he could not walk and had to be carried. He had been savagely beaten and tortured. The director of the Treasury Police said it had been a mistake, that they had confused him with another suspect. We took him immediately to a hospital. There he received physical and psychiatric treatment because some of the beatings had been to the head and he had partially lost his memory. But it was useless. There had been internal injuries to his vital organs, and, in his weakened state, he was unable to withstand the potent drugs they administered. After fifteen days he died.

Then in 1985, seven months after I arrived in the United States, I received information about the capture of my son Joaquin Caceres. Upon leaving his office at the Commission of Human Rights in El Salvador, he was followed by a car with tinted windows. The car of security police dressed in civilian clothes abducted Joaquin when he got off a bus. In a park, he was tortured and interrogated almost to the point of death. Then they took him to the National Police, where he was interrogated for five consecutive days. Before transporting him to Mariona Prison, they took photos and published them in the newspaper accusing him of being a subversive and guerilla. After one year, thanks to International Solidarity he was released.

These are the injustices my family has suffered and these are the motives that led me to become a part of the Committee of Mothers.

There is a great power in this testimony: the empowering force of village organization behind the idea of cooperativism, the humble duties of the catechist ranging from matrimonial advice to money management and health care. Against this innocent framework of self-help are massed all the paraphernalia of state terror, the whole array of army, security force, national police, the dreaded Treasury or political police, clandestine prisons, the tinted one-way windows of Cherokee Chiefs behind which so many have disappeared, the official denials; detention, torture, death. In defense, only the solidarity of other unfortunate women, the slender organization of human rights groups, the hope of justice.

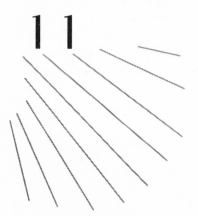

STATE TORTURE AND RELIGION. THE TORTURE OF CHILDREN

In Iran, torture moves from its familiar use as dictatorial policy toward the force of divine or otherworldly punishment. Despite differences in geographical or cultural locus, torture in Iraq, for example, is similar in "meaning" to torture in South America: a military regime is breaking opposition, imposing its force, intimidating dissent. In terms of the mechanism of state power, the same is true in the Islamic Republic of Iran. But another dimension has been added: the authority from which the torture emanates is divine rather than human. The supernatural has been added to the political.

Iranian torture has also been very much complicated by becoming legal as well as remaining, as elsewhere, forbidden and secretive. Iran's Islamic Constitution actually enjoins certain forms of judicial torture such as public flogging, the stipulated sentence for the crimes of fornication or blasphemy. Religious law has been subsumed into the secular code. At the same time, in a gesture toward the contemporary and international (Iran has signed the 1984 UN Conventions Against Torture), it forbids extra-judicial torture, the torture of prisoners to extract confessions, for example.

Although technically forbidden, the torture of prisoners through falaka, beating on the soles of the feet or the back of the legs, is very widely practiced in Iran. However, falaka is rarely acknowledged as torture but accepted instead as yet another "Islamic punishment." It is routinely inflicted after arrest and frequently repeated in detention or even later when prisoners are serving sentences. Falaka is a diabolic torment, the victim's legs swell, clothing is bloodstained from the trouser cuff to the thigh; many are unable to walk at all when the beatings end and must drag themselves back to their cells along the floor. Scars last for years, walking is impaired, and in some cases people are even paralyzed. Prisoners are often suspended during falaka or bound in contorted postures. In the Amnesty International report on Iran of January 1992, a woman prisoner describes this agony: "The position my hands were in was exhausting, it affects the body's entire nervous system. After a while even if they don't beat you hard you feel it acutely. If they tap you with a pencil it feels like a hammer."

Iran is unusual in having legalized certain tortures in its criminal code, and in the case of other tortures technically illegal having managed to come to view them as punishments of the same religious order, expressions of the will of God. Torture plays a great part in Iranian repression, both in public flogging and in the falaka carried out in the secret of prison, where the victim is tied to a bedstead and beaten with cables for hours by guards taking turns, until the feet and legs are swollen and bleeding or the back is cut with lashes and the kidneys are injured.

This is the torture of the political suspect which we have come to see taking place in so many corners of the world—but with one difference: the authority for his/her suffering here has been elevated to the divine. Iranian theocracy has provided a different referent and dimension. The sense of hopelessness and solitude are enlarged now in the dim light of Evin or Qasr

Prison where so many suffered under the old regime of the Shah. The victim is more overwhelmed than ever: condemnation is no longer human but sacred; omnipotent, omniscient.

Judicial or legalized torture in Iran is administered before a member of the clergy; to oversee the act, witness, and regulate it. But a mullah or clergyman is often also present during technically illegal or surreptitious torture, falaka. The presence of a physician during torture generally represents a desecration of values in Western contexts; the presence of a "man of God" may do so still more. The only parallel we have for comprehension here is the memory of the Inquisition. In each case deliberate torment expresses not only the will of the state but a divine will as well. Fate is expanded and grows heavier. The burden upon the victim is increased exponentially; so too is the authority of the state, magnified now by having enlisted supernatural powers and added them to its formidable array of physical controls.

THE effect of torture, its "meaning" for all parties—tortured, torturer, the public who are informed of it in whatever manner so that they may be edified and controlled—is greatly altered when it emanates from and expresses the will not merely of the state or the army, temporal government or a political faction in power, but the supernatural itself. Pain is punishment now: meted out and appropriate. The infliction of pain is no longer a transgression against law and civilized custom. Judicial torture (particularly flogging) was never relinquished by Islamic canon law and its recent formal reassertion is a victory for theocracy. Indeed, the total restoration of *shari'a,* the Islamic legal code, complete with its *qissas*—amputations for thievery, flogging for sexual license, and stoning for adultery—was an essential goal of religious will expressing itself politically. This would bring peace and harmony to human society.

A different force now mediates. The supernatural is not

comprehensible to temporal government but only to those trained to interpret the divine will, the clergy. It is the reemergence of the clergy as an authoritarian force and ruling class that distinguishes the Iranian experience, constitutes its originality, forecasts the possibility of theocracy as a form of modern statecraft, an unlooked-for development.

But then, everything in the Iranian revolution has been a surprise. It began as an insurgent's dream, the longed-for and improbable *levée en masse,* the miracle of non-violent and spontaneous opposition toward an old and finally insupportable tyranny—one that had suppressed dissent so thoroughly that this explosion of political will could never happen again. No organized parties were permissible, censorship was efficient. How could this even come about, this birth of consciousness, these waves of protest building upon each other? Beginning with the readings of outspoken rebel poetry at Teheran's Goethe Institute in 1977, leading to a series of defiant protests that could not be put down, gradually expanding to larger and larger street demonstrations, then the great coordinated strikes through the winter of 1978–79, each link in the popular front seeming to be almost fortuitous, a wonder. The Shah had killed the people's political will, created a desert and mined it with the secret agents of Savak. After twenty-five years of despotic monarchy, the political fabric had been either so damaged as to be useless or a material stored away so long as to have no strength or texture left. But now this flowering, this insistence, this general awakening: everyone demonstrated, bank clerks and bureaucrats went out on strike, the post office ground to a halt and the oil refineries, commerce stopped and life went into the streets. There it would occur, the miraculous showdown, a general confrontation with the last agencies of force. The people faced the army. On February 12, 1979, the army gave way to the people.

Iran: its mysterious revolution, that great unarmed population rising together against one of the largest and best-equipped armies in the world, this new historic precedent daring to oppose such visible force, winning through its courage and insistence, its own cavalier attitude toward death, its ability to accept martyrdom. Even more effective—the psychological warfare that the demonstrators carried out, tempting the soldiers to join them, baiting them only so far, maintaining careful discipline. The insurgents were restrained throughout, even when finally armed; the air force giving in to the demands of the people, refusing to shoot into the crowd any more, handing out guns.

But then, at the moment of its success, the insurrection is coopted, the revolution is taken over by the clergy. It was planned, a conscious theft, the open and loosely organized democratic forces no match for the superb manipulation of the clerical network, its brilliant if meaningless rhetoric of anti-imperialism. Cities had been organized by neighborhood committees; these in turn were linked with the mosques, places of safety and protected assembly, centers of news, information, coordination, and finally, through the device of the cassette tape and loudspeaker, the locus of clerical inspiration, the noble exiled voice of Ayatollah Khomeini, long persecuted by the Shah, speaking benignly from France—the moral arbiter of the insurrection praising democracy and sexual equality, piously reiterating the very principles for which the demonstrators had risked their lives.

First of all, the guns must be returned, handed in at the mosques. This was done. The popular front is doomed now. When arms were distributed again, they went to a section of the populace completely under clerical control, the "disinherited," unemployed migrant workers on the fringes of society, a lumpenproletariat empowered now through arms, euphoric with deputized authority, ubiquitous in street patrol, roadblock. Counterrevolution.

Everything changes: guns are everywhere, an irresponsible force in the hands of bullies; and behind this arbitrary macho one makes out the unlikely figure of the priest. The police, the army, and the gendarmerie have been replaced by these new creatures of the clergy: the *pasdaran,* the revolutionary guard, and, most shadowy of all, the paramilitary and ostensibly secret bands of men in the *Hezbollah* or Party of God. Power has come to the have-nots, whose only saving identity in city shanty towns was their religious affiliation, their loyalty to Islam and the clergy. Conservative, largely illiterate, feudal in their notion of order, they have nothing to lose and everything to gain as the clergy turns against democracy and tightens its control, using this new and intensely loyal militia to enforce increasingly authoritarian policies, alternately admitting and denying the violence which this "mass base" of "popular will" represents.

These bands are bused to demonstrations in order to fall upon and attack peaceful participants with chains, bricks, and clubs, acting out of an intense and carefully manipulated hatred directed early on toward targets like feminists and democrats, and later toward freedom of the press or political opposition groups like the People's Mojahadin. With the suppression of the women, half the task of consolidating power was achieved at one stroke. One gender was put over the other now, females were humbled, diminished, reduced beneath citizenship; male compliance was in good measure assured through this bribe of undisputed hegemony. Finally all power was concentrated in the divine person of the Ayatollah Khomeini, the Imam or Prophet.

A theocracy is a specific variety of authoritarian life with a characteristic emotional climate and feel, its fears and anxieties different in quality from those experienced under other forms of despotism, military dictatorship or absolute monarchy such as the Shah's regime which had come before. The very currents of power that flow through these systems are separate, unlike each other, as is their costume, manner, artifact. Their arrogance, their rejoicing in power is a different elation, a different euphoria. In feeling righteous, the minions of each system feel righteous in their own way.

The terror each invokes is a different terror. Consider that particular inner sensation of the gut and heart in the experience and exploitation of guilt under theocratic auspices: the one accused is, as it were, more accused, because indicted before a greater audience and by a higher power than the local and merely human. In Islamic theocracy, there is much sexual politics and sexual polarity since its first premise is a revitalized male supremacy upon which all other hierarchal thinking rests, the division between the sexes as central as sex itself is catastrophic.

For example: A woman accused of sexual license because she is without a veil is being assaulted on a number of charges, the most basic of which is her gender itself, and that gender is automatically and arbitrarily sexualized so that no act is really necessary to prove her guilt; it exists in her existence. The forces in contest are not simply the two sexes at their familiar odds in patriarchy, eternally in struggle even if statically dominant and subordinate. Now there is a higher presence using a loftier standard, which has already judged the issue, given its blessing to the male element, and brought the news of her defeat and unworthiness to the female with a certainty, a finality so great it has the force of surprise—as well as that of inevitability. The truth is now indisputable. There is no recourse now. Whatever had been potentially arbitrary in her fate, whatever might possibly be relative, local and parochial, different in other cultures, is now monumentally constant, immutable.

This is how she perceives it. How it is perceived from outside, by others, is clearer still, the puzzle of her guilt or innocence has been solved without reference to the two constituencies of male and female, each colored by their own interests, even by their sexual potential, itself compromising, tainted. In the permanent judgment of the supernatural the issue is decided almost by being raised: the temptation which the female represents to the male is a state known to exist, proven fact, so immanent in femaleness itself that the individual female need commit no act to be part of this, participates in it by her very existence. Innocence is impossible. Guilt is destiny, inherent in female being itself, unchangeable.

ALL decisions in theocratic circumstances are magnified, cut in stone. Even the smallest factions and disputes are intensified and enlarged when viewed in the prism of the eternal; a multiplication of power and significance takes place merely by the addition of the timeless dimension of the sacred. Everything now has the greatest possible import, implication, resonance. Crime becomes sin, and in so becoming it changes its nature utterly. Political crime is an already specious form of crime, and where it has no parallel in the criminal code, actually imaginary: for instance, an indictment for distributing pamphlets. But as crime is transformed into sin, political dissent becomes an offense of terrifying dimensions, no longer directed at the momentary character of those in power but an offense against power itself, eternal power, the very opposite of temporal government—holiness itself takes umbrage.

Everywhere under theocracy, the ephemeral becomes the eternal; petty event augments, distorts, aggrandizes itself. Authority may be deceptive, fraudulent, but now, under religious auspices, as hard to refute as any imponderable. Triumphant, inscrutable, disproportionate in its claims, in its imagined parallels between cause and effect, human activity and divine ordination. And what scope it affords for crimes of the mind, crimes of attitude, belief, opinion.

Interior as all criteria will be henceforth, as resolutely psychological, the smallest intention is equivalent to the action taken, the deed done. The potential and the real are no longer distinguishably different. Attitude and act are finally indissoluble. Because the heart is at issue, the will, intention—there is no privacy, no place to hide, even to hide a thought, a passing impulse. Control is absolute.

Theocracy is the most entire form of government, and life in Iran seems to prove this, day-to-day living since the proclamation of the Islamic Republic is affected even to the most minor details of personal experience and private behavior. Alcohol is absolutely forbidden and under pretext of searching for it any house may be entered at virtually any moment, so that what are customarily private social gatherings have acquired a novel "political" meaning. So too has the sanctity of private homes and apartments, liable to be invaded at any moment, invasions that routinely discover other offenses than the ones for which they were undertaken.

The state has not only taken a stand on alcohol—generally something most government regulates but does not proscribe, content to permit its use as part of civil or personal life—but in Iran it has taken a stand on music too, proscribing nearly all varieties except for the religiously correct or the nationalistically classical. Other sorts of music, as well as dance and film, are criminalized, and punishment is often swift and intrusive. Sexuality is also a carefully state monitored event in Iran, with dire penalties and considerable surveillance.

Claims to privacy and private life have little meaning since the Islamic Republic is only realized when *shari'a,* Islamic canon law, is fully implemented in every detail and facet of life—and not one of these is outside the purview of religion. No separation of church and state is ever intended. Instead, their unity is meant to be ensured by all public legislation. In fundamentalist thinking, the public and private spheres are never mutually exclusive, never even bifurcated: they are meant to be the same, one seamless whole before the relentless eye of sacred authority.

The law is immutable and does not bend, it can be honored at home as well as in the public court. In cases of sexual crime, a trial at home is preferable in that it avoids scandal and protects the family name. *Shari'a* may extend permission to hold a family court, even to execute its sentence in private. Enormous powers are then directly conferred on the male members of the family, virtually the power of life and death. In the final scene of Jane Rawlinson's novel *The Lion and the*

Lizard,* the son of the house, an ambitious young Islamic guard, takes it upon himself to execute a sentence of death on his sister for having borne an illegitimate child. The idea of family is mocked as they sit around the kitchen table, parents and siblings, their unity destroyed by this travesty of judgment. Islamic principle carried to its logical conclusion is grotesque and barbaric; the brother imagines himself entitled to shoot one sister pointblank with a revolver and then bestow a younger sister upon an aged priest in "temporary" marriage or concubinage. It is a sordid conclusion to the hope the revolution had inspired. It is also an anatomy of the forces that bore that hope away.

IN the clerical courts themselves, sentences of execution may be delivered after a few moments hearing before a single Islamic judge. There is no provision for appeal. Trials are held in secret, defendants have no attorneys and are not permitted to call witnesses. Prisoners may be held for years without trial; Amnesty International reports on Iran even refer to cases where prisoners have been tried and then not informed of their sentences. From the beginning, revolutionary justice was swift and in a hurry: Khomeini's Prosecutor-General, the cleric Sadeq Khalkhali, worked "round the clock" to send the "enemies of Islam" before firing squads, aware that this "wave" of public feeling would "recede" and then his activities would be limited: "Therefore while we had the opportunity and the time," and Khomeini's own urgent mandate, "I executed them all for their crimes. According to the letter of the Qur'an they were 'corruptors on earth' and had to be killed."†

Thousands of Iranians have since been executed for their political beliefs. Over seventeen hundred executions took place

---

*(New York: St. Martin's Press, 1986).
†Quoted in Ali Rahnema and Farhad Nomani, *The Secular Miracle: Religion, Politics and Economic Policy in Iran* (London: Zed Books, 1990).

in the last six weeks of the Iran-Iraq War between the end of July 1988 and the beginning of January 1989. In the five months that followed, another nine hundred executions took place, criminal or political, the difference often lost in sexual politics where a death sentence is awarded for adultery or homosexuality. The execution of homosexuals has now taken on a public and ritual character meant to stamp out such behavior forever.

If one survives political imprisonment in Iran it is often only after a lengthy and humiliating self-denunciation on public television; tortured or otherwise intimidated, one is forced to renounce one's principles and associates after having signed statements of loyalty to the Islamic Republic. Prisoners may then be released into a kind of cat-and-mouse parole whereby they, or a relative who must serve as their substitute, can be recalled and imprisoned at any time. Prisoners are also forced to sign statements that they will never disclose their experiences in prison to anyone, thereby protecting their torturers. Even after serving one's term, release is conditional on signing a vow of repentance.

It is all so entire. Added on to the prescriptive and prohibitive forces of the state are all those now of virtue and vice, sin and damnation, honor and lies, false vows and secrecy. Moral territory is usurped and conquered by official authority and the social strategy of religious devotion. When legal or physical control over the person is added to all this through arrest and detention—the traditional powers of the state now vastly increased by the addition of the supernatural—the result is awesome, total, more entire than anything we have known for centuries. It may be a new departure. Perhaps Iran is only a precursor, the first of what may come to be a number of Islamic Republics, founded on a political interpretation of the fundamentalism spreading throughout the Muslim world in groups like the Muslim Brotherhood and Hezbollah, Iran merely the harbinger of a new theocratic state.

/   /   /

ONCE established, the practice of torture seems to become applicable to any group or situation. A convenience, a way of dealing with certain elements, certain social problems, a brutality that establishes itself as expedient. Disappearance, for example: begun on "politicals," it has spread in many places to the treatment of criminals. The idea of human "trash" takes hold in the minds of security and police authority. Perhaps its most tragic use at the present is against children.

There are locations where such abuses became extraordinary, as in the widespread torture of children in South Africa following the uprisings in Soweto; there are also places where the torture of children is routine and consistent, that is, governments that torture suspects will torture suspected children as well.

This is the case in Turkey. Helsinki Watch attorney Lois Whitman, in an Op-Ed piece for *The New York Times* (Friday, January 3, 1992), describes several cases of the torture of children apprehended on both criminal and political grounds such as distributing leaflets; for this offense a sixteen-year-old Turkish girl was badly beaten and held for two months. Whitman herself interviewed nine children between the ages of thirteen and seventeen, all of whom had been abused in detention. Helsinki Watch has reports of dozens of other cases of the torture of Turkish children in custody. Their families were never notified of their whereabouts; all of them were incarcerated in adult prisons, none were permitted to see lawyers during their interrogations. A child of fifteen accused of robbery was detained for four days, during which he was subjected to falaka, the soles of his feet beaten, then his whole body beaten with clubs while he hung suspended upside down, naked and blindfolded. He was then handcuffed to the door of his cell and beaten again, suspended again by the arms and given electric shock. This child then signed a confession, since repudiated. Turkish authorities consistently deny allegations of torture: Turkish attorneys charge that torture is routine in 80 to 90 percent of political cases and 50 percent of criminal cases. Turkey is a signatory state both to the European and the United Nations Conventions Against Torture.

There are indications that the torture of children may become more specific. Destitute and defenseless, children of the street are becoming targets of disappearance and death, the victims of what are now habits of cruelty, established practices of dealing with the unwanted human being. At first there were only scattered press references and reports of this phenomenon in Guatemala, although the numbers of children murdered by death squads, the police, and the military in Brazil and Iraq had indicated a disturbing pattern; by now UNICEF has gathered information on the torture and disappearance of children in many countries which indicates strong tendencies in some, emergencies in others.

Death squad culture has created a scenario now, a manner of locating and apprehending a target, the scapegoat vanishing only to reappear as the mutilated example of an existence that will not be tolerated: communism, destitution, overpopulation, feral childhood. These are street children, beggars, some of them addicted to "glue," some of them migrants or refugees of counter-insurgency, some abandoned—place, land, and parents lost, no longer even remembered. Their numbers grow, they are a "problem," an increasing social phenomenon perceived as an offshoot of criminality and addiction throughout the region; drugs a familiar excuse for police brutality whereby the desperate condition of these children may be construed as corruption rather than poverty. Their presence is offensive in the eyes of security: conspicuous, a blemish to the public image, not only an embarrassment before visitors but a threat to tourist income.

Their very being suggests the stray, an insult to order and ownership and family cohesion. There is about them an inevitable lawlessness because they are also utterly indigent and dependant for sustenance upon garbage or petty crime, sleeping in the open in ditches, ravines, culverts, or protected only by cardboard and other scraps of material. The children of no one, wandering outside a social order where children are dependent for existence upon being the acknowledged property of adults. Unacknowledged, then, without public resources of any kind, deprived of any type of collective support that might constitute "permission" to exist, they exist anyway; without permission, that is without parents or sponsors. It is an existence increasingly precarious in authoritarian society, and in view of the growing brutality of police methods and the hardening of attitude that accompanies the use of torture in social policy, increasingly perilous as well.

In Guatemala, these children are being subjected to police brutality which ranges from casual torture during round-ups to mutilation, disappearance, and death. According to Amnesty International sources and W. E. Gutman's report in *Omni* magazine (November 1991), which includes information supplied by the child advocacy group Casa Alianza and is accompanied by a large number of photographs of disfigured and mutilated young corpses, the perpetrators of these crimes against children in Guatemala are police and security personnel. Sometimes police patrols operating in plainclothes or hiding their badges; at other times police officers working second jobs, "moonlighting" by operating as executioners "on behalf of local municipalities and private businesses." A third type are members of private security corporations that are licensed by the national police and the Ministry of the Interior. For all the evidence of their crimes, these men are rarely tried or indicted.

There is little outrage or sentimentality over these deaths, since the lives in question are not those of beloved offspring but understood to be a kind of public nuisance. In view of the "delays, irregularities and blatant reversals connected with official inquiries" into these cases, Amnesty feels that children's rights have been continuously subordinated to trade and diplomatic concerns. Meanwhile worldwide there are some 100 million street children living in fear of their lives, many of whom "disappear, are beaten, illegally detained and confined, sexually exploited, tortured and systematically killed by agents of the state." Gutman and Amnesty list twenty-two countries where children are systematically sexually exploited, as in the Philippines, Taiwan, Sri Lanka, and Thailand, or illegally imprisoned and tortured, as in Argentina, Brazil, Bolivia, El Salvador, Iraq, South Africa, and Turkey, and where they may also be executed either extra-judicially or legally, as in the United States, where fourteen states have juveniles on death row.

In Guatemala, there is much evidence of a police policy of unrelenting brutality toward homeless and addicted children. Gutman describes the murder of one such child called Nahaman, an adolescent glue addict fatally beaten by a policeman and casually left to die in the street:

> When the children returned about 30 minutes later, Nahaman had managed to move a few feet. He had lost bowel and bladder control. He was unconscious. Someone had covered him with paper flowers and a piece of white crepe, as is customary in Guatemala when children die. Nahaman was taken by ambulance to San Juan de Dios, a state-run hospital. No police report was filed—he was registered as "XX" (unknown)—nor was a medical exam performed. Comatose, Nahaman was suffering convulsions and urinating blood. In addition to six fractured ribs, the boy sustained two broken fingers and open wounds to his cheeks and head. . . . He also had a three-inch gash on his back. Surgery was performed in an attempt to repair Nahaman's liver and save his life. Despite recurring convulsions, no brain scan was ever done. He never regained consciousness and died ten days later.*

*W. E. Gutman, *Omni* magazine (November 1991).

Gutman also reports that Bruce Harris of Casa Alianza, who filed the charges against Nahaman's murderers, was afterwards so harassed by Guatemalan police he had to leave the country and now lives in Mexico. Four officers were actually convicted of the child's murder, but there are now government efforts to invalidate those proceedings on the grounds of an alleged typographical error in the court documents.

Forty Guatemalan children have been killed by the police in 1991–92, some bodies showing particular signs of torture, the ears cut off, the eyes gouged out or burned. As if in admonition, tongues were cut out as well. The terrible impunity, the dizzying possibilities of death squad activity must be very strong in crimes against such children. Anything can be done to them, there is no hindrance; consider the void that surrounds homeless youth, the absence of friends and protectors. Look again at their physical vulnerability, their small stature.

This is perhaps also how the police think of women and girls as incidents of rape by the police become widespread; in a recent Amnesty report, this abuse is now said to have reached epidemic proportions: there is the most recent example of mass rape in Bosnia. All throwaway children are sexually victimized, but girls are aggressed upon with disproportionate frequency under patriarchy, where a deliberate conditioning toward passivity and fatality has rendered them extraordinarily vulnerable. Two generally separate categories, political torture and the "apolitical" customary sexual assault and domestic torture of women so routine within patriarchy, not only intersect here but even merge at times in a new perception of sexual politics. When the police themselves are the agents of rape, even the rape of minors, one begins to see unmeasured opportunities for impunity, a terrible power set loose upon the helpless condition of childhood before state authority. We are in Closet Land once again, staring at the ranked hierarchies of state and gender and age, hemmed in by the cloying air of domination, the dynamic of cruelty.

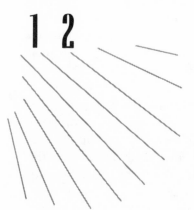

12

CONCLUSION

ULTIMATELY, as individuals we are all helpless before the state, the collective power of armies and governments, the voices that order us to halt in the street. Or command that we push the buzzer and let them up the stairs. When the group that has come to get us is at the door, it is late to begin considering the possibilities of organized opposition. But the knowledge of torture is itself a political act, just as silence or ignorance of it have political consequence. To speak of the unspeakable is the beginning of action.

One of the ways we discuss torture is ask the question: what to do with the torturers when dictatorial regimes give way to democracy? The torturer remains in the midst of those he has wronged. Shall he be accosted, accused, and judged? Imprisoned, or merely removed from office? Or forgiven? Or awarded a total amnesty? One wonders why the last choice is even considered, but in fact it is frequently the chosen course. Why? Because democracy is fragile still, because the army could stage a coup, because civil rule is not yet consolidated and exists only on the sufferance of the military caste.

Because the politics of cruelty is understood to be only in abeyance, hidden behind a curtain for a while. One catches sight of the telltale army shoes, an image registered on the collective optic screen, a presence stamped upon consciousness, pervasive beneath the nervous politician's rhetoric. The officer corps responsible for torture will ultimately stand together, refuse to permit its membership to be convicted, and insist on some form of amnesty. In challenging its infallibility, one challenges force itself, perhaps even state power and legitimacy.

Lawrence Weschler's *A Miracle, a Universe* deals with these questions directly in the case both of Brazil and Uruguay. As its subtitle, *Settling Accounts with Torturers,* suggests, the question of the army's obedience to civil authority leads to the greater question of the legitimacy or the necessity for an army of this size and power—given the depravity of which it has been capable. If there were real trials, if accounts were settled, the results would be very significant: "A military which would be shown—not just known, but shown—to have indulged in such systematically dishonorable, disfiguringly dishonorable activities" might not only lose its honor, Weschler speculates, "which had always been a sort of fiction," but even "the populace's suspended disbelief in that fiction." Questioning this far, one stumbles upon "potentially *magic* truths" with very real consequences as to the military's "budget, assigned mission, continued control over its own indoctrination and promotion practices, its tutelary power over the wider population." After all, *"Who finally knew how far the military would go to prevent such things from being said?"** The meaning and future of militarism itself might be at stake. But, in fact, accounts are not being settled.

There is not merely saying, there is doing. There is the publication of the truth of what really happened in the days of

---

*(New York: Viking Penguin, 1990), p. 217 (italics in the original).

dictatorship and there is the possibility of trial and judgment of those events. This is a great range of consequence, all of it ultimately dependent upon how much power the military still holds and what it will now permit civil society to experience of either truth or justice. This is a dilemma in many places: Argentina, Guatemala, Brazil, Chile, Uruguay. Only Argentina actually put its torturers on trial, and of all those hundreds it accused, convicted only a handful. Even this caused such military resentment that there have been a number of attempted coups since the trials began in 1975. Upon taking office in 1989, President Carlos Menem extended executive pardons to officers still facing trial while indicating that the few who had been convicted might be pardoned as well.

If not justice, then truth? The military would thwart either one. But of the two, the desire for truth is the more basic and urgently felt by all the victims of a society which has undergone torture. As Weschler puts it: "People don't necessarily insist that the former torturers go to jail—there's been enough of jail—but they do want to see the truth established." Even though it is known (people know who the torturers are and the torturers know it too), the truth must be investigated in a formal way, socially recognized. Or, as Weschler quotes Professor Thomas Nagel of New York University, the distinction is between "knowledge and acknowledgement, that is, what happens to knowledge when it becomes officially sanctioned, when it is made part of the public cognitive scene," a transformation that is "sacramental."*

This is certainly true of the accounts of victims which both Argentina and Uruguay have published under the title *Never Again (Nunca Más)*. It is also true of the great Brazilian version of events, *Nunca Mais,* the Report of the Archdiocese of São Paulo, compiled (as we saw earlier) in secret during five years of lingering repression, and using, for once, not the testimony of victims but the records of the Supreme Military

*Weschler, p. 4.

Court itself, the torturers convicting themselves in their own words and from their own files, through 1 million pages of transcript "borrowed" surreptitiously so that it could be Xeroxed and analyzed by members of a group led by Cardinal Arns and Jaime Wright. It was a dangerous project and necessarily secret, so secret that the identities of its members are still largely unknown. To prevent discovery and destruction of the documents, they were stored in several places and microfilmed in Geneva. The raw data is an invaluable archive of government misdemeanor, and the two finished products of the study—a thirty-volume version for university research and a single volume for the public—will stand as permanent sources of life under such a regime. The latter has a wider readership than any book in Brazilian history and is meant to be such a definitive account of the years 1964–79 that there may be no reoccurrence.

But reversion is a constant danger. Once a society becomes as regimented as Argentina, Brazil, or Uruguay, as dominated by inquisitorial ideology and security controls and surveillance, reversion is always possible, remains as near as the resumption of military rule—for which civilian politicians have frequently been responsible. They are so again in voting for blanket amnesties which grant the military virtual impunity. The party and the army cut deals, the politicians forgive all, playing it safe, propitiating the armed forces. The victims lose their rights, so do the people at large. Consider Uruguay, where there was an attempt, by popular plebiscite, to overturn the congressional vote whereby professional politicians had extended total amnesty to the previous military regime. A grass-roots campaign was organized to reverse this gift of impunity through a popular referendum. Every obstacle was put in the way of obtaining the referendum: a staggering number of signatures (one sixth of the population) was required just to initiate the ballot. Then a year passed while government contested the signatures on the most specious grounds and harassed those who had dared to sign. But enough had, and it came to a vote. However, by that time the citizenry had been muddled and intimidated, unremitting propaganda and advertising had created a majority who, through exhaustion and confusion, would finally endorse the government position that to grant amnesty to the army for its crimes would preserve the new peace of democracy.

The amnesty itself had violated Uruguay's own commitments to the UN Conventions Against Torture. Then the results of the referendum, in permitting crime to be excused by a special plebiscite, violated the principle of equal protection before the law, which is fundamental to it. So is the principle of governmental accountability: rebels and criminals pay dearly; the state is increasingly unaccountable. It is as if the Germans had voted after the war to excuse Nazi crimes against the Jews. In Uruguay, too, the new "democratic" government had now come to be the protector and apologist of the previous military regime.

And the torture never ends, because it is never admitted to, the torturer's famous boast—"no one will ever know, no one will ever hear you, no one will ever find out"—continues, holds true. One asks, what is torture, and of course it is being roused out of bed and put in a hood, and taken away to beatings and drownings and shocks. But, as victims point out, one could also be abducted and imprisoned somewhere to hear others scream for weeks on end . . . and, even if they didn't beat you, you had been tortured—you signed a false confession. For all coercion that leads to confession is torture. And most of all torture is fear: if you knew it would last only a stated interval, perhaps you could bear it; it's the not knowing, the uncertainty of menace, that drives you to panic. Not just what they do to you, but what they may do to you next, what they have the power to do to you, at any moment, at every moment. Torture is all potentiality, endless possibility. And if the world keeps silent afterward, torture is not only victorious but permanent, eternal. Continuous.

Elaine Scarry, in her wonderful essay on the "structure of

torture" in *The Body in Pain*,* calls torture a dialogue between the voice of the interrogator asking the question and the flesh of the prisoner absorbing that all-consuming pain, which blots out the whole world and all perception, thought, memory, past, principle—covering every inch of consciousness until the victim is nothing but the pain he/she experiences. The confession, which even sympathetic observers take to be a betrayal, is nothing less than the loss of the prisoner's world and values in that pain, a destruction, a torture and crime in itself. It is to pain that one loses the soul when the whole wide world is reduced to the body, the victim's world shrinking as the torturer's expands into the fiction of his political power, a fiction built upon nothing but the actual suffering of a victim. But as Weschler comments upon Scarry, here lies the dilemma: for those who live for others and for social ideas, the body defeats them with its pain and despair before the absolute solitude of human existence, essentially a solitude before death. A terrible knowledge is born of this pain. The scream of the victim is the body calling out to the soul, the self calling out to others. Both will go unheard, unanswered. The lesson of torture is this silence. Just as the torturer boasts—no one will ever hear you, no one will ever know, no one will ever discover.

For that reason, then, the silence must end, must be broken, the victim's voice be restored, since otherwise the torturers are never negated or defeated or even counterbalanced, they are merely in or out of power. The moments when they are out of power hardly absences at all since their message is not really refuted during those periods, only softened. And as the torturer comes back into power or remains amnestied quietly on the sidelines, awaiting his chance again—against his world of force there is no saving equivalent in expression. The silence, continuing, continues the injustice and thereby prolongs the torment, for the essence of torture is its deliberate cruelty, its

---

*Elaine Scarry, "The Making and Unmaking of the World" in *The Body in Pain* (New York and London: Oxford University Press, 1985).

willed immorality, its conscious inequity. A laughter that mocks.

AND how easy it is to become complicit. To share this laughter, or the smile that breaks across our face unconsciously, against our will—the way we laugh at someone falling down. Not really because it's funny, but because it surprises, catches us off guard. We smile this way too when afraid, when not really amused but nervous. Such smiles often become a complicity with what we hate; they betray us, or we betray ourselves in smiling, the response almost an involuntary reaction, a spasm. With impressive honesty Lawrence Weschler describes an occasion when he is betrayed into such a smile while interviewing General Medina, the former military dictator of Uruguay, now its minister of defense. It is an occasion when Medina admits to his regime's policy of torture: "A man after being arrested was interrogated, according to his characteristics, energetically or mildly," Medina puts it, still careful of his language. "Energetically?" Weschler pursues, a reporter after all.

"Energetically in the case of a man who refused to speak."
"Energetically, meaning what?"

> He was silent for a moment, his smile steady. For him, this was clearly a game of cat and mouse. His smile horrified me, but presently I realized that I'd begun smiling back. (It seemed clear that the interview had reached a crisis; either I was going to smile back, showing that I was the sort of man who understood these things, or the interview was going to be abruptly over.) So I smiled and now I was doubly horrified by the very fact that I was smiling. I'm sure he realized this, because he now smiled all the more, precisely at the way he'd gotten me to smile and how obviously horrified I was to be doing so. He swallowed me whole.

The smile is everything, for humor slides into neutrality, even approbation. We become complicit below the rational level, below speech or admission—like a drug or music or movement to rhythm. In a fine and now neglected novel of totalitarian life in Romania, *Incognito,** Petru Dumitriu describes the same phenomenon of the smile. A Socialist invited some Soviet officers to dinner. They got roaring drunk and raped his wife and daughter. "The unfortunate thing," the standard Party apologist explains to the narrator the next day, "is that they rammed a bottle into his wife, and she had a hemorrhage and died a few hours later." The narrator listens, the Party member smiles. "It is the smile of a man no longer capable of any pleasure, natural or perverse, except that of acquiescing in a will outside himself." The narrator has seen it often on the faces of Party workers through a lifetime of Byzantine intrigue, betrayal, investigation, and denunciation. Coming from an entirely different direction it approaches Weschler's smile, the able reporter of *The New Yorker* momentarily impaled by the will of a military dictator; perhaps he too experiences what Dumitriu calls "the sensation of absolute power and at the same time the pang of abject submission."

Another of Dumitriu's characters, a philosophic torturer, rhapsodizes over his "science": "the most ancient of the fine arts, older than the so-called art of love and certainly richer and more varied. The art of love is nothing but a dozen positions and a couple of dozen refinements, but torture has a thousand varieties. All animals can couple, but man is the only animal that tortures." For torture is social, a case of the group against the individual: "All you need is a collective, constituted group operating on a man in isolation. The group, as we know, is stronger than the individual and torture is the first way of proving it."†

The smile then is a kind of a social reflex; we smile in identifying—even if involuntarily or momentarily—with the society which force has brought into being. It is a smile of

---

*Translated by Norman Denny (New York: Macmillan, 1964), p. 208.
†Dumitriu, p. 299.

coerced but irresponsible complicity, a scared, frozen smile; intimidated, it "goes along"—which is enough. Dumitriu's narrator comes to realize that terror is "a generalized state affecting all society," but also a collective responsibility: "It is the work of all members of society, who accept it, tolerate it, acquiesce in it, more or less consciously and openly" . . . and finally it envelops as society envelops the individual. By then of course it is too late. And the individual is nothing against torture; that is the whole point of its practice: to annihilate the single objector.

One may not even need to smile in collusion; perhaps the conditioned tendency to obey authority is sufficient for most citizens. In Stanley Milgram's classic study *Obedience to Authority,** naive college students cast as "teachers" in a university experiment on learning and memory delivered massive amounts of electric shock to other students cast as "learners," simply because they were repeatedly ordered to by an "experimental scientist." Abridging his book for *Harper's* magazine in an article entitled "The Perils of Obedience," Milgram states that most of his subjects who delivered shock did so out of a "sense of obligation," which leads him to agree with Hannah Arendt's contention that evil is essentially banal and to conclude that directed cruelty does not require a sadistic personality: "That is, perhaps, the most fundamental lesson of our study: ordinary people, simply doing their jobs, and without any particular hostility on their part, can become agents in a terrible destructive process. Moreover, even when the destructive effects of their work become patently clear, and they are asked to carry out actions incompatible with fundamental standards of morality, relatively few people have the resources needed to resist authority."†

If one adds to this the force of state permission, patriotic service, and the motivation of special training, the incentives of

---

*(New York: Harper & Row, 1974).
†Stanley Milgram, "The Perils of Obedience," *Harper's* (December 1973).

increased status, privilege, and rewards, one comes to see how routinely the sadistic energy of the professional torturer is the creation of circumstance rather than personal inclination or special predisposition.

WHY does one study torture? Read about it, think about it, analyze and "obsess" over it. Because of hating it, fearing it, having felt or imagined or somehow experienced it. Because of wanting to see it end. How does one end torture? One doesn't—the question is as hopeless as asking how one ends war. Yet, on the simplest level this essay was embarked upon out of just such an absurd desire, wish, impetus—as if speaking up in outrage were a a way to "do something about it." But having surveyed the devastation of torture in so many places, its growth, its future, its habitual use by government on the one hand, and the blasé acceptance of torture by populations who are not directly affected on the other—one begins to experience a certain futility, the sensation of shouting against the wind.

And yet . . . Amnesty's emblem is a candle in the wind wrapped in barbed wire, the wire encircling, the candle flame bent but not blown out; maintaining itself. One doesn't end torture, it is brought to an end. Slowly and with enormous effort, friction, energy, like a locomotive brought gradually to a standstill. For we are dealing with momentum here. There are moments when it seems futile and yet, as the old freedom song reminds us, "one and one make a million," suggesting an effort of vast numbers, worldwide, something that large. A collective will. Something missing still or only being born and as yet too young, and small. Despite the efforts of Amnesty, World Watch, Helsinki Watch, Americas Watch, and all the other non-governmental groups that monitor or take action; the term "non-governmental" itself a clue.

One is almost tempted to go further and use the phrase "anti-governmental," since it is the governments—even the governments who are signatories to the UN Conventions Against Torture—who offend. The United States, for example, which offends more abroad than at home, though it is not without offense there as well, has been extremely slow to ratify.* A Special International Tribunal convoked at Hunter College in 1990 concluded that the United States does in fact violate the conventions in holding political prisoners, sentencing them disproportionately, and violating their rights through cruel and degrading treatment in its prisons, particularly the U.S. Federal Penitentiary in Marion, Illinois, and the Women's High Security Unit at Lexington, Kentucky, object of popular outcry for its program of ¢ensory deprivation in underground cells, constant illumination, and absolute isolation. Numbers of notable American political prisoners such as Leonard Peltier serve outlandish terms, some in solitary under inhumane conditions.

While governments must truly concur in abolition, it is unlikely they will do so without popular pressure. Conventions against torture, like all pledges and promises, are only as good as the power to enforce them and the means of redress when violated: means of an international court or authority to whom any citizen might apply—means presently not at hand. Implementation is crucial: guarantees of extradition to safety, indictment of the offending authorities, power of appeal against one's own nation state. The sovereignty of the nation state itself is a great obstacle to the abolition of torture.

There is nationalism at the popular level, and on the level of government itself, multinational or transnational economic power—these forces put torture in place and keep it there. As long as we identify culture and language and love of place with nation and national government, we are vulnerable to patriotic manipulation; as government's power increases, there is a concurrent increase in manipulation. To have any effect on state

*The United States did not ratify the 1984 UN Conventions Against Torture until the fall of 1992.

power, even to see and apprehend it, one must, as a first step, transcend nationalism. Amnesty and the other non-governmental groups are effective just because they ignore borders and identify through common humanity.

The term "citizen"—which historically followed the term "subject," a new term once and full of a sense of "rights" and "prerogatives"—now often serves to remind us how these entitlements have wilted under the state's greater and greater amassment of power in modern centralization of control, technically facilitated with computerlike speed: records, files, information itself becoming a hand closing over the arm of any one of these citizens. The feeling of subjection returns.

One may plausibly "take" this situation or "leave it," accept or deny, if not in exile, then in "ixile," that state of inner retreat people inhabit when public life is unendurable. But in today's "one world," there is no place to go. Since one cannot really leave, leaving must be transformed into changing, a change so beneficial to the majority of people on earth it seems strange it is not already in place. Yet dealing with power means dealing with what has gone on for a long while and with great cumulative energy. And when energy gathers finally on an opposite pole it comes in some circumstances to revolution, reversal, an overturning. This often begins a new series of abuses, tortures, excused by new "necessities."

Reason and the rule of law seem better and better guides, in the long run, both "revolutionary" and "radical" by virtue of the rights they have won for us in the past, rights jeopardized on so many fronts in the present. Already eroded in some quarters, they may be overwhelmed in the future. Torture is an index of unfreedom; it calls out to us in its essential obscenity: frenzied, passionate, in search of revenge, cruelty wanting repetition, its mirror image. Law transcends this, reason refuses to repeat. Reform may initiate a movement, a wide campaign for abolition.

Hope is crucial here. Despair is submission to the threat of unendurable torment, if not our own, then another's. But it is, after all, another's fate and not our own. Whom would we not betray to escape torture? Whom would we not substitute in our place on the parrot's perch? Better that one than me, we say in our hearts; even the best of us know this much self-interest. The politics of cruelty applied to you or me through its inherently extreme and exaggerated circumstances will obtain as long as we can be isolated, made to feel separate or alien, as long as we can be intimidated one by one. Knowing, each of us, that before the prospect of our own torture, we would betray.

Therefore we must prevent that prospect from ever occurring. Or reoccurring. Here or elsewhere. Torture cannot be prohibited without an attack upon state power, limiting it, pruning it back to democratic proportions, imposing strict limitations upon its increasing luxuriance. One wonders if the time for that has already passed. Or has not yet come into being.

MEANWHILE, one deals with immediate suffering, attending to the greatest harm first, listening for and heeding the cries, reacting humanly, sensibly, efficiently, even objectively as does Amnesty, taking no sides except that of the victim, acting "without politics" in the ordinary sectarian sense. Yet only politics itself, in the profound sense, can deal with torture at its root, the assumption of the power to torture by the state, or perhaps the reassumption of this power as prerogative. Given its unquestioned powers to incarcerate—which is everything, or nearly everything: sequestration and secrecy, physical restraint and the shaping of physical and psychic experience (expanded by detention, particularly if detention is clandestine)—given these powers, the exercise of torture is only a logical extension of power itself. When the individual is so controlled and hemmed in, so easy to isolate and oppress, although torturers tend to be lazy people in a hurry, to carry this power over into torture is inordinate indulgence.

How does the state come by its powers? Through its monopoly on force and its capacity to incarcerate. Therefore it has always had them, relinquished them only after long campaigns of agitation produced certain restraints which eventually curtailed them. But only for a while, since vigilance is the price of this type of freedom. In a sense, therefore, the state has simply reassumed these powers, slipped back into them as its claims were permitted to grow and magnify themselves through unchallenged arguments of revolutionary necessity, military necessity, counter-insurgent necessity, the complex necessities of national security—for all of which one must read its own self-interest, its hold on power.

A consolidated power, not merely of this particular government, regime, administration but the state itself, its accumulated force as it would be passed on to the next cast of military officers or even law-abiding civil bureaucrats. That power has advanced steadily and we have permitted it. To curtail it now may be late and difficult. Uncontrolled, it is terrible and has produced the present, this growing nightmare of force, torture only its most obvious excrescence. There is the prospect of it proliferating or going on untrammelled; yet even continuing as it does, it produces crime from which only the accident of place removes one.

Certain governments now "get by with murder" because the fortunate citizens of other governments completely fail to identify with their unfortunate fellows, are effectively "nationalized," confidently imagining "these people" deserve their fate. Anyway it's not their affair, they are the happy citizens of State A, which does not torture its citizens; as for the woeful conditions in State B, they are something else again. Imagining the two unrelated, accidental, a matter of luck. Or as Page duBois explains the dynamic in *Torture and Truth,* "Torture has become a global spectacle, a comfort to the so-called civilized nations," their proof of the "continued barbarism of the other world," the Third World "which has become, beside the site of torture, the spectacle of the other tortured for us."*

THE collective will toward abolition, small and weak as it is, is likely to succeed first at the abolition of physical torture, somatic torture, torture to the body itself. But this success would not prevent the growth of psychological torture. In Uruguay, for example, prisoners brought out of clandestine detention and interviewed by reassuring psychologists upon their admission to acknowledged public prisons were promised they would not be mistreated any more. In fact, their every confidence was systematically betrayed by a highly sophisticated behavioral psychology completely at the service of the state. As Lawrence Weschler describes Libertad Prison in Uruguay, the declared purpose of the regime was to drive one mad, a deliberate manipulation of sanity and suffering.† All punishment was in relation to the rules, but the rules are secret and are changed every day. The declared purpose is to break the prisoner by destroying his mind, and every effort of behavioral science is brought to bear to accelerate this. Guards are trained to show aversion, films are projected out of focus, it is forbidden to sing, laugh, smile—everything has emblematic meaning, to draw a rose brings a month in solitary as ideological punishment. There are two prisoners to each cell but only one chair; since it is forbidden to sit on the bed, one prisoner must pace or stand at all times.

The prison itself is a panopticon, where everything is visible; the larger society begins to replicate a panopticon as well. The logic behind all this surveillance and imprisonment is generally economic; in this case, the military government had put its hopes in the free market theories of Chicago economist Milton Friedman, or as the Uruguayan writer Eduardo Galeano put it,

*(New York: Routledge, 1991), p. 157.
†Weschler, p. 147.

people were in prison so that prices could be free. With governments, one thing leads to another.

The potential to abuse the person inherent in the power to
arrest and confine expands with special powers legislation and
the practice of using secret places—prison itself becoming a
magic location, the house next door, anywhere at all. Torture
may be secret, but the news of it leaks out; people know.
Unsure as they are, they know something. But when legal and
constitutional protections have been lost or eroded, progress
against torture is likely to be a contest between state power
and aroused public opinion, a new and difficult campaign
merely to recover what has been lost. People hear in fear, in
horror, in dread. But not in outrage, not in sufficient numbers
of effective anger. Not yet.

THOSE who have undergone torture return now to become
a special category of persons, either our source of information
or "victims," exceptional cases originally attended with heroic
compassion by pioneers like Dr. Inge Kemp Genefke of the
Research Center for Torture Victims in Copenhagen. There
even the dialogue of therapy had to be reexamined for its
resemblance to the structure of interrogation. But as the idea
spreads, one sees its humane potential diluted by a neglect of
the social and political meaning of torture. In a new center for
torture victims in Minneapolis, the care extended is both physical and psychological, the damage sometimes including certain permanent physical effects as well as psychological damage—which is a constant—but in Minneapolis this is dealt
with in a peculiarly American way. In order to "qualify for
benefits," that is, state and public assistance in food, housing,
and treatment, the victim first has to be "diagnosed" by American standard psychiatric practice—as it were for an illness, a
mental illness, a psychiatrically mediated "disorder."

The psychiatric explanation of torture as "post-traumatic
shock syndrome" comes to replace a political and social under-

standing of torture. And with considerable political effect, moreover. And so the victim of governmental brutality, a physical brutality committed upon political and ideological grounds, becomes the disordered mental condition of another government's begrudging psychiatric charity in a void where politics have ceased to exist. So have ethics. In their place a mysterious disease model has taken over, the victim victimized again, diminished again. Since most of the torture victims of this American center are from South American dictatorships, client states of the American government, there is a poignant irony in the "diagnosis and treatment" model here, a quality of imperialism in action, an aspect which its practitioners fail to notice.

In fact, torture is becoming more and more a "branch of medicine," twofold for either for good or ill, like black and white magic: on the one hand, medical personnel assist the torturers inflicting pain; on the other, medical personnel assist the tortured in their recovery once torture has ceased. The psychologists and psychiatrists who "define" the experience of torture to those who have in fact experienced it can also change and manipulate its meaning. Increasingly, the mind as well as the body is at issue in torture, and tormenting the mind grows into a wider and wider field, expanding rapidly through behavioral modification and drugs. The greater sympathy lies with the body in general, the more popular feeling, and harm to it is clearly acknowledged as harm, a brutality to be dispensed with. The blow is material, unarguably real, and therefore may be cleanly dispensed with, whereas any assault upon the mind is so much more subtle, ambiguous.

The very medicalization of torture is part of this. The psychiatric diagnosis, presented as mere bureaucratic necessity, is of the essence, for in this place psychiatry has assumed the role of government and authority, delegated, licensed to act as its agent, and in its scientific and objective judgment the victim is in some way impaired (rather than aggressed upon or wronged by) his (or her) experience. The idea of justice is removed from the discussion, the activities of the interrogators and security forces. Everything that made sense of the prisoner's suffering, his principles, his innocence, the injustice done to him. Instead, the victim approaches now not for vindication but to solicit psychiatric expertise, facing another authority, another judge, another questioner. He faces medicine, not law, an important distinction since law would exonerate him and medicine has yet to decide his case. And so the victim of state brutality in a client state applies not for redress or restitution but for healing in the place from whence his harm emanated. There is an imperial circularity here. Short-circuitry as well: the political has been psychiatrized, privatized, personalized into marginality; the social reality of dictatorship, the politics of cruelty have been banalized into a "case." Telescoped, trivialized, shrunken.

THE enormity of torture on the other hand, its eternity of pain, can be inferred on every side. Two instances haunt me, both from Uruguay: the fates of the Tupamaros Mauricio Rosencof and Raúl Sendic, both of whom endured more than a decade of total solitary confinement. Following his arrest, Rosencof, a playwright, was subjected to nine months of continuous torture, requiring four different hospitalizations. For the next ten years he and Sendic were held hostage, subject to immediate execution if there were any signs of Tupamaro resistance. Both men were kept in tiny cells three by six feet. For years Rosencof was not permitted to stand or walk, but ordered to sit on a bench facing the wall all day long.

Sendic was kept at the bottom of a dry well. "We were beginning to think we were dead, that our cells weren't cells, but rather graves, that the outside world didn't exist, that the sun was a myth," Rosencof told Weschler. "Seriously, in over eleven and a half years, I didn't see the sun for more than eight hours altogether. I forgot colors—there were no colors. The impact after all that of seeing green again was truly amazing."

So are the resources of the human mind. Rosencof explained that he survived

By dreaming . . . Imagination. Taking long walks with my daughter. Sometimes, when the guards weren't looking, I'd stretch myself out for a sunbath on the beach. After a while I'd get hot and go off and get a nice, cold drink. Then the problem became hiding the bottle, because the cell was searched daily. You can imagine the trouble I'd have been in if the guards had suddenly uncovered a Coke bottle. Hiding objects acquired in my fantasies became quite a chore.*

A Coke bottle, litter of empire, the American fetish, the subject of Pop art, now a relic—transformed utterly: pleasure conjured into being, a terrible beauty in its ironic metamorphosis.

*Weschler, p. 145.

ACKNOWLEDGMENTS

OVER the six years I undertook this study I was supported materially and spiritually by the Hamburg Institute for Social Research, whose continued demonstration of faith in my project, however tardy and unproductive it must have seemed at times, made it possible. Although I had started on this alone, I doubt I would have had the nerve to finish without them; I would surely never have had the means.

It was a strange and lonely way. Friends were an enormous help because they were interested, read or listened to the manuscript as it was written: particularly Sophie Keir, Naomi Dodds, Eleanor Pam, Linda Clarke, and Joan Casamo. I am especially grateful to Jennifer Floryan, who watched me live with the subject the last four years, and to Linda Kavars, who managed the farm so that I could. Anne Keating taught me how to use a computer and gave me access to a university library. My friend Robin Morgan put me in touch with Mary Cunnane, who could edit and publish the text. I owe a great deal to my mother, who set much store by this book, kept after me these years to complete it, ninety years old when I read the first chapters to her in her armchair in St. Paul—chapters on the Gulag and the death camps: "I am not sure I wanted to know this much before I died . . . but then, imagine what they knew."

PERMISSIONS

INDEX

accountability, necessity for, 296–302
Aden, British torture discovered in, 102
Ad extirpanda, 99
African National Congress, 143
Afrikaans, compulsory education in, 124, 125
Akkache (Algerian rebel), 92
Algeria, French military in, 79–98, 110
  British control of Ireland compared with, 102, 109
  clandestine detention procedures of, 81–82
  national pride and, 97–98
  political censorship by, 79–80
  public opinion mobilized against, 79, 102
  torture practiced by, 82–95
Alger Républicain, 80
Ali, Muhammad, 207
Alianza Anticomunista Argentina, 226
Alipore Jail, 195
Alleg, Gilberte, 93

Alleg, Henri, 79–98, 99, 102, 105, 106, 110–111
  arrest of, 80–82
  background of, 79–80
  physical torture of, 83–90
  psychological torture of, 91–95
Alport, Catherine, 138–143, 161
Amandla (Tlali), 123, 124
Amaya, Rufina, 275
American Connection, The (McClintock), 267, 271
Americas Watch Committee, 275, 305
amnesty, accountability vs., 296–302
Amnesty International, 137
  apolitical stance of, 308
  book by French members of, 145
  on British torture in Ireland, 102
  collective effectiveness of, 107
  disappeared persons listed by, 231
  emblem of, 305
  on Guatemalan death squads, 266
  on Iranian criminal procedure, 281, 289

Amnesty International *(continued)*
    nationalism transcended by, 307
    number of governments accused of
        torture by, 18, 113, 173
    on sexual exploitation and
        brutalization of children, 294, 295
*Amnesty International, the Human
    Rights Story* (Power), 113
And Night Fell (Pheto), 36
Anitar, 200
Ao-Han-Ouan, Prince, 158
apartheid system, *see* South African
    apartheid system
Arbenz Guzman, Jacobo, 259, 260
Arendt, Hannah, 59, 304
Arévalo, Juan Jose, 259
Argentina:
    disappearances in, 225–226, 227,
        228–229, 231–232, 236–237
    military junta in, 228–230
    mothers' opposition movement in,
        237, 275
    prison conditions in, 227–228,
        232–234, 238–241
    torture practices in, 227, 230–232,
        233–234, 240, 298
    torturers prosecuted in, 229–230, 298
Argentinean Mothers of the
    Disappeared, 275
Armaugh Jail, 201
Army, U.S., 265, 271, 272, 273
Arns, Cardinal, 299
Atlacatl Battalion, 274, 275
Audin, Maurice, 80, 85
Aumeyer (SS Officer), 62–63
Auschwitz:
    crematoria at, 59
    gas chamber facilities at, 59
    Levi's survival in, 54, 69–73
    slave labor system at, 54–56, 57
    victim-financed transport to, 47
authority, obedience to, 304–305
"Autobiography" (Sosa), 276n

Bacry, Daniel, 145, 148
Base Christian communities, 263, 275,
    276

Basement, The (Millett), 11, 155
Bataille, Georges, 155, 156, 157–162,
    165–167
Bay, André, 145
beatings, systematic, 248
Beatles, 36
Beauvoir, Simone de, 110
behavior psychology, 310
"Believe It Or Not by Ripley," 150,
    151–153
Bergen-Belsen, 149
Bettelheim, Bruno, 72
Bharadwaj, Radha, 168–193
Birkenau, 59, 61–64, 71
Bismarck, Otto von, 176
Black, George, 260n
blindfolding, 175, 181, 232–234
bodily integrity, violation of, 173–174
Body in Pain, The (Scarry), 301
Bosnia, 11n, 295
Boumendjel, Ali, 81
Bourgois, Phillipe, 274
Brasil, Nunca Mais (Report of the
    Archdiocese of São Paulo)
    (Torture in Brazil), 242, 246, 247,
    249, 251, 298–299
Braunstein, Saundra, 225n
Brazil, national security state in,
    241–252
    anticommunist sentiment in, 242
    courts of, 246, 247, 249, 251–252,
        298–299
    military training system and,
        242–243, 246–247
    neocolonialism and, 243, 252
    organization of, 243–245
    torture institutionalized by, 245–252,
        298–299
Breci (Italian regicide), 199
Breytenbach, Breyten, 130
British Shell, 211
Brownshirts, 144
Brutus, Dennis, 201
Bukharin, Nikolay Aleksandrovich,
    40
Buna Camp, 57
Butyrki Prison, 32

Cadets (Constitutional Democrats), 39

Caistor, Nick, 202*n*

Calder, John, 80*n*

Cambodia, crucifixion victim in, 145–148

capital punishment, ritual quality of, 156, 157, 161

captivity:
absolute powerlessness experienced in, 30, 114
defiance eroded in, 31–32
inhumanity of, 31, 113
as interruption of life, 194–195
isolation in, 32, 42, 156, 195–201, 204–209, 313–314
volition suspended in, 31–32
in voluntary erotic activities, 113–116
see also detention; prison(s)

Carpeaux, Louis, 158

Casa Alianza, 293, 295

Castello Branco, Marshal, 244

Castilla, Juan Carlos, 231

Castro, Fidel, 144

Catherine, Saint, 150–153

Catholic Church:
martyrdom and, 150–153
Salvadoran resistance backed by, 269

Cavalcante, Jose, 250

Center for Internal Defense Operations (DOI-CODI), 244, 246, 251, 252

Cheka, 39, 50, 144

Chelmno, genocidal procedures at, 47–48, 58

Chen Boda, 210

childbirth, pain of, 184

children:
among the Argentinean disappeared, 227, 231–232
on death row, 294
as metaphor for powerlessness, 190, 191
as military targets, 274, 275, 277
sexual violation of, 181, 187–188, 189
in Soweto uprising, 123, 124, 125–126, 291

of the street, 292–295
torture of, 125–126, 129, 145–148, 291–295

China, People's Republic of, 209–221
constitution of, 219, 220–221
leadership changes in, 210, 219–220
People's Council actions in, 144
prison tortures in, 215–217
propagandistic penal system in, 209–221
ritual confessions required in, 209–210, 211, 213, 214, 215, 219

Chinchilla, Norma Stoltz, 260*n*

Chinese torture of the hundred pieces, 155–159, 160, 161, 164–167

Christianity:
religious martyrdom and, 150–153
South American regimes and, 236, 263, 269, 275–276
torture practices legitimized by, 99;
see also Inquisition

CIA, 259, 271

citizenship, immunity from torture provided by, 98, 99

Clements, Charles, 273

Closet Land, 168–193, 234
formal futuristic setting of, 169–170
imagination as escape mechanism in, 176–177, 178, 180, 185–186, 187–188, 192
women's subordination symbolized in, 173–175

Cold War, 242, 260

colonialism:
Brazilian neocolonialism and, 243, 252
racism at root of, 99, 108–110

Color Bar Act (1926), 123

Co-Madres (Committee of Mothers and Relatives of Political Prisoners, Disappeared and Assaulted of El Salvador), 275, 276, 277, 278

communism:
Latin American military regimes against, 242, 255, 260, 262, 263, 270
U.S. Cold War policy and, 242, 260

Communist Party:
  in French Algiers, 87
  purges within, 40, 107
  torture resistance code for, 87
  see also China, People's Republic of;
    Russia, Soviet
complicity, 302–305
Conciliatory Act (1924), 123
confession:
  as betrayal, 91, 301
  false, 43, 104, 179, 209–210, 211, 213,
    214, 215, 219, 249–250
  after time gained for comrades,
    33–34, 87
  see also resistance
Confession, The (London), 107
Congress, U.S., 274
Connor, Peter, 157n
Conquest, Robert, 75n
Constitutional Democrats (Cadets), 39
counter-insurgency:
  in El Salvador, 268–279
  in Guatemala, 260–268
  national security state vs., 260–261
  paramilitary forces and, 265–266,
    269, 271–272, 275
  state authority ultimately
    undermined by, 273
  violence escalated to massacres in,
    273–275
crematoria, Nazi, 59, 61, 62, 71
criminal procedure, proscription of
  torture tactics in, 16–17
crucifixion:
  in Cambodia, 145–148
  of Jesus, 151
cruelty, complicity with, 302–305
cruelty, erotic character of, 155–167
  identification with victim and,
    163–164
  patriarchal sexuality and, 160
  power of taboo and, 160, 161
  in punishment for sin, 116, 189
  religious aspect of, 161–162
  voluntary sadomasochism and,
    113–116
Cultural Revolution, 210, 214, 218, 220

Dachau, 149, 154
Dalton, Roque, 268
Dante Alighieri, 72
Darkness at Noon (Koestler), 76
Dassin, Joan, 242n
Dawidowicz, Lucy, 52
Day in the Life of Ivan Denisovitch, A
  (Solzhenitsyn), 56
death:
  bogus threats of, 34, 107, 128
  from crucifixion, 147
  as escape, 91, 106
  fear of, 30
  Nazi extermination procedures and,
    47–48, 54, 58–73
  as result of torture, 33, 34, 91, 129,
    211, 248, 252
  from slave labor conditions vs. mass
    extermination, 56–57
Declaration of Human Rights, UN, 102
Declaration of the Rights of Man, 16
Declaration on the Protection of All
    Persons from Torture, UN, 13,
    229n
Decree Against Subversive Activity in
    the Rear (1920), 39
dehumanization:
  of imprisonment, 31, 113
  in Nazi camps, 54–56, 71–73
  suicidal despair engendered through,
    91
democracy, military prosecutions
    under, 296–300
Denny, Norman, 303n
DEOPS (State Departments for Political
    and Social Order), 244
De Profundis (Wilde), 209
Detained: A Writer's Prison Diary
    (Thiong'o), 200–209
detention:
  conventional state facilities vs.
    undiscovered locations for, 81–82
  state psychiatric authority for,
    113–114
  without trial, 41–42, 201–203, 205
  see also captivity; prison(s)
Didion, Joan, 269–270

Diplock Courts, 101
disappearance, 228
  see also specific South American regimes
dissent, total suppression of, 74, 244, 264, 270
Divine Comedy, The (Dante), 72–73
Dlamini, Moses, 130, 131–133
documentation, governmental, 38
DOI-CODI (Center for Internal Defense Operations), 244, 246, 251, 252
domination, patriarchal aspect of, 34–35
Don Quixote (Cervantes), 209
Dostoevski, Fyodor, 56
dragon chair, 247
drawing and quartering, 164
drugs:
  capitulation under, 94–95
  for protraction of torture, 249
  for punishment vs. psychiatric treatment, 95
duBois, Page, 309–310
Dugin, Itzhak, 60
Dumas, Georges, 158
Dumitriu, Petru, 303, 304

Eberl (SS Officer), 58–59
Einaudi, Giulio, 54*n*
Einsatzkommando, 59
electric shock, torture with, 83–84, 85, 87, 89–90, 227, 247
electroconvulsive therapy, psychiatric use of, 89–90
Elias y Barahona (Guatemalan press representative), 266
Elizabeth I, Queen of England, 108
El Mozote massacre, 274–275
El Salvador, 268–279
  death squad victims in, 269–270, 272–273
  military massacres in, 268, 273–275
  oligarchy of elite families in, 270
  popular resistance in, 268, 273, 275–279

U.S.-assisted counterterror in, 269, 270, 271–275, 276
emergency powers, 18, 52, 101, 311
Emergency Provisions Act (1973), 101
Emergency Provisions Act (1978), 101
End Papers (Breytenbach), 130
Enlightenment, 19, 99
Epicurus, 30, 34, 42
erotic practices:
  voluntary captivity used in, 113–116
  see also sexuality
ESA, 266
espionage, technological enhancement of, 27–28
Europe, statutory abolition of torture in, 16
European Court, 102
evil, banality of, 59, 304
Evin Prison, 188, 281–282
executions, public, 155–159, 161, 164, 166–167, 256–257

Fahrplananordnung 587, 46, 47
falaka, 188, 281, 282, 291
fascism, endurance of, 85
Fascist Party, 49–50
Faul, Denis, 103
Federal Penitentiary, U.S. (Marion), 306
fingerprinting, 38
First Circle, The (Solzhenitsyn), 23–34, 37–39, 41–43, 44–45
Flecha, Victor Jacinto, 202
flogging, public, 280, 281, 282
Ford Motor Company, 244
Fornazari, Juan Pablo, 231
Foucault, Michel, 156
Fou-Tchou-Li, 158
France:
  Nazi occupation in, 79
  see also Algeria, French military presence in
French Resistance, 79, 87
Friedman, Milton, 310

Galeano, Eduardo, 310–311
Gandhi, Mohandas K., 143, 193
Gang of Four, 210, 211

Garrison Guatemala (Black, Jamail, and Chinchilla), 260*n*
gas chambers, 48, 58–59, 61–64, 66–68
Genefke, Inge Kemp, 311
General Motors, 244
Genet, Jean, 201
genocide:
  Nazi program of, 40, 46–48, 58; *see also* Nazi death camp system
  of Russian kulaks, 40
Geopolitica do Brasil (Golbery), 245
Germany (Third Reich):
  anti-Semitism legislated in, 51–52, 123
  Eastern European massacres executed by, 59–60
  final solution embarked on by, 46, 53
  French Resistance members tortured by, 79
  Stalinist genocidal policy vs., 40
  state power increased through ideological necessity in, 49, 50–51
  torture protocols authorized by, 51
  variety of political/racial enemies of, 51, 52, 53, 69, 91
  Volk ethos of, 50
  see also National Socialist Party, Nazism; Nazi death camp system
Ghana (Nkrumah), 205
Ghose, Aurobindo, 195–200
Ghose, Sisur Kumar, 196*n*
Gĩkũyũ, 206
Gilbert, Martin, 52
Glazer, Richard, 64
Goethe Institute, 283
Golbery do Conto e Silva, General, 245
Gonzalez de Junquera, Maria Eugenia, 231, 236–237, 240
Good Friday, 151
Göring, Hermann, 46, 53, 245
Goulart, João, 243
Grabner (SS Officer), 62
Great Britain:
  India ruled by, 196
  in Kenya, 203
  see also Irish dissidents, British dealings with

Great Terror, The: A Reassessment (Conquest), 75*n*
Greece, military torturers prosecuted in, 229*n*
Grossman, Vasily, 74–75
groups, revenge actions of, 144–145
Guatemala:
  brutal counter-insurgency developed in, 260–268
  deaths and disappearances in, 264, 266, 267
  health workers persecuted in, 264–265
  Indian communities destroyed in, 255, 267–268
  intelligence organization in, 265–267
  land distribution in, 259–260
  rural villagers militarized in, 253–259, 264
  street children brutalized in, 293–295
Guatemala, A Cry from the Heart (Schwantes), 265
guilt, presumption of, 42
Gulag:
  fugitives from, 29
  Nazi death camp system vs., 40, 45, 52, 56–57
  public works programs and, 40, 57
  secrecy maintained about, 27, 78
  sleep deprivation tactics used in, 33
  ten million persons affected by, 39
Gulag Archipelago, The (Solzhenitsyn), 56
Gutman, W. E., 293, 294–295
gypsies, Nazi actions against, 52, 53

habeas corpus, suspension of, 18, 101, 250
Hamilton, Alistair, 107*n*
Harper's, 304
Harris, Bruce, 295
H Blocks, The (Faul and Murray, eds.), 103–104
Hell-Hole Robben Island (Dlamini), 130*n*
Helsinki Watch, 291, 305
heroism, active vs. passive, 111

Herzog, Wladimir, 248
Heydrich, Reinhard, 46, 53, 58
Hezbollah (Party of God), 285, 290
Hilberg, Raul, 45, 46, 47, 52, 53, 58
Himmler, Heinrich, 51
Hinduism, 196
Hitler, Adolf, 74, 78
    Lenin's totalitarian model advanced
        by, 18
    mystical omnipotence ascribed to, 50
homosexuals, persecution of, 52, 53,
    77, 290
Hossler (SS Officer), 62
Hugo, Victor, 16
Human Rights Commission, 269, 278
humiliation, sexual, 34–35
Hungarian uprising, 154
hunger strikes, 103
Hunter College, 306

ice box, 247
Ilaqua, Carlos Maria, 231
imagination, as escape mechanism,
    176–177, 178, 180, 185–186,
    187–188, 192, 314
imperialism:
    racism at root of, 99
    see also colonialism
Incognito (Dumitriu), 303
Index on Censorship, 202n
India, solitary confinement experience
    in, 195–200
Innocent IV, Pope, 99
Inquisition, 15, 18, 76, 99, 148, 171, 282
International Solidarity, 278
interrogation(s):
    of children, 125–126
    cinematic depiction of, 168–193
    in Communist China, 212–219
    deceptive tactics used in, 92–93,
        170–171, 175–176, 181–182, 183
    duration of, 33
    Himmler's Third Degree methods
        for, 51
    as impersonal state search for truth,
        171–172
    sensory deprivation during, 100–101

sleep deprivation and, 33, 42, 100, 101
by South African police, 125–126,
    127–129
in Soviet Russia, 33, 42, 43, 171
Iran, Islamic Republic of, 280–290
    clergy as ruling class in, 283,
        284–285, 289
    criminal prosecution in, 287, 289–290
    falaka torture used in, 188, 281, 282,
        291
    legal torture vs. secret torture in,
        280–282
    police system of, 284–285
    popular democratic revolution
        superseded by, 283–285
    private life outweighed by moral
        authority of, 287–289
    Shah's regime vs., 282, 283–284, 285
    women subjugated in, 285, 286–287
Iran, Shah's regime in, 148, 282,
    283–284, 285
Irish dissidents, British dealings with,
    100–105
    emergency legislation for, 101
    European Court decisions on, 102
    French Algeria compared with, 102,
        109
    pacifist tactics and, 111
    prisoner of war status withdrawn in,
        102
    in prison protests, 102–103
    psychiatric drugs used in, 95
    racial hatred behind, 108
    sensory deprivation used in, 100–101
    writing by prisoners forbidden in,
        103, 201
isolation, 32, 42
    see also solitary confinement,
        solitude
Italy, Fascist, ideological focus for state
    power in, 49–50
"It's No Use" (Flecha), 202
Izurieta, Zulma "Vasca," 236, 238–239

Jamail, Milton, 260n
Japan, torture in criminal procedures
    abolished in, 16

Jesus Christ, crucifixion of, 151
Josephson, Helen, 140
judicial procedure, ideological necessity
    for suspension of, 48–49, 50–51
Junquera, Néstor, 231, 236–237, 240
jurisprudence, dual system of, 48–49

Kaffir Boy (Mathabane), 119n–123
Kafka, Franz, 75
Kamiti Maximum Security Prison, 200,
    203
Kariuki (Mau-Mau), 207
Kenya:
    arrest procedures in, 201–203, 204,
        205–206
    Kenyatta government in, 203–205,
        207–208, 209
    Mau-Mau uprising in, 140, 203, 207
Kenyatta, Jomo, 200, 203, 204, 206,
    207, 209
Kenyatta University College, 201
Khalkhali, Sadeq, 289
Khmer Rouge, 147
Khomeini, Ayatollah Ruhollah, 176,
    188, 284, 285, 289
Koestler, Arthur, 76, 171
Krishnamurti, Jiddu, 107
Kristallnacht, 220
Kronstadt sailors' uprising, 39
kulaks, resettlement of, 39, 40
Kuttner (SS Officer), 67

labor camps:
    death camps vs., 56–57
    see also Gulag; Nazi death camp
        system
Land Act (1936), 123
Lanzmann, Claude, 45, 69
Lawrence, Saint, 150–151
legal system:
    ideological necessity for suspension
        of, 48–49, 50–51
    preconditions for torture established
        within, 51–52, 123, 272
    revolutionary reforms within, 307
    Roman, 18, 98–99
    torture tactics abolished in, 16

legislation, of special emergency
    powers, 18, 52, 101, 311
Leme, Alexandre Vannucchi, 251–252
Leng-Tch'e, 158
Lenin, V. I.:
    as arbiter of revolutionary
        correctness, 50
    political incarceration instituted by,
        17
    torture tactics restored by, 17, 74
    total state power developed by, 18,
        41n, 74
Leningrad, Stalinist purge of, 40
Levi, Primo, 54–56, 57, 69–73, 88
liberation theology, 236, 275
Libertad Prison, 310
Life, 149, 154
Life and Death in Shanghai (Nien), 210n
Likens, Sylvia, 154–155
Lin Biao, 210, 217, 219
Lion and the Lizard, The (Rawlinson),
    288–289
Little School, The (Partnoy), 225–241
Liu Shaoqi, 210
London, Artur, 107, 171
Long Kesh, 103
Louis XIV, King of France, 38
Loup, Elyette, 92
Lubyanka, 30–32, 37–39
Lucy, Saint, 151
Luxemburg, Rosa, 74

Maathai, Wangari, 206
McClintock, Michael, 267, 271, 273,
    274
Maisonave, Ana Maria de, 231
Maisonave, Rodolfo, 231
"Making and Unmaking of the World,
    The" (Scarry), 301n
Malraux, André, 79
Mandela, Nelson, 56, 132, 133
manhood, in torturer's brutality vs.
    victim's silence, 110–111
Mao Zedong, 210, 211, 214, 219, 220,
    221
Marmol, Miguel, 268
Martinez, General, 268

martyrdom, religious, 150–153
Marxism, Nazi *Volk* ideology vs., 50
masochism:
   voluntary captivity and, 113–116
   woman's acculturation toward, 152, 160
Massera, Emilio, 229
Mathabane, Mark, 118–123, 124, 125
Mau-Mau, 140, 203, 207
Mauriac, François, 79
Mavrino, 27
Mayan communities, military indoctrination of, 253–259
medical personnel, torture attended by, 51, 94, 178, 246, 248–249, 282, 312
Medici, Emilio, 244
Medina, General, 302
Mellors, Alec, 51
Menem, Carlos, 298
Mengele, Joseph, 94
Mensheviks, 39
mental illness:
   compulsory drug therapy and, 95
   electroconvulsive treatment for, 89–90
   political dissidents misdiagnosed with, 95–96
   state power of detention for, 113–114
   torture victims rehabilitation considered as, 311–313
   unprotected singularity of, 90–91, 95–96
Miete (SS Officer), 64
Miguel Marmol (Dalton), 268
Milgram, Stanley, 304
military, special powers of legislation for, 52
military regimes:
   accountability vs. amnesty for torture in, 296–300
   fugitive Nazis in, 85
   U.S. assistance given to, 242, 243, 259, 261–262, 265, 269–275, 276
   see also specific countries
Miracle, a Universe, A: Settling Accounts with Torturers (Weschler), 297

Mitrione, Dan, 247
Mittel Europäisch Reisebüro, 45–46
Mohammad Reza Pahlavi, Shah of Iran, 282, 283, 284, 285
Moi, Daniel, 206
Mommsen, Theodor, 98–99
Monteiro, Affonso, 250
Montejo, Victor, 254–259
Morte D'Arthur (Malory), 209
Moscow purge trials, 40, 76
Muller, Filip, 61–64
Murray, Raymond, 103
music, torture accompanied by, 36–37, 55–56, 87
Muslim Brotherhood, 290
Muslims:
   fundamentalist, 290
   shari'a legal code of, 145, 282, 288–289
   see also Iran, Islamic Republic of
Mussolini, Benito, 49
Mutual Support, 264

Nagel, Thomas, 298
Nahaman (Guatemalan street child), 294–295
Nairobi University, 201
nationalism, transcendence of, 306–307
national security state, 242
   counter-insurgency vs., 260–261
   Soviet model for, 41
   see also Brazil, national security state in
National Socialist (Nazi) Party, Nazism:
   as model for gangsterism, 131
   South African apartheid vs., 123–124
   in South American military, 85, 242
   Volk ethos embodied in, 50
   see also Germany (Third Reich);
   Nazi death camp system:
National War College, 242
Native Administration Act (1927), 123
Nazi death camp system, 44–73
   bureaucratic banality of, 46–48, 59
   cremation used in, 59, 61, 62

Nazi death camp system *(continued)*
 dehumanization efforts in, 54–56,
  71–72
 extermination program at, 47–48, 54,
  56–58
 financial arrangements for, 45–47
 gassing facilities of, 48, 58–59, 61–64,
  66–68
 legislative preconditions for, 52,
  123
 marching bands used in, 55–56, 71
 official secrecy maintained about, 45,
  46, 47, 53, 59–60, 61, 64
 organizational structure within, 54
 photographic images of, 60–61,
  149–150, 154
 psychological tactics of, 54–56
 resistance in, 71–73
 scientific experimentation in, 52–53
 slave labor system in, 54–55, 56–57,
  59, 60
 Stalinist precedent for, 40
 systematic corruption within, 55
 transport procedures for, 45–47,
  65–66
 victims duped in, 62–63, 65, 66–67
necklacing, 138–144
Never Again (Nunca Más), 298
New Italian Encyclopedia, 49
New Yorker, 303
New York Times, 291
Nien Cheng, 209–221
 background of, 211–212
 release of, 212, 213, 220–221
Night and Fog, 60
Nkrumah, Kwame, 205
NKVD, 39
NOA, 266
Nomani, Farhad, 289n
Northern Ireland, *see* Irish dissidents,
  British dealings with
Notes from the Underground
  (Dostoevski), 56
Nunca Mais, see Brasil, Nunca Mais
Nunca Más (Never Again), 298
Nuremberg Trials, 78, 229
Nürnberg laws, 52

OBAN (Operation Bandeirantes), 244,
 246
Obedience to Authority (Milgram), 304
Ochoa, Colonel, 274
Okhrana, 17
Omni, 293, 294n
Opinión La, 237
ORDEN, 271
Ortiz Luna, Octavio, 276
Our Lady of the Flowers (Genet), 201

Pan African Congress, 132
Panama Canal Zone, U.S. forces in,
 265, 274
Pandolfi, Dulce, 246–247
paramilitary groups, 253–259, 265–266,
 269, 271–272, 275
parrot's perch, 246, 247
Partnoy, Alicia, 225–241
 background of, 236–237
 disappearance of, 225–226, 228
 fates of fellow prisoners discovered
  by, 230–232
 prison conditions endured by, 227,
  232–234, 238–241
 on trials of former leaders, 229–230,
  251
Party of God (Hezbollah), 285, 290
patriarchy:
 female denigration and, 34–35, 77–78
 Iranian theocracy vs., 286
 in penal procedures, 98–99
 sexual patterns drawn from, 34–35,
  152, 160, 164–165
Pekin qui s'en va (Carpeaux), 158
Peltier, Leonard, 306
People's Mojahadin, 285
Perera, Victor, 254n
"Perils of Innocence, The" (Milgram),
 304
Péron, Juan, 236
personal search procedures, 32
Peters, Edward, 16, 18, 48–49, 50–51,
 98, 99
Pheto, Molefe, 36
photography, 137–167
 of Cambodian crucifixion, 145–148

emotional power of, 153–154
of erotic aspects in cruelty, 155–167
factuality of, 146, 148–149
of mob vengeance in South Africa,
138–144
of Nazi concentration camps, 60–61,
149–150, 154
of Salvadoran death squad victims,
269–270
for state recordkeeping, 38
physicians, torture attended by, 51, 94,
178, 246, 248–249, 282, 312
Pilgrim's Progress (Bunyan), 209
political necessity, normal legal
protections transcended by, 48–49,
50–51
political prisoners:
captivity as test for, 206–208
as prisoners of war, 102
psychiatric drugs tested on, 95
in United States, 306
political subversion:
as broad and inclusive charge, 17,
270
criminal offenses vs., 17–18
state power at war with, 234–236;
see also counter-insurgency;
national security state
Pollsmoor prisons, 130
Popular Socialists, 39
pornography:
children in, 181
disapproval expressed in, 174, 175,
189
distant tone of, 87–88
post-traumatic shock syndrome,
311–312
power:
obsession with, 112
torture as logical extension of,
308–309
see also state power
Power, Jonathan, 113
Prevention of Terrorism Act (1975),
101
prison(s):
comradeship in, 90–91, 238–240, 241

feminine role-playing by men in, 132
Irish dissidents' protests in, 102–103
medical treatment in, 208, 217
psychological torture program in,
310
regimentation in, 56
in secret, 81–82, 226–227, 229,
250–251, 311
in United States, 306
writing in, 201, 205, 206, 209–210
prisoners of war, Irish dissidents as,
102
*Prisoner Without a Name, Cell Without
a Number* (Timerman), 237
private life, state invasion of, 177–178,
181, 287–289
prolyxin, 95
Promparty, 39
public executions, 155–159, 161, 164,
166–167, 256–257
purity, masculine obsession with, 189

Qasr Prison, 281–282
qissas, 282
Question, The (Alleg), 79–96
Sartre's introduction to, 91, 97–98,
99, 108–112

racism:
against Asians, 147
educational restrictions based on,
123–124
imperial/colonial dynamic built on,
99, 108–110
Nazi policies of, 51–52, 53, 69, 91,
123
of South African apartheid system,
117–133
of U.S. policy in Latin America,
261–262
Rahnema, Ali, 289n
rape:
of children by police, 295
as expression of, 112
humiliation of, 34
as patriarchal sexual pattern, 160
in prison, 132

Rastgeldi Report, 102
Rauff, Walter, 47
Rawlinson, Jane, 288–289
Reagan, Ronald, 274
recordkeeping, technology of, 38
regimentation, 54–56
Regional Center for
    Telecommunications (La
    Regionale), 265–267
religious belief:
    erotic sadism and, 157–158, 161–162
    martyrdom and, 150–153
    prison experience and, 196–200
    sexual repression and, 116
    state torture policy based on,
        280–290
Report of the Archdiocese of São Paulo
    (Brasil, Nunca Mais) (Torture in
    Brazil), 242, 246, 247, 249, 251,
    298–299
Research Center for Torture Victims,
    311
resistance:
    to drugs, 94–95
    in Nazi death camps, 71–73
    physical vs. mental, 86, 91, 187
    rewards of, 92, 93, 128–129, 192
    time for confederates gained by,
        33–34, 87
    torturers angered by, 88–89, 191–192
Resnais, Alain, 60
revolution, ideological necessity linked
    to, 49, 74, 307
Richopo, Neide, 251–252
Ride on the Whirlwind, A (Sepamla),
    126–129
Right Socialist Revolutionary Party, 39
Rios Montt, Efraín, 255, 261
Ripley, Robert, 150, 151–153
Rise and Fall of the Third Reich, The
    (Shirer), 220
Robben Island, 56, 130–133, 201
Rodley, Nigel, 16
Romania, totalitarian regime in, 303
Roman law, torture practices addressed
    in, 18, 98–99
Romero, Maria Elena, 231

Romero, Oscar Arnulfo, 268–269, 270,
    276n
Romero de Metz, Graciela Alicia,
    230–231
Rosencof, Mauricio, 313–314
Ross, Kathleen, 268n
Royal Ulster Constabulary, 108
Russia, Soviet:
    Criminal Code of, 41
    dissidents given psychiatric
        misdiagnoses in, 95–96
    domestic espionage in, 27–28, 41
    interrogation procedures of, 33, 42,
        43, 171
    official secrecy policies in, 41
    political purges in, 40, 76, 107
    revolutionary necessity in, 49
    Romanian regime under, 303
    secret police established in, 39
    slave labor system in, 27, 40, 57; see
        also Gulag
    state terrorism established in, 40–41
Russia, tsarist:
    labor camps in, 56
    torture in criminal procedures
        abolished in, 16, 17

Sade, Marquis de, 88, 166
sadomasochism:
    captivity employed in, 113–116
    patriarchal sexuality vs., 152, 160
Saint-Just, Louis, 144
saints, martyrdom of, 150–153
Salvador (Didion), 269–270
Salvadoran Human Rights Commission
    (Socorro Juridico), 274
Sanctuary, 276
Sands, Bobby, 103–105
sans-culottes, 144
Sartre, Jean-Paul, 79, 80n, 91, 97–98,
    99, 108–112
Savak, 283
Scarry, Elaine, 300–301
Schaaf, Richard, 268n
Schwantes, David, 265
search procedures, 32
secrecy, 18

bureaucratic language used for, 47
of detention places, 81–82, 226–227, 229, 250–251, 311
national security rationale for, 41, 245
on Nazi death camp system, 45, 46, 47, 53, 59–60, 61, 64
pretense of, 245–246
Stalinist, 78
subsequent accountability vs., 300–302
of torturer's identity, 105, 107–108
of torture with no mark, 33
Secular Miracle: Religion, Politics and Economic Policy in Iran, The (Rahnema and Nomani), 289*n*
Sendic, Raúl, 313
sensory deprivation, 99–101
Sepamla, Sipho, 126–129
sexuality:
  as aspect of cruelty, *see* cruelty, erotic character of
  female denigration and, 77–78
  patriarchal patterns of, 34–35, 152, 160, 164–165
  religious sacrifice and, 161–162
  shaming of women connected to, 34–35, 152, 153, 154–155, 173–175, 180–182
Sexual Politics (Millett), 11, 155
sexual torture:
  dignity of privacy violated by, 173–175, 180
  humiliation of, 35
  sadomasochistic ritual vs., 115
Sharashka, 27, 33
shari'a, 145, 282, 288–289
Shirer, William, 220
Shoah, 45, 58, 60, 61–69
shock response, 141, 142, 155–156, 157–158, 159
Sijeyo, Wasonga, 206
Silva, Ednaldo, 250
Sisulu, Walter, 132, 133
slave labor:
  extermination facilities built by, 56–57, 59

in Nazi death camp system, 54–55, 56–57, 59, 60
in Russia, 27, 40, 56, 57
of South African prisoners, 130, 131, 132
slavery, 16, 98
sleep deprivation, 33, 42, 100, 101
smiles, complicity expressed through, 302–304
Sobibor, 60
Sobukwe, Robert, 132
Social Democrats, 39
Socorro Juridico (Salvadoran Human Rights Commission), 274
sodium pentathol, 94
solitary confinement, solitude, 194–222
  in British-ruled India, 195–200
  imaginative visualization employed in, 314
  insanity engendered by, 199, 200
  invention of, 156
  in Kenya, 200–201, 204–209
  spiritual development pursued in, 195–200
  as torture, 42
  in Uruguay, 313
Solitude (Storr), 100–101
Solzhenitsyn, Aleksandr I.:
  on arrest procedures, 23–30
  Gulag experience chronicled by, 39, 41–43, 44–45, 56
  imprisonment and exile of, 41
  Lubyanka imprisonment described by, 30–34, 37–39
  Soviet interrogation described by, 171
Sondergerichte, 51
Sosa, Joaquin, 277–278
Sosa, Juan, 277
South Africa, photograph of burning policeman in, 138–144
South African apartheid system, 117–133
  black work force in, 118, 123
  children terrorized under, 118–123, 125–126, 291

South African apartheid *(continued)*
  educational restrictions within,
    123–124, 125
  gangsterism in, 131, 132
  initial legislation of, 123
  land distribution under, 117–118
  mob reprisal against black policeman
    in, 138–144
  passbook system of, 118, 119
  police raids in, 118–123
  prison conditions of, 56, 126–127,
    130–133
  student rebellion against, 123–126
  townships developed under, 118
South America, Nazism in military
  establishments of, 85, 242
Soviet Russia, *see* Russia, Soviet
Soweto, student protests in, 123,
  124–125, 291
Soyinka, Wole, 201
Spanish Inquisition, 15, 18, 76, 99, 148,
  171, 282
Special Forces, U.S., 261, 274
Special International Tribunal, 306
Special Powers acts, 101
Speck, Richard, 165
Spenser, Edmund, 108
Stalin, Joseph, 43
  as arbiter of revolutionary
    correctness, 50
  Gulag system and, 27, 40, 56, 57, 78
  ideological aspect of torture under,
    74
  Lenin's totalitarianism advanced by,
    18
  primacy of state power stressed by,
    41
  public works programs of, 40, 57
State Departments for Political and
  Social Order (DEOPS), 244
state power:
  in counter-insurgencies, 260–279
  over criminals vs. political
    subversives, 17–18
  emergency legislation for, 18, 52,
    101, 311
  erotic mimicry of, 114–116

ideological rationales for enlargement
  of, 48–51
individuals' fears of, 74–77
national security justifications for,
  41, 242, 309
over private life, 177–178, 181,
  287–289
progressive enlargement of, 309
recordkeeping procedures and, 38,
  266–267
self-preservation of, 74
technological omnipresence of,
  27–28, 38, 177–178
of theocracy, 280–290
torture as absolute manifestation of,
  18, 30, 42
Storr, Robert, 100–101
Story of O, The (Réage), 88
street children, brutalization of,
  292–295
Suchomel, Franz, 58–59, 65–69
Superior War College, 242–243
surveillance, technological enhancement
  of, 27–28, 38
Survival in Auschwitz (Levi), 54–56, 57,
  69–73
Surviving and Other Essays
  (Bettelheim), 72n

Tales from Prison Life (Ghose), 196–200
Tambov peasants' rebellion, 39
Tears of Eros, The (Bataille), 157–162,
  165–167
technology, state power extended
  through, 27–28, 38, 177–178,
  266–267
telephone surveillance, 27–28
témoignage, 15
Ternisien, Michel, 145, 148
Testimony (Montejo), 254–259
theocracy, *see* Iran, Islamic Republic of
They, Lois, 225n
Thiong'o, Ngũgĩ wa, 200–209
  arrest of, 201–203, 204
  in solitary confinement, 200–201,
    204–209
Third Degree, 51

Third World, nationalist disdain for, 309–310
Thuku, Harry, 207
Tiananmen Square, 217
Timerman, Jacobo, 237, 251
Tlali, Miriam, 123, 124, 126
Torture (Peters), 16, 98
torture:
  behavioral psychology used for, 310
  categorization issues reawakened with, 77–78
  cinematic depiction of, 168–193
  clerical witnesses to, 282
  collective public conscience mobilized against, 78–79, 305, 310, 311
  compassionate response to accounts of, 69, 88
  comradeship in, 90, 238–240, 241
  confession elicited by, *see* confession
  confinement as, 32–33
  as contest of wills, 33, 111–112, 185, 192
  in criminal procedure, 16–17
  of crucifixion, 145–148
  death threats used in, 34, 107, 128
  defined, 13
  drugs utilized in, 94–95, 249
  electricity used in, 83–84, 85, 87, 89–90, 227, 247
  family relationships exploited for, 92–93, 103, 208, 248
  fatalities caused by, 33, 34, 91, 129, 211, 248, 252
  fear of, 30, 300
  female responses to depictions of, 162–163
  first-person accounts of, 88, 104–107
  historical precedents set for, 53
  history of, 15–18
  ideological justification for, 48–51, 74
  imagination as escape from, 176–177, 178, 180, 185–186, 187–188, 192, 314
  international agreements against, 306; *see also* United Nations

legislative preconditions for, 51–52, 123, 272
  as manifestation of absolute state power, 18, 30, 42
  medical personnel involved in, 51, 94, 178, 246, 248–249, 282, 312
  as mob action, 138–145
  modern reinstitution of, 16–19
  mundane associations linked with, 37, 104
  music played during, 36–37, 55–56, 87
  in national security state, 245–252
  new governments' acknowledgment and prosecutions of, 296–302
  non-governmental efforts against, 305–308; *see also* Amnesty International
  old French phrase for, 85
  oppressor/victim dualities and, 35, 111–112
  "other" subjected to, 51–52, 77, 99, 309–310
  passivity induced by, 87
  photographic records of, 60–61, 137–167, 269–270
  post-World War II repudiation of, 78
  psychological insult of, 34–35, 92
  in public executions, 155–159, 256–257
  rape vs., 34
  readers' reactions to accounts of, 104–107
  of religious martyrdom, 150–153
  Roman establishment of protocol in, 98–99
  sadomasochistic mimicry of, 113–116
  as science, 246–247, 248–249, 303, 310, 312–313
  secrecy maintained about, 18; *see also* secrecy
  sexual, 35, 115, 173–175, 180
  shock reaction to images of, 141, 142, 155–156, 157–158, 159
  of slaves, 98
  state religion as basis for, 280–290

torture *(continued)*
  time gained by resistance to, 33–34, 87
  two western revivals of, 98, 99
  with water, 85–86, 248
  worldwide incidence of, 15, 18
  see also torturers; victims of torture
Torture, La (Mellors), 51*n*
Torture, La: La Nouvelle Inquisition (Ternisien and Bacry), 145
Torture and Truth (duBois), 309–310
Torture in Brazil (Report of the Archdiocese of São Paulo) *(Brasil, Nunca Mais)*, 242, 246, 247, 249, 251, 298–299
Torture in the Eighties, 113
torturers:
  deception practiced by, 62–63, 65, 66–67, 92–93, 170–171, 175–176, 181–182, 183
  identity protection for, 68, 105, 107–108
  individual sensibilities indulged by, 35–36
  legal accountability of, 229–230, 251–252, 296–302
  Nazi Gestapo admired by, 85
  power as obsession for, 112
  sadistic humor of, 36, 82–87
  state permission for taboo behavior granted to, 35–36
  torture as sport for, 83
  training of, 246–247, 310
Traité de Psychologie (Dumas), 158
Treatment of Political Prisoners Under International Law (Rodley), 16
Treblinka:
  extermination facilities at, 58–59, 64, 65–69
  railroad transport of prisoners to, 46, 65–66
  singing compelled in, 68–69
Trotsky, Leon, 74
Tupamaros, 313–314
Turkey, torture of children in, 291–292
Tzalala, Mayan Indians militarized in, 253–259, 267

UNICEF, 292
Union of Soviet Socialist Republics (USSR), *see* Russia, Soviet
United Fruit, 260
United Nations:
  Declaration of Human Rights, 102
  Declaration on the Protection of All Persons from Torture, 13, 229*n*
  torture practices alleged for members of, 113
  torture prohibited by, 78
United Nations Conventions Against Torture:
  amnesty for torturers precluded by, 300
  establishment of, 229*n*
  signatories in violation of, 280–281, 292, 306
United States:
  Cold War defense policies of, 242, 260
  foreign military trained in, 242, 261, 262, 274
  juveniles on death row in, 294
  Latin American military regimes assisted by, 242, 243, 259, 261–262, 265, 269–275, 276
  UN conventions violated by, 306
Uruguay:
  accounts of torture practiced in, 298, 302, 313–314
  economic policy of, 310–311
  psychological torture program in, 310
  torturers granted amnesty in, 299–300
  training programs for torture in, 247, 310

vengeance, mob actions of, 138–145
victims of torture:
  children as, 125–126, 129, 145–148, 291–295
  comradeship among, 90–91, 238–240, 241
  disorientation of, 168–169, 175–176, 233

false confessions given by, 43, 104, 179, 209–210, 211, 213, 214, 215, 219, 249–250
female identification with, 162–163, 165, 190
other victims heard by, 92, 183, 248, 250, 251–252, 300
psychiatric disease model applied to, 311–313
readers' empathy with, 104–105
social programs for, 311, 312
threats about family members of, 92–93, 103, 208, 248
torturers' admiration for, 188
see also torture
Victoria 82 Plan of Campaign, 261
Videla, Jorge, 229
Vietnam, U.S. counter-insurgency strategy in, 261
Vilna massacres, 60
voice prints, 27–28
Volk, 50–51
voyeurism, 166

Wannsee Conference, 46
Warsaw ghetto, 58
water tortures, 85–86, 248
Weschler, Lawrence, 297, 298, 301, 302–303, 310, 313, 314*n*
Western eroticism, female embodiment of sexuality in, 166

White Hand, 266
Whitman, Lois, 291
Whitney, Thomas P., 24*n*
Wilde, Oscar, 209
Wirth (SS Officer), 59
Witness to War (Clements), 273
women:
in Iranian theocracy, 285, 286–287
male prisoners in roles of, 132
masochistic acculturation fostered in, 152, 160
patriarchal denigration of, 77–78
sex as responsibility of, 166, 174
shaming of, 34–35, 152, 153, 154–155, 180–181
victim identity linked with, 162–163, 165, 190
Women's High Security Unit (Lexington), 306
World Watch, 305
Wright, Jaime, 242*n*, 299

xenophobia, 41

"Yellow Submarine," 36
Yoshimura, Fumio, 147, 148
Yoti, Gustavo Marcelo "Benja," 231

Zaidl, Moke, 60
Zhou Enlai, 210, 211
Zyklon gas, 48, 63